Management Research Challenge

Management Research Challenge

Selected Readings

Edited by
Lynn Thurloway

SAGE

Los Angeles | London | New Delhi
Singapore | Washington DC

SAGE

Los Angeles | London | New Delhi
Singapore | Washington DC

SAGE Publications Ltd
1 Oliver's Yard
55 City Road
London EC1Y 1SP

SAGE Publications Inc.
2455 Teller Road
Thousand Oaks, California 91320

SAGE Publications India Pvt Ltd
B 1/I 1 Mohan Cooperative Industrial Area
Mathura Road
New Delhi 110 044

SAGE Publications Asia-Pacific Pte Ltd
3 Church Street
#10-04 Samsung Hub
Singapore 049483

First published 2014

Typeset by C&M Digitals (P) Ltd, Chennai, India
Printed and bound by CPI Group (UK) Ltd, Croydon, CR0 4YY
Printed on paper from sustainable resources

British Library Cataloguing in Publication data

A catalogue record for this book is available from the British Library

MIX
Paper from responsible sources
FSC
www.fsc.org
FSC® C013604

At SAGE we take sustainability seriously. We print most of our products in the UK. These are produced using FSC papers and boards. We undertake an annual audit on materials used to ensure that we monitor out sustainability in what we are doing. When we print overseas, we ensure that sustainable papers are used, as measured by the Egmont grading system.

ISBN 978-1-4739-0709-6 (pbk)
E-ISBN 978-1-4739-0788-1 (e-book)
E-ISBN 978-1-4739-0789-8 (pbk with e-book)

Contents

Introduction

Welcome to the *Management Research Challenge: Selected Readings*.

This book contains many of the key readings for qualitative methods (Section 4) and multi-strategy methodologies (Section 5). These readings offer an introduction to different options that you may like to consider for your own research project. They will be useful in supporting you in terms of making your initial choices about your method(s) of data collection but they should also help you after this phase in terms of developing an understanding of the requirements of the method(s) as you begin the collection and analysis phases. Hence you should use the key readings in this book and, of course, other resources linked to the module as part of the overall support for your chosen approach to your investigation.

As you work through the learning material you will be guided to the appropriate readings for that section or approach. Once again you may find it useful to skim through the articles as you consider the different options for your investigation and then read the appropriate articles in more detail once you have decided on your approach and are designing your fieldwork.

We do hope that you find the readings in this book useful in developing your learning of business research and helping you to develop and apply it more effectively in your project and work.

Lynn Thurloway

1 Researching your own organization

Susanne Tietze

Introduction

The purpose of this chapter is to introduce and discuss the involvement of the researcher in the research scene and with the research participants in a specific scenario, i.e. where the researcher's employing organization provides the context for the research project. Such contexts also include settings where the researcher might be the owner of a small business, in particular where family businesses are at the core of the research venture. It has always been of interest to academic researchers and scholars to understand researchers' involvement in the research scene. Yet recent trends, in particular in doctoral studies, have made an exploration of the ties of researcher and researched in the context of researchers exploring their employing organization more prevalent. Here, the emergence and continued growth of professional doctorates (Doctor of Business Administration) degrees in the UK and Europe (Fisher and Tietze, 2010) has also seen an increasing number of research projects where managers and practitioners will bring the problems and issues of their employing organization to the research agenda and articulate research plans that are set in the context of their employing organization. While there is a body of literature exploring the notions and processes of auto-ethnography and writing the self into the research texts (Reed-Danahay, 1997; Watson, 1995; and see also Humphreys and Learmonth, in this volume), there is not much literature and guidance available for students who are researching their own and colleagues' practices in the context of their employing organization (Costley et al., 2010). The chapter therefore presents some ideas about the nature and dynamics of the researcher–researched relationship when research is located in the employing organization.

Any research project is, of course, situated in particular contexts, which will shape and inform the parameters and questions a researcher might venture to address. Researchers, too, are 'situated', i.e. they will bring a particular socio-political, historical, gendered, generational, ethnic and racial background to their research projects. In this regard research questions, research interests, choice of method and research instruments are interlinked with the researcher herself, with her life experience, and her development, background and values. Thus, becoming aware of the researcher's role in the research process is vital to understanding how such involvement shapes the generation of knowledge. In other words, the researcher 'is the research instrument par excellence' (Hammersley and Atkinson, 1995: 19) and appreciating his or her role in the research process is also vital to appreciating the trustworthiness and authenticity of qualitative research and accounts produced by the researcher (Guba and Lincoln, 1981; Lincoln and Guba, 1985).

Understanding the relationships between researchers and those they research is therefore a key part of appreciating the situatedness of all knowledge. Yet in contexts of researching one's employing or own organization issues of researcher involvement are particularly pertinent, as the boundaries between researcher and researched, as well as the spatial and temporal confines of where and when data are collected and when the research project is completed, become more ambiguous and open-ended.

My experience of conducing a social science research project set in my employing organization informs much of this chapter, as coping with the ambiguity of roles and boundaries turned out to be a conflict-ridden personal experience. As a researcher defined by the interpretive tradition, which stresses the importance of meaning in all social processes, I have put great value on understanding how meaning is generated in organizational contexts and in the interplay between social actors (see Tietze et al., 2003: 17–31). Writing this chapter is therefore a way of (re)articulating for its readers as well as for myself how the relationships and bonds between researcher and researched are part of the 'meaning' researchers make of their findings and of the research accounts they write and make available to a wider audience.

In the following, I will first discuss the relationship between the researcher and the researched, focusing on the issues that arise when researching one's employing organization. This includes a commentary on field roles and ethical involvements (see also Holt, in this volume). A section on 'reflexivity' (see also Haynes, in this volume) as central to qualitative-interpretive research then follows, and again, the discussion focuses on issues that are particularly pertinent when researching contexts one is familiar with. These discussions include a commentary on the precariousness, dilemmas and emotions that inform such 'bonds' of researcher and the researched in the context of researching one's own organization. From there on there follows an account of my own experience of conducting an ethnographic study set in an organization where I was both researcher and employee. This account will focus in particular on relationships with colleagues.

The Researcher–Researched Relationship

Work by scholars such as Becker (1967) and Berger and Luckman (1966), as well as the increasing involvement of women in academic research projects, had contributed to the dismantling of 'impartiality' and 'objective neutrality' as the only basis for investigating the social world. Instead, this had been increasingly seen as an intersubjective creation (Burr, 2003). This now being accepted, it is no longer possible to treat people as 'research objects', as 'mere mines of information' to be exploited by the researcher as the neutral collector of facts. Arendell (1997), for example, reports from her experience of interviewing men and argues that the relationship that evolved during the research process was influenced by the identities and histories of those involved and was activated as the researched asserted gendered hierarchies during the interview process. Cotterill (2002) also recounts issues of friendship, vulnerability and power as part of the process of interviewing women. In other words, these researchers started to pay attention to the notion that researching 'the other' always involves reflections on one's own position, purpose and sources of power as pre-knowledge and presuppositions are activated in establishing relationships with the researched. Imbued in such a stance *vis-à-vis* the researched is an ethics of involvement, which attempts to avoid potentially exploitative relationships; rather the researcher lays open to the respondents her/his dependence to provide access to their meaning-worlds and interpretations of circumstance. Establishing a deep relationship with the researched as people and agents in their own right is therefore a key task of qualitative reflexive researchers. Watson (1994), for example, begins his ethnography of managerial work by reproducing a piece of banter between himself and a manager who was employed by the organization Watson observed. This piece of banter is used as a rhetorical device to introduce the reader to the characters and people within the ethnography. In particular, the author, Watson, introduces himself as an active agent in the research process and uses the authorial voice 'I' and also refers to the person he exchanged banter with as 'my management friend' (Watson, 1994: 1) – pointing to the different roles and identities people take on or are given in such involved research.

The issues of involvement and establishing relationships with the researched are a key topic for all qualitative-interpretive research projects – one that comes more clearly and urgently to the fore when researching one's own organization or social context. In other words, it magnifies the issues that all qualitative researchers face when seeking close, sometimes even intimate involvement with the people whose meaning worlds they want to access and understand. Frequently, researchers will indeed focus their inquiry on aspects of their own work organization or professional setting – this is particularly so for (junior) researchers who may conduct empirical research for their thesis or dissertation in the context of their employing organization. In this regard they will bring their pre-understanding and preconceptions of organizational issues to the research scene. Importantly, they will have also already established a relationship with their potential respondents, i.e. their colleagues, because as researchers/employees they will carry particular organizational roles and positions in the organizational hierarchy. They will be – sometimes deeply – embedded in the organizational context they research. One could argue that this position makes it difficult to research one's own organization, as it has been argued that (qualitative) researchers should be like 'professional strangers' (Agar, 1980) – yet researchers who research their own organizations are already aware of their routines and practices, people and processes. They are not strangers. In this regard researching one's own organization, inclusive of pre-formed relationships, is a precarious balancing act between 'strangeness' and 'familiarity'. Researchers will have to find the means to render strange what is established as 'normal', that will find mechanisms that will distance themselves from what they already know. Such close engagement with the research scene and the researched can be an advantage, of course, as pre-existing ties could ensure access to organizational niches and nooks, which may remain hidden otherwise. Having a good network of accessible colleagues and (work) friends can also provide depth and colour to a research project. While not all projects focusing on one's own organization are necessarily auto-ethnographic in character (making the life experience of the ethnographer central to the ethnographic work; Coffey, 1999), all fieldwork conducted in a setting the researcher is familiar with evokes emotional and intellectual work, which is different from the emotional-intellectual work associated with 'normal' research projects (i.e. researching a 'strange' setting). As the engagement of the researcher with the researched is likely to last beyond the temporal boundaries of the research project, the stakes of the relationship between the two parties are higher than in more detached modes of engagement.

Reflexivity

Reflexivity challenges the notion that it is possible for researchers to be neutral automatons and implies that the orientations of researchers are shaped by their socio-historical location and in this regard the biography of the researcher informs the research. This is inclusive of the values and emotional dispositions that they bring to the research setting – indeed, some scholars would argue that research projects pose serious questions of 'identity' and 'self' for the researcher (Etherington, 2004). In this regard, part of the research process is to ask questions about one's own personal interest in the topic, one's presupposition and pre-knowledge; how do gender, class, ethnicity and nationality influence one's positioning in relation to the topic and the respondents? Cohen et al. (2009) provide a recent example of how researchers' sensibilities and circumstance inform the topic choice, reflection and theorizing on an issue of topical relevance, i.e. the relationship between home and work. The authors use their own lives and conversations they have with each other as fellow academics and friends to conduct a metaphorical analysis of their circumstances. Of interest here is the way the authors break traditional academic conventions about how to integrate examples and experiences from one's own life to make sense – and even theorize – institutional relationships (between home and work) from a personal yet also a theoretical perspective.

In work contexts, one might consider the impact of one's hierarchical position, one's degree of technical expertise, subject specialism or occupational knowledge as aspects that may influence how one is perceived as a researcher by the researched and how this might influence the interactions of the research process.

Ethics

The intersubjective nature of social and organizational life means that the researcher and the researched have shared meanings and that the researcher brings her methodological understanding to the research scene to develop this shared meaning into collective knowledge. Meaningful engagement and understanding between the two parties involved in academic inquiry can only happen if a degree of closeness, understanding, trust and openness is developed. Yet in this there also lies a danger or at least a dilemma: fieldwork, in particular ethnographic studies set in one's employing organization or such like, is 'up close and personal'. It has to be in order to be successful and meaningful. Yet, such 'closeness' breeds complications and conflict and poses some serious ethical dilemmas.

Fieldwork is a deliberate interruption of the respondents' lives with a view to generating understanding and knowledge. Indeed some anthropological scholars speak of the 'violence' of fieldwork, even if that violence is symbolic (e.g. Hastrup, 1992, quoted in England, 1994: 249; Okely and Callaway, 1992). In particular if relationships between researcher and researched are pre-established, friendly and personal, the greater the risk is for them to be potentially even more exploitative compared to more traditional methods, as such relationships are more open to manipulation and betrayal – by the researcher as well as by the researched. The line between gossip, chat, a research interview, the exchange of information and opinions melts into 'data'; the formal parameters of the research interview can burst boundaries as interviews are continued via chats by the coffee or photocopy machine. These encounters provide an opportunity to achieve genuine insights into the unfolding nature of organizational processes and human projects. Yet, ultimately, such words and talk become 'data', in that the 'lives, loves, and tragedies that fieldwork informants share with a researcher are ultimately data, grist for the ethnographic mill, a mill that has a truly grinding power' (Stacey, 1988: 23). The opportunities to blur relational and spatial boundaries in a research setting where the researcher is already an established member are manifold and tempting.

In other words, the researcher's task is to 'appropriate' the words and meanings of 'other people' with a view to turning them into written texts (thesis, reports, papers, articles). In my own experience, I have (not in my own organization) researched the consequences of flexible working from the perspectives of flexible workers and their families, their team leaders, senior managers and a host of other organizational stakeholders. There were occasions during this research project when, while listening sympathetically to the stories of flexible workers, I found myself thinking: 'this is a great quote for the paper on the hidden consequences of flexible work'. It is, in my view, inevitable that a researcher will 'objectify' a research participant at the very latest when 'data' are turned into written texts. As researchers who are researching their own organizations, such appropriation and objectification can be even more problematic as relationships continue to exist beyond the end of the research project, i.e. 'exiting the field' is not an easy option to evade potential conflicts and the complexities of 'tangled' relationships. On the contrary, the political and emotional dimensions of fieldwork and writing up fieldwork (Atkinson, 1990) become highlighted as the 'detachment' of the researcher from the research scene and its inhabitants is non-existent. Also, in transforming one's observations and interview data into written texts, the thoughts and meanings of the researched are opened up to public gaze and the scrutiny (and not even in 'their own words' and on 'their own terms', but through the interpretive filters of the researcher) not only of scholars and academics, but potentially also of their managers and bosses, their peers and (work) friends. This exposure is inevitable as the purpose of research will be to produce permanent, systematic and written accounts of the (empirical) study.

Field Roles – Between Familiarity and Strangeness

The question of which role to take on when conducting empirical research is of crucial importance for the researcher as this choice will influence how to engage with the researched or which parts of the organization one has access to or not. For researchers whose inquiry is set in their own organizational contexts, there are automatically several roles to be considered here. They are researchers as well as employees, managers, bosses, occupational experts, colleagues and friends. These different roles are sometimes hard to keep apart and in terms of conducting research in one's own setting it is not possible to enter and exit the field in the same way as an 'outsider' could do. Typologies for field roles for the researcher have been identified and discussed for many years (Gold, 1958; Junker, 1960; Adler and Adler, 1987). It is still useful to consider which role is appropriate along a continuum of conducting covert/overt research, to assess degrees of engagement/detachment from the research scene and subjectivity/objectivity in the production of research accounts (see Hammersley and Atkinson, 1995: 80–124 for an in-depth discussion). These roles can be dotted along a continuum between 'complete participant', 'participant-as-observer', 'observer-as-participant' and 'complete observer'. Scholars researching their own organization may be complete participants in terms of their employee roles and in this regard they will bring their experiences and perspectives to the scholarly inquiry. Indeed, in many instances there will have been a public announcement or acknowledgement that they are conducting a research project in the organization, so that a complete (and thus covert) participation is not possible. As researchers they are therefore more likely to 'participate and observe'. This juggling of an employee role with a researcher role requires a degree of emotional and intellectual flexibility in terms of handling researcher engagement with the research scene. Yet such flexibility needs to be balanced with having a firm stance about modes of engagement with the researched who may have developed different perspectives of what it means to be both a colleague and a research participant. They, for example, might differentiate between information provided in a research interview that can be used for research purposes, and informal exchanges over a cup of tea or coffee that they assume are 'personal' and not meant to be reproduced as 'quotes' in papers and texts.

Returning to Agar's (1980) notions of familiarity and strangeness, these can be drawn on to appreciate the precarious balancing act researchers in their own organizations have to maintain in order to gain access to the information/data/meaning they require so that they can address their research concerns while maintaining good relationships with their respondents. Familiarity is linked to a pre-engagement with the research scene and its inhabitants, with perceptions, perspectives and views that have been acquired through processes of occupational and organizational socialization. Strangeness is usually associated with entering the research setting as an outsider and the research process is seen as a process to render what is puzzling, new and 'strange' into something that is understood, meaningful and to be made sense of within selected academic conventions and traditions. Being both employee and researcher this process is somewhat different and less linear compared to entering a field as an 'outsider-researcher'. Researching one's own organization requires managing a simultaneous familiarity and strangeness in a way that focuses on addressing research issues. The researcher process entails asking questions about what is familiar and why; and how to render the familiar strange and novel in order to deepen the understanding of organizational processes. If the 'normal' (researcher entering research scene as stranger) process of research is to transform the 'unfamiliar' and 'strange' into the 'known' and 'familiar', the research process for the researcher-employee is reversed: the challenge is to transform the 'familiar' and 'known' into the 'strange' and 'unknown', with a view to generating a different and more informed understanding of the issues under investigation.

Isn't This a Bit Too Close to Home?[1] Experiences of Researching One's Own Organization

'Isn't it a bit close too home?' was a comment a colleague made when it had been announced via the email system that I was going to conduct research work for my doctoral thesis within my then employer, a university in the UK. This was uttered in passing as part of a corridor conversation; it nevertheless made me reflect about my involvement with the research scene and the organization I was about to explore in depth.

The background and rationale for my research were based on a deeply personal purpose, which was to resolve the 'linguistic confusion' I experienced at the time of entry into the organization and for many years afterwards. Both private and professional reasons had brought me, a German national steeped in the traditions of the humanities and the arts, to the UK, and my professional socialization fell into a period of change in the UK higher education sector as it expanded from an elite system to a mass education system. I experienced my socialization time as long and difficult as I could not make sense of certain words such as 'the student-customer', 'internal markets' or 'portfolio of activities'. Today I can theorize such introduction of new words and concepts as a discursive shift concomitant with a redefinition of the purpose of higher education and universities. However, back then I was not able to 'theorize' my confusion, despite being technically competent in the use of the English language and functioning well at work. Thus, my experience of trying to make sense of my own sector and circumstances provided the motivational basis for the selection of my broad research topic, which was to find out how 'language work' was essential to an understanding of organizational and cultural processes. My aim was to observe and record language use over a prolonged period of time. In the early stages, my main intent was to combine the pursuit of doctoral studies with the resolution of my 'puzzlement' and 'linguistically confused state'. In doing so, I also intended to make a contribution to the then expanding field of language-sensitive studies set in the context of work organizations.

[1]No talk data that are directly related to my PhD thesis will be used in this chapter. Narrating my account of the research process, I draw on memory only. This does reflect the meaning of what was said, rather than using the words that were uttered. This is partly to protect my former colleagues, but also to make the point that much of what we write about we retrieve from memory.

Initial perceptions of research

Following the announcement of my intent to research language-based organizational processes colleagues commented on my project. These remarks were mainly expressing interest and support, with some 'mild fun' being dispensed at times as my research interest in language was seen to be curious and intriguing as well as a little bit 'odd' and 'unworldly'. My position as a junior member of the faculty, together with my choice of research which was seen as slightly out of sync with the faculty's ambition and strategic drive, resulted in my being perceived as 'non-threatening' in terms of the information I might require. In many regards this worked to my advantage as observing quite senior management meetings, gaining access to documentation and arranging to talk to colleagues were easy to organize. In making field notes and conducting my research, my data collection proceeded nicely. Concomitant with the empirical work, my reading of the literature progressed and in particular David Lodge's (1977) *The Modes of Modern Writing* and Lakoff and Johnson's (1980) *Metaphors We Live By* provided theoretical trajectories that proved invaluable for the latter stages when I began to theorize my experiences and findings in terms of metaphorical (learning, developing, changing) and metonymical (ordering, categorizing, normalizing) processes.

Relationship with the researched

I want to use three examples that brought to the fore some dilemmas I faced in conducting my research. Partly, these experiences – and some difficulties – reflect a degree of naivety when I embarked on my project as I genuinely thought of my doctoral work as 'only' seeking understanding and developing conceptual advancement, rather than being embedded in political and power structures. However, let it be stated here that overall the experience of conducting research into my own organization was a positive one and colleagues were generous with their time, their willingness to speak freely, and also their desire to be quoted and 'heard'.

Relationship with senior managers

I sat in and observed senior management meetings in order to understand how 'words and meanings' were used and generated, by whom and in which contexts. Here, the relationship worked quite well. Being a junior member of staff (and female as opposed to the all male senior management team at the time) was helpful as colleagues liked to chat before or after meetings; sometimes they offered their particular interpretation of events or people or even added further comments and views. In one instance, it was expressed to me that my work ought to contribute to 'getting the message across' (i.e. how faculty needed to change), which I saw as a mild form of using my research to suit a particular interest. However, in my view no stronger or more direct attempts to influence my research were made.

At the stages of writing up my research and consequent publications however there was more interference, as I had to provide, for example, papers to a particular senior manager to be inspected. There was never a direct attempt to change or even comment on my papers, yet I was also asked to ensure that my written thesis would remain confidential for a period of two years as a minimum. Towards the end and nearer the writing-up period of my research, a degree of 'edginess' surrounding my research became more tangible and my realization grew that a language-focused project was no longer perceived as innocent and harmless as it had been in its early stages. At a 'PhD student conference' at which I presented some findings, the attending professors commented about the academic merit of the work. Afterwards I remember being advised to be careful about how I would handle the data and how I would use these. While relations with senior managers I met with at other times to discuss the written outputs remained cordial, there was also an undertone of wariness and nervousness in the conversations I had with them.

Peer relationships

Mainly, I worked with colleagues and peers; happily drifting between my research and employee identity, both developing and changing in the light of their mutual enactment.

There were two such relationships with colleagues, which triggered in me feelings of unease and tension. The first instance relates to two colleagues who were of similar age to me, yet much more advanced in career terms, as they had achieved senior and strategic positions in the faculty. They were using 'words' in different ways from other colleagues and therefore I wanted to understand their perspectives on the faculty and the university. My internalized norms required me to see them as peers and equals, friendly colleagues with whom I shared a certain socialization experience. Yet, mainly I felt inadequate and somehow 'not up to scratch' when comparing myself to them. In one case I decided not to seek this colleague out for a further interview – although she clearly symbolized a new model of career and 'talk' in the newly emergent faculty structures. I can now look at my choice and see it as an unease about or inability to deal with the simultaneous existence of hierarchical differences, peer relationships, gender and age dimensions. Yet, at the time I simply decided 'not to go there' and in research terms my decision implied the exclusion of particular perspectives and interpretations from my work.

Another emotionally fraught relationship concerned a colleague with whom I taught on a module. My 'problem' was that I did not respect this colleague very much, as the teaching relationship was difficult and characterized by differences about assessments. However, this colleague was helpful to the extent of volunteering himself as a potential interviewee. I felt unable to decline his offer. The specific interview with him was long and long-winded, in my view. Yet from this interview I used many of his interpretations and views later on when revisiting my scripts and when theorizing this experience, as some of his views entailed almost poetic comments and summaries on his painful experiences of changing contexts and meanings in the context of higher education.

Peer relationships: betrayal

In the final stages of my research I asked some female colleagues whether they would work with me to capture the particular view of women on the change process in higher education and the university. I had made it clear to them that I intended to take notes and write a conference paper based on my findings. The meeting went well, it was cordial and chatty, many a story was told and views were exchanged freely. Having turned my interpretation of this event into a conference paper and before submitting it to the conference convenors, I sent it to these colleagues for their perusal. Not expecting much in terms of comments, I was taken by surprise by some of the reactions, which were bordering on the fierce and requested changes to the paper or for particular contributions and involvements to be completely removed. There were also arguments pointing out that the paper was 'only' my interpretations and therefore not a 'true' account of what my colleagues had said and in particular what they had meant by their words. While relationships did not break down in the context of the 'group interview', there was a definite 'cooling off' and a general increase in wariness between colleagues and myself. I remember having to work hard at the time in order to appease and alleviate their fears, while feeling at the same time misunderstood and hard done by. Ultimately, this paper was never made publicly available.

Reflections

Overall and with hindsight these events point to the emotional, gendered and political nature of fieldwork – a fact I had read about as part of my literature review, but that I had not associated with my 'harmless' study of words and meanings.

First, my 'juniority' in the hierarchy of the faculty helped me to gain access to meetings, information and participants' perspectives. Here, my relatively junior status was overall helpful and in particular for capturing the views of senior management. Yet, the insecurities related to my junior status when talking to two particular colleagues similar in age, yet much senior in terms of their hierarchical position, resulted in my decision not to seek a closer collaborative relationship with one of them – thus potentially limiting a source of useful and meaningful information. It is only in writing this chapter, many years after the completion of my doctoral thesis, that I have realized it was the female of these two colleagues whom I found more troublesome to work with – a reflection of gendered relationships, perhaps, in particular the female–female ones?

Second, the further my work proceeded and took shape, and the nearer thoughts and ideas came to be expressed in a thesis and papers, the more complicated and precarious the research process became. Writing research accounts is part of the scholarly project and it renders permanence, consequence and substance to 'insubstantial talk' and 'ideas'. This transformative process makes research potentially dangerous to participants as their words and speech translate into interpretations and written accounts. They become re-appropriated in contexts that are embedded in political and power structures. Frequently, issues of the re-appropriation of meaning come to the fore at the early stages of research when access is negotiated (and frequently declined). Yet in my particular case, it was at the later stages of the research process when the 'permanence' and 'consequence' of the written text provoked reactions. Also, these reactions at the time appeared to me exaggerated, unfair even, because after all I had informed all participants that I was working as a researcher and that therefore their spoken words might be turned into written accounts. Yet writing today, I can see colleagues' reactions as being informed by a different rationality: when reading my written interpretation of their words, they responded within their particular contexts, which went far beyond the confines of the chatty, animated meeting with colleagues as the written account evoked the political, ongoing and precarious contexts of their everyday lives. They also responded epistemologically by pointing to the notion of my account 'only' being my interpretation and as such 'not true'. The reactions were emotional, possibly driven by nervousness, yet they also indicated a sense of the betrayal my interpretation had caused, as colleagues felt that I had used their personal involvement and friendly relationships for academic gain without taking their positions and contexts into account.

Third, emotions, my own and those of colleagues, played a continuous part in the research process. In this regard the research process is an emotional process, which using reflective hindsight is related to the blurring of boundaries between myself as researcher and as employee, each of which required different dispositions and modes of engagement with the researched. At the same time the researched made themselves available as informants and participants, but they also remained colleagues, allies, friends or foes. In blurring such boundaries interesting data may be collected – albeit too easily at the expense of relationships that will have to last beyond the temporal parameters of a research project.

In addition, my own emotional disposition *vis-à-vis* colleagues was laid bare as the research process forced me to face some home truths about my own gendered behaviour and my sometimes contradictory position about balancing my academic and organizational ambition with a tempered view of preserving some scepticism and distance about career advancement. With hindsight, I can see myself now at a crucial stage of my career and life, where I had to decide what kind of academic I wanted to become and at what cost. Thus, my own precarious sensibilities were played out through the enactment of the dual role of researcher/colleague for a while.

In my view the greatest challenge of this mode of engagement is to establish and protect meaningful and authentic relationships in the light of the possibility of exercising 'symbolic violence' that implies the manipulative engagement of those one involves in the research.

Generating Knowledge: Experiences Recollected in Tranquillity

In my work, past and present, acts of theorizing have helped me to achieve a degree of detachment from the emotional dilemmas and encounters of fieldwork.

In the case of my doctoral work, theorizing was not only a necessity to make sense of the data, it also removed me from the research setting, from colleagues, from politics, and an emotional entanglement with people. The process of developing conceptual understanding requires abstracting oneself from the immediate context, so that in writing one oscillates between experience, pure and raw, and reflection, pure and calm. In my doctoral work, I experienced an aloofness when analysing my fieldwork notes. To an extent, the analytic process was a more peaceful period in which the emergence of conceptual understanding replaced the immediate experience of relationships and vested interests. Briefly, my theorizing addressed the budding interest of organizational scholars in rhetorical figures, in particular metaphors, but also in metonymy and irony. Thus the development of a 'tropological approach' in order to understand language use and meaning making in one organizational setting was my theoretical contribution to knowledge. Personally, at the end of my doctoral thesis, my initial experience of linguistic confusion had been addressed. I could now describe my confusion more concisely and in terms that allowed me to resolve it. A year after my completion of the thesis, I left the organization as part of a career move. Most of the relationships I formed in these early and difficult years have remained cordial and conflicts and tensions have become part of a mutually shared past.

Guidelines for Qualitative Researchers

Following on from the lessons learned, there is some advice I can offer to researchers embarking on a project set in the context of their employing organization. It mainly entails aspects for developing awareness of the emotional aspects of relationships, their management over time and beyond the research project's temporal boundaries. It also relates to the acknowledgement of one's own views, as well as emotional and social dispositions.

- Your research is informed by your background and situation and these form the bedrock of your research from the articulation of themes, topics and questions to the design and execution of the empirical work and also to writing your accounts. As you are the research instrument par excellence, you form part of your own inquiry. Be aware and honest about how such involvement may frame how you formulate and execute your research and also how you write about it.

- Researching includes the production of written accounts and making them available to the world. There are two issues to consider here: a) which authorial voice you will adopt, i.e. from which position will you write your account; b) how any written account bestows permanence to your research and is subject to readers' interpretation. This renders a written account potentially dangerous to participants and to yourself. Other than adhering to the ethical guidelines of your employer/professional body (e.g. adhering to the rules about confidentiality and anonymity), how will you protect those involved in the research (see also Holt, in this volume)?

- Following on from there, your engagement with the researched will bring into play dual identities played out by yourself, the researcher-employee, and the researched colleagues. The blurring of boundaries between roles and identities is perhaps the most beneficial aspect of researching one's own organization. At the same time it is also the most difficult one as such blurring may lead to unclear situations, implicit expectations and assumptions about the research process and outcome.

- Emotions form part of the research process. At times the 'emotionality' of engagement may take forms that can be both highly conducive or highly detrimental to the achievement of your research aims. In the first instance, you need to be aware of your own emotions and manage them as a normal and sensitizing process of your research.

- The role of theory and conceptual work is part and parcel of the academic project. In addition, the abstracting and analytical framing of data in the vocabularies and meaning systems of particular traditions can assist in rendering 'strange' the 'all-too-familiar' and the 'all-too-emotional'. The use of theory can be activated almost as a Brechtian alienation effect to counter-balance the familiarity and closeness concomitant with researching one's own organization with a measure of intellectual detachment.

Conclusion

Research enquiry is positioned in the tension between what is 'familiar' and what is 'strange'. Much of our understanding of what good research is about centres on the assumption that good research makes the 'strange' more 'familiar' and known. This assumption is, perhaps, in itself debatable as one always brings pre-supposition and pre-knowledge to the research scene, so that what the researcher already knows and assumes is an intrinsic part of any enquiry. Yet, in cases where researchers investigate their own (employing) organization, the research process is to an extent reversed, i.e. it is about making the 'familiar' 'strange'. In doing so, research questions, issues and objectives become entangled in blended identities and relationships within social, emotional and gendered contexts of hierarchy and power. Developing the reflective awareness and ability to address such contexts is part of becoming a researcher and is particularly so in the context of researching one's own organization.

Further Reading

In his (1994) book *Language Shock: Understanding the Culture of Conversation* Michael Agar proposes that language and culture are inseparably linked. Understanding one's own assumptions about language use, conversation and knowledge is linked to an understanding of language use as a social and cultural practice. The book is helpful in introducing different theoretical approaches to understanding language and developing language-sensitive, theoretically grounded approaches to research projects.

Paul Atkinson's (1990) *The Ethnographic Imagination* points to the importance of writing research accounts and the construction of texts as deliberately shaped knowledge accounts. This includes the conventions and expectations of audiences who might read these accounts. It is helpful to appreciate the importance and processes of writing research accounts.

Howard Becker's volume of essays, *Sociological Work* (1970), contains one essay titled 'Whose side are you on?'. Here, Becker proposes that every researcher takes sides and that this is a normal, but often denied part of social science research. This essay helped me to acknowledge and accept my involvement and the perspectives in my research.

In Bridge and Baxter's (1992) 'Blended relationships: Friends as work associates', the authors provide interesting examples, based on their empirical research, about working with friends, who are also research respondents.

Jennifer Moon's (2004) *A Handbook of Reflective and Experiential Learning* is an instructive text on learning and reflection and can be related easily to the researcher's experience. It also provides useful inputs on reflective writing, including the use of diaries and logs – these may be techniques that can be drawn upon to keep a record of the research process.

For a good variety of chapters on different aspects of the researcher and author-self and their involvement in auto-ethnographic writing, see Deborah Reed-Danahay's (1997) edited volume, *Autho/Ethnography: Rewriting the Self and the Social.*

John Van Maanen's (1988) *Tales of the Field: On Writing Ethnography* offers different approaches to writing ethnographic accounts, based on different epistemological positions and therefore employing different rhetorical means of persuasion. It is a stimulating text to read and helpful in providing ideas about how writing research accounts, and how to cope, rhetorically, with issues of researcher involvement.

T.J. Watson's (1995) 'Rhetoric, discourse and argument in organizational sense making: a reflexive tale' is a research account based on an ethnographic study of a company in the UK. The author worked there for a long period of time and the account is a good example of a style of writing which makes the author's voice central to the account and also 'reveals' how his thinking shaped the interpretation and analysis of data.

References

Adler, P.A. and Adler, P. (1987) *Membership Roles in Field Research*. Newbury Park, CA: Sage.

Agar, M. (1980) *The Professional Stranger*. Chicago: University of Chicago Press.

Agar, M. (1994) *Language Shock. Understanding the Culture of Conversation*. New York: William Morrow and Company, Inc.

Arendell, T. (1997) 'Reflections on the researcher-researched relationship: a woman interviewing men', *Qualitative Sociology*, 20 (3): 341–368.

Atkinson, P. (1990) *The Ethnographic Imagination: textual constructions of reality*. London: Routledge.

Becker, H. (1967) 'Whose side are you on?', *Social Problems*, 14 (3): 239–247.

Becker, H. (1970) *Sociological Work*. London.

Berger, P.L. and Luckman, T. (1966) *The Social Construction of Reality: A Treatise in the Sociology of Knowledge*. London: Penguin.

Bridge, K. and Baxter, L.A. (1992) 'Blended relationships: Friends as work associates', *Western Journal of Communication*, 56: 200–225.

Burr, V. (2003) *An Introduction to Social Constructionism* (2nd edn). Hove: Routledge.

Coffey, A. (1999) *The Ethnographic Self: Fieldwork and Representation of Identity*. London: Sage.

Cohen, L., Duberley, J. and Musson, G. (2009) 'Work-life balance? An autoethnographic exploration of everyday home-work dynamics', *Journal of Management Inquiry*, 18 (3): 229–241.

Costley, C., Elliott, G. and Gibbs, P. (2010) *Work-based Research: Approaches to Enquiry for Insider-Researcher*. London: Sage.

Cotterill, P. (2002) 'Interviewing women: issues of friendship, vulnerability and power', *Women's Studies International Forum*, 15: 593–606.

England, K.V.L. (1994) 'Getting personal: reflexivity, positionality, and feminist research', *The Professional Geographer*, 46 (1): 80–89.

Etherington, K. (2004) *Becoming a Reflexive Researcher: Using Our Selves in Research*. London and Philadelphia: Jessica Kinsley.

Fisher, C. and Tietze, S. (2010) 'Doctor of Business Administration: DBA Programmes in the UK', in T. Fell, K. Flint and I. Haines (eds), *Professional Doctorates in the UK*. Staffordshire: UK Council for Graduate Education, pp. 40–45.

Gold, R.L. (1958) 'Roles in sociological fieldwork', *Social Forces*, 36: 217–223.

Guba, E.G. and Lincoln, Y.S. (1981) *Effective Evaluation: Improving the Effectiveness of Evaluation Results through Responsive and Naturalistic Approaches*. San Francisco, CA: Jossey-Bass.

Hammersley, M. and Atkinson, P. (1995) *Ethnography: Principles in Practice* (2nd edn). London and New York: Routledge.

Hastrup, K. (1992) 'Writing ethnography', in J. Okely, and H. Callaway, (eds), *Anthropology and Autobiography*. London: Routledge, pp. 115–132.

Junker, B. (1960) *Field Work*. Chicago: University of Chicago Press.

Lakoff, G. and Johnson, M. (1980) *Metaphors We Live By*. London and Chicago: University of Chicago Press.

Lincoln, Y.S. and Guba, E.G. (1985) *Naturalistic Inquiry*. Beverly Hills, CA: Sage.

Lodge, D. (1977) *The Modes of Modern Writing: Metaphor, Metonymy and the Typology of Modern Literature*. London: Arnold.

Moon, J. (2004) *A Handbook of Reflective and Experiential Learning: Theory and Practice*. Oxford: Taylor and Francis.

Okely, J. and Callaway, H. (eds) (1992) *Anthropology and Autobiography*. London: Routlege.

Reed-Danahay, D. (ed.) (1997) *Autho/Ethnography: Rewriting the Self and the Social*. Oxford: Berg.

Stacey, J. (1988) 'Can there be a feminist ethnography?', *Women's Studies International Forum*, 11: 21–27.

Tietze, S., Cohen, L. and Musson, G. (2003) *Understanding Organizations Through Language*. London: Sage.

Van Maanen, J. (1988) *Tales of the Field: On Writing Ethnography*. Chicago: University of Chicago Press.

Watson, T.J. (1994) *In Search of Management: Culture, Chaos and Control in Managerial Work*. London: Routledge.

Watson, T.J. (1995) 'Rhetoric, discourse and argument in organizational sense making: a reflexive tale', *Organization Studies*, 6 (3): 805–821.

2 Focus Groups

Binna Kandola

Introduction

The use of focus groups in the social sciences waxes and wanes depending on the prevailing attitude towards them and the popularity of alternative approaches. Although the last 20 years have seen an increase in their use for research purposes, they have been used as a research tool for nearly a century. Stewart et al. (2007) identify three influences on focus group methodology:

- Sociology and social psychology.
- Clinical psychology.
- Market research.

Researchers with a sociology or social psychology background tended to use the method to gain insights into group-related topics such as social interaction and cohesion. These applications broadened out in the 1940s with the advent of radio. Broadcasters and researchers were interested in finding out why some programmes were more popular than others. Technology was created that enabled group participants to press buttons while listening to a programme indicating whether they liked or disliked something. Modern versions of these devices are still in use today. There was, in other words, a focus on the research, as all data were obtained from groups of people. The clinical psychology approach was less direct, preferring people to discuss whatever it was they wanted to give expression to. This type of approach was more influenced by psychotherapy and facilitators tended to have a psychotherapeutic background. Market researchers, however, tended to be less concerned about the theoretical background and would use whatever technique and methodology they felt was appropriate. This might sometimes be less rigorous but it shows us that the focus group is a versatile and adaptable method, which can be fun as well as informative. Following these traditions, the roots of focus groups can be traced back to the early twentieth century.

However, if you look beyond the social sciences to other disciplines you will find methods that appear remarkably like focus groups but are called something else. In design, architecture and engineering circles there is a technique called the charette. This enables stakeholders to have their say in, for example, the design of a building. This approach has its roots in the nineteenth century and possibly earlier. So focus groups, or other variations, have a long history.

Now before going any further it is important to recognize here that my own approach to focus groups owes more to the sociological and social psychological tradition than to the others. And while not being a market researcher I do believe that we can apply different formats to focus group discussions and data gathering.

Projects using focus groups as the primary source of information can run into a number of difficulties. These include:

- Clarifying what the project is about and how focus groups can help.
- Identifying who you would like to have attending the groups in the first place.
- Communicating the purpose of the group to ensure people turn up.
- Ensuring that everyone participates in the meeting.
- Having a clear methodology.
- Analysing the results.
- Having facilitator skills.

In other words, running focus groups successfully requires much more than just facilitating sessions: there is a lot of planning, communication and persuasion involved. So unless these factors are considered, no matter how good the facilitation itself is, the overall result will not be a good one. In the remainder of this chapter each of these issues is addressed in turn.

Clarity of Purpose: Why Would You Use Focus Groups?

Focus groups are almost an everyday tool in marketing and political circles, typically being used to provide in-depth insights into, for example, products, brands and policies. When skilfully handled, they can tease out how people feel about a given topic and these data are clearly useful in advertising, presenting and generally communicating information to the general public. There are also many other uses for focus groups (Schafer, 1990).

Focus groups work particularly well when researchers are trying to explore people's feelings and experiences in more depth than can be obtained from a survey, for example. They can help to determine the mood or climate regarding a particular topic and can also help in providing ideas for future actions that an organization can take.

The first step towards having focus groups requires researchers to know why they are being used. It also means they must think through the alternatives to using them. It then requires that they be clear about what the purposes of the study are and how the data are going to be used.

Sampling

This can be a tricky area. Occasionally there will be few or no restrictions about the number of focus groups that are to be carried out but this is rare. Usually there will be restrictions on time and budget, which means thinking carefully about the number of focus groups to be conducted, where they will be held, and the number of people that will need to be involved. As with a lot of things regarding focus group these questions will be answered more through art than science. Political considerations will often come into play, e.g. all functions will expect to be involved; all the regions will need to be covered.

Apart from that the numbers to be seen will really depend upon the nature and complexity of the topic being investigated. If, for example, this is the experiences of women in non-stereotypical roles, it may be necessary to carry out focus groups with women at different levels in the organization – those in general management positions as well as those in specialist positions – and at different office locations. Such analysis, however, will require increasing the number of groups. Mixing the focus groups in terms of levels, geography, etc. is also an option but this requires the facilitator or moderator to be able to dissect the opinions of the different people involved rather skilfully. It needs to be acknowledged, however, that such fine-grain analyses are very difficult to achieve a high degree of reliability from focus groups. Ideally what researchers really want to achieve is to be able to call a halt when they think they are gaining no new insights or information from the focus groups they are conducting.

This of course means that they are analysing the focus groups as they are being conducted rather than waiting for all the data collection to be completed before examining them.

Communication

The focus groups obviously need sufficient numbers of people to attend them to make them effective. This means not having so many that people feel intimidated or unable to contribute because of the sheer numbers involved. But it also means not having so few so that researchers become concerned that their opinions and views do not reflect those of the wider population.

Communication therefore is of great importance. People need to be aware of:

- The purpose of the meeting.
- The outputs of the study.
- The reason why they have been chosen.
- The practicalities and logistics of the session, e.g. where it is being held, timings, etc..

Sometimes inducements may be necessary and even when not needed, these may be offered. This could be as straightforward as offering a nice lunch, inclusion in a prize draw or even some financial reward, e.g. money or vouchers. The idea behind doing so is, of course, to ensure people turn up rather than to persuade them to reflect a particular point of view (which of course would be bribery!).

Communicating the project to the intended participants needs to be done in good time so that they can put the dates in their diaries. Four to six weeks notice is typically about what is needed, with a reminder closer to the event. There should be a contact point for participants to get in touch regarding confirmation of attendance and to answer any queries that people may have.

If researchers are conducting focus groups for research purposes within an organization it is always helpful that they get the support and sponsorship of someone senior. Ideally the communication should then come from both individuals, i.e. the researcher and the sponsor, but not necessarily jointly. A message from the senior sponsor could say, for example, that a piece of research is going to be carried out by an independent academic. It could also say why the research is important to the organization and that people's participation would be welcome. At a not too distant point later, say a few days maximum, a message from the researcher would build on the sponsor's comments, providing more detail on the method and reinforcing the confidential nature of the project. Separating this communication helps to establish this independence of the research.

It is not uncommon at the start of a session to find that people will complain that they have no idea what the focus group is about and that they were told by their line manager that they needed to attend. In other words, this is not the ideal start. Clear, timely information will therefore help to create the right impression before the session itself starts. Once people are in the room it is important that the facilitator establishes their credibility, confidence and confidentiality.

Credibility is partly about sharing relevant experiences with the participants and it is also partly about communicating with confidence. This sharing of experience, in my view, needs to be done relatively briskly – namely walking the fine line between conveying expertise and bragging. On the one hand, the participants need to feel they are in capable hands in this session, with someone who knows what they are doing and will guide them expertly through the next few hours or so. This helps to allay any potential anxieties the participants may have. On the other hand, they must not come across as someone who considers themselves superior to the people in the room, which will only serve to create a gulf between facilitator and participant and this will mean that people will feel too inhibited to participate. This may sound a little harsh but academic researchers can sometimes let themselves down by not appearing professional enough early enough.

By confidence I mean that people should feel able to speak up. This is dependent on the skills of the facilitator, the process that is being operated and the general behaviour of the other participants. In short it is about the environment in which the discussion takes place. The facilitator needs to ensure that everyone understands that all views related to the topic are welcome. This will mean that early on in the discussion it is established that all views and opinions are going to be taken seriously and that nothing will be considered frivolous or silly: there will be no value judgements made about their comments. Clearly, this is partly connected to the process being followed and we will come to this shortly. However, it is mainly due to the skills and style of the facilitator. A dismissive style, misrepresenting what people are saying or allowing people to criticize the comments from others are just some of the things that can inhibit discussions.

Having said this, it is important that the discussion is not dominated by one or two people, which if researchers are not careful can be a fairly typical occurrence. In such situations the facilitator will need to ensure that they remain in charge of the discussion, encouraging the talkative members to rein themselves in for a moment in order for other people to have their voices heard. The facilitator will need to make it clear that while the individuals' contributions are welcome it would be good to hear from others in the room. It requires a degree of firmness to carry this out while at the same time ensuring that the vocal person is still encouraged to participate.

Confidentiality is part of the way in which the facilitator can create a confidence in others to talk freely but it is also of such importance that specific reference needs to be made to it. It sounds like a straightforward topic: everything that is said in the room will be treated in confidence. As with most things though it is not necessarily as simple as it may seem. For example, the rules of confidentiality should not apply if the facilitator hears of any illegal activity or action that could be a hazard to health and safety. Outside of these circumstances though it is difficult to think of a situation where the facilitator would have to break the confidentiality rule: indeed it is most important that they abide by it.

Sometimes the organization may ask for information about what happened in a focus group, who said what and what is emerging from the research. Through conversations like this, especially if it is with someone researchers trust, it would be easy to let their guard drop and divulge information that was given in good faith by participants. Researchers may sometimes feel the pressure because it is the sponsor who is asking the question and the research is dependent on their continued support. Despite this it is critical that the desire to please does not override their better judgement. In a meeting recently, the contact, a very rigorous and scrupulous individual, asked me whether it might be possible to have the transcripts of the things people had said in the groups. He wanted these so that he and his team could analyse them further. He also wanted to see whether they could identify any differences between ethnic groups, gender, etc. When we said he would be unable to do this because we had promised the participants that the material would be handled in confidence he immediately recognized the error he had made and apologized.

Confidentiality among the participants, however, is a different matter altogether. Facilitators can only ask participants to agree to keep things in confidence, but they cannot ensure that this will be the case.

On one occasion a colleague conducted a focus group and gained participants' support for the need to maintain confidentiality. During the discussion a member of staff, who was not present in the room, was referred to. Although no names had been shared another participant was able to recognize who was being discussed and on leaving the focus group told her friend what had been said about her. This person, unhappy at what had been discussed, then issued a grievance against the person making the remarks. This was subsequently not upheld on investigation, but it does show firstly the importance of laying down the ground rules and secondly the difficulties of ensuring participants do not divulge confidences themselves. It also highlights the fine line that one needs to tread between encouraging a discussion but not allowing other people to be criticized, particularly those who are not present.

Ensuring Everyone Participates

The whole point of a focus group is to hear the views of a number of people, not just one or two of them. If the discussion is dominated by a small group of individuals this clearly defeats the object of the exercise. It is important therefore that a good process is employed, which ensures that everyone feels able to participate and their views are considered to be valued and legitimate.

A simple process, introduced to me by Sylvia Downs, a former colleague, has proved to be enormously effective. The focus group participants should be asked to work in pairs (this is usually done by working with the person next to them, but does not have to be). Questions that need to be responded to are then introduced one at a time. Participants are given time to discuss and record their responses on paper or flipcharts. Once the question has been considered the facilitator asks for each pair in turn to give one of their ideas, observations or comments. The facilitator writes down what they say onto a flipchart before asking the next pair for their comments. This process continues until all the pairs have exhausted their comments. At this point, the facilitator can ask for an elaboration of some of the remarks made or specific examples to illustrate what was said.

So that is an overview for what the process is, but the thing that makes it effective is the micro behaviour of the facilitator and an understanding of why things must be done in a certain way.

Pairs

People work in twos for the simple reason that a conversation needs to take place. In small groups with even as few as three people, one person could take a back seat and not participate at all. In a pair, even if one person does all the talking the other at the very least has to listen. So working in pairs is an effective way of getting people involved without feeling exposed. Allowing them to discuss their thoughts and ideas first also enables people to get their voices heard and to rehearse what they are going to say before sharing it with the wider group.

Asking each pair in turn

This is important and each pair must be given the opportunity to speak without being interrupted by others. Giving them this space establishes the ethos that everyone is going to be heard. Furthermore, as it is a response from a two-member team, no person is necessarily personally exposed.

Writing comments onto a flipchart

The idea here is that the participants can see how their comments are being recorded publicly. As far as possible the facilitator must always use the words that the participants use. Too often facilitators can summarize, or see what they do as summarizing, but in doing so can subtly alter the meaning of what is said. If views are to be condensed it is important that the facilitator first checks with the participants to ensure that they are happy with the paraphrasing. Not only does this maintain the integrity of the data collection it also helps to create an atmosphere of openness and transparency.

Moving onto the next pair

Researchers should always ask people for a comment. They must be careful when people say, 'Our idea is already up there' as this may indicate a reluctance to speak up. If they say this then they should ask them to share their thoughts anyway as sometimes these can be subtly but distinctively different even though superficially they appear to be the same.

Continuing until all the points are collected

Often we will find that we must do two more rounds of the room to get all the ideas and comments out. After a couple of rounds we may just ask if there are any other points people want to make that haven't been captured already.

Asking for examples or further elaboration

Once the ideas have been collected researchers can ask people to provide a clarification of anything that appears unclear. They could also ask for examples to illustrate what is meant by a particular comment. It is important that these examples are specific and have been witnessed by the people themselves, i.e. not based on hearsay (I will discuss below how such examples can be collected using the Critical Incident Technique).

Having a colleague to act as a scribe

In order to record the examples correctly it is useful to have a colleague present who can act as a scribe. They should note down what the person says in their own words as far as possible. The facilitator and scribe should repeat back the example to ensure that they have understood and recorded the example in a way that the participant understands and agrees with.

Moving on to the next question

The above process can be followed for all subsequent questions; however, facilitators should start with a new flip chart page when getting the feedback.

The above process is deceptively simple but it enables:

- A climate of openness to be established.
- Trust to be conveyed by and developed with the facilitators.
- Everyone to participate.

- Views to be aired.
- The recording of comments and views to be correct.

Methodology

The above process and principles can be applied to almost any focus group methodology. In this section I would like to discuss some different approaches that can be used in focus groups: keys to understanding; the critical incident technique (CIT); the repertory grid; and appreciative inquiry.

Keys to understanding

The 'keys to understanding' (Pearn and Mulrooney, 1995) are essentially a framework for asking questions, which has been shown to be highly effective. Designed to be used to help people learn new concepts, the keys can be usefully applied to focus groups settings. There are five keys:

1. *Purpose* – exploring the possible purposes of something.
2. *Comparison* – how it compares and contrasts with something already familiar to the participants.
3. *Viewpoints* – how it is seen from different people's perspectives.
4. *Problems* – what problems will or might arise?
5. *Checks* – how can we check or evaluate our understanding?

So, for example, if the focus group concerned employee wellbeing, the keys could be used to shape the questions to be asked.

1. What purposes do you think are served by focusing on the wellbeing of our employees? (Purpose).
2. How does our approach to wellbeing compare with other organizations' approaches? (Comparison).
3. How is the wellbeing programme viewed by different groups of people, e.g. front-line staff, management, senior management? (Viewpoints).

4 What problems have arisen in the implementation of the programme? (Problems).

5 How could you tell if the programme was working effectively? (Checks).

A final question could be: 'What actions would you suggest we take to make the programme truly effective?'

This is an example but it shows how the keys to understanding can be used to set both breadth and depth around a specific topic. When used in conjunction with the process for facilitation outlined earlier, it can prove to be very effective.

Critical incident technique

This methodology was designed shortly after the Second World War by John C. Flanagan (1954). The focus of this method uses specific examples relevant to the topic that the participant is directly involved in or observes first hand. The example or incident has to be *critical,* i.e. the outcomes are either very successful or unsuccessful.

The key steps involve describing:

- The background to the incident, e.g. when and where.
- What exactly happened in the situation and why it was so critical.
- The feelings of different people and the actions taken.
- The outcomes.

Again the sequence of steps makes this easy to follow in focus group settings. Using the wellbeing study, the question asked of the group could be: 'Think of an example where something occurred in the organization that you witnessed which had a significant impact either positively or negatively on your own personal wellbeing or someone you work with'.

Participants are then asked to share the example or examples with their partner and focus on:

- What action was taken.
- How people felt about it.
- The outcomes and effect it had on the participant and the people around them.

This technique differs from the others in that it provides detailed examples rather than pithier observations, which can be more easily bullet pointed on a flip chart. It also requires the facilitator, while the incident is being recalled, to be thinking about what further information is required to ensure that the example is as full and complete as it can be.

When CIT is used in interview situations it is dependent on the interviewee's perception of the incident. A benefit and potential drawback of the group discussion is that others may chip in with their views on what happened and why. This is acceptable and to be encouraged only insofar as the original contributor agrees with the others' view. The advantage of this method is that it involves real situations and as a consequence can provide a genuine insight into actual behaviours that are either effective or ineffective. The storytelling approach also means that it is inherently interesting.

In group settings of course extra effort has be taken to ensure anonymity and confidentiality. However, the nature of some critical incidents will mean that other people, who are not directly involved, may either have heard of what happened and/or know the principal characters involved. The rules around confidentiality therefore need to be stressed. It can also suffer from the recency effect, i.e. people remembering events that occurred more recently. If incidents are recalled from longer ago, however, some information may be forgotten and may be mis-remembered and distorted.

Repertory grid technique

The repertory grid (RG) technique is the methodology devised as part of George Kelly's (1991) personal construct theory (PCT). In essence the theory says that we all make sense of the world in different ways. The way we analyse events, perceive people, etc. is determined by our schema, or constructs, and these are individual and personal. The theory is of less relevance here but the method of eliciting the constructs is important and this is known as the repertory grid technique.

The facilitator has a number of elements related to the topic being discussed. Elements are examples of what is being examined and they should be as concrete as possible. There could be eight to twelve of these (it is likely that some preparatory work will have been needed to establish which elements would be the most relevant).

In the focus group three elements will be chosen, either by the facilitator or one of the participants. The participants must then identify the way in which two of the elements are similar and different from the third. As the process is personal, different combinations of elements will be made and different constructs will emerge. This is all fine, fun and interesting. It is the role of the facilitator to explore the constructs in more detail to find out what exactly is meant. A scribe is also of great use here. It is not suprising if only three or four iterations of the process are all that can be carried out in a three-hour session.

The elements for a wellbeing study could include different types of initiatives or benefits, e.g. head massages, gym memberships, home working.

A final step could include creating a grid with the elements across the top and the constructs down the side. Each element would then be rated against each comment. Every person would do this and the grid would be analysed using specialist software designed for this purpose. In practice this can often be very time consuming and may not be possible in time constrained consultancy assignments, but the academic researchers may find this a worthwhile exercise.

The RG is a good technique to enable a discussion around specific elements of the topic in question, which other methods do not do. It can, with the right group, produce a wealth of information, which can of course then create problems of its own in terms of getting this analysed. It requires strong facilitation to get the best out of it and to ensure that the group stays on track.

Appreciative inquiry

The basic tenet of 'appreciative inquiry' (Watkins and Mohr, 2001) is to focus on what is good and effective about an organization and use this as the starting point for any future change. The approach is based on what is known as the four Ds:

- *Discover*: trying to find out what works well currently.
- *Dream*: visioning what perfection would be like.
- *Design*: creating the perfect process.
- *Destiny*: what we are going to do next to ensure that the design is delivered.

As with the keys of understanding, the four Ds are readily translatable into focus group formats. So, using the same wellbeing topic as earlier, the questions would be:

- In terms of employee wellbeing, what works well currently? (Discover).
- What would your vision be of an organization that is the best at looking after the wellbeing of its employees? (Dream).
- What processes would we need to have to ensure we improve the wellbeing of all employees? (Design).
- What do we need to do next to put these processes into place? (Destiny).

The appreciative inquiry approach quite deliberately and consciously makes people think very positively about the organization and, as it says in the title, appreciate the good things that are happening. It is used as a starting point for further investigation and exploration. In contrast to the keys of understanding, there is no real discussion about the problems, which could lead to a somewhat overly optimistic view of what is achievable. On the other hand, it may also prevent the disgruntlement that can occur when problems are being discussed. It fits in with the current thinking on positive psychology and its emphasis on upsides and making the most of them.

Analysing the Data

Whatever method is employed there is still the difficulty of analysing qualitative data. Content analysis is the most straightforward way of doing this, identifying, classifying and categorizing themes. This could be done by hand or by using specific software designed to be used with qualitative data, such as NVivo (see Sinkovics and Alfoldi, in this volume).

Ideally each focus group would be analysed separately rather than combining all of the data together. Separate analysis will be more laborious but it pays dividends in the end as it will enable a comparison of the groups to take place so that researchers can see if different locations have different priorities, problems or situations. Care needs to be taken not to over-interpret these differences.

With many of the methods we can end up with lists of ideas and observations and it can be difficult to identify priorities. This can be particularly galling when looking at the actions people think an organization should take. A simple way around this is to give each person five self-adhesive dots. These represent five votes and they must apply these to the actions (or whatever question is being considered) in whatever way the participant sees fit. If, for example, there are five actions of equal importance they can cast one vote for each of these. At the other extreme they may see one action that is, for them, the greatest priority, in which case it will receive all five votes. This is not an exact science but it is surprising how quickly priorities can emerge for a group. This can help academics and consultants alike to determine what employee priorities are.

Facilitator Skills

We can have a clear purpose, a great method, and a good turnout, but still have a poor outcome from a focus group, i.e. little or no information, poor participation. This highlights the importance of good facilitation. It is an exercise that requires some skill and we can really notice how important this is when we are able to compare poor and expert facilitation. A good facilitator will exert a subtle, unobtrusive yet firm control of the group, enabling individuals to feel they have a valued part to play in the process.

In the main, the facilitator will be non-judgemental and welcoming.

Table 15.1 shows the various things, both verbal and non-verbal, that a good facilitator will do, while Table 15.2 shows the things they need to avoid.

Table 15.1 Things a focus group facilitator should do

Verbal	Non-verbal
• Acknowledgement – e.g. 'yes', 'uh huh'	• Smiling
• Open questions – e.g. 'who', 'how', 'what', 'when', 'where' and 'why'	• Nodding
• Summarizing and reflecting – e.g. 'So what you're saying is …'	• Eye contact
• Allowing time for people to respond	
• Referring to people by name	

Table 15.2 Things a focus group facilitator should avoid doing

Verbal	Non-verbal
• Criticizing or disagreeing – e.g. 'I disagree', 'You're wrong'	• Frowning
• Agreeing – e.g. 'That is correct'	• Looking bored
• Owning personal opinions	• Shaking head
• Making recommendations – e.g. 'You should …'	• Gazing away from the group
• Using 'closed', 'leading' or 'double-headed' questions	• Fidgeting
• Interrupting	• Pointing at people

Over and above this, however, the facilitator needs to ensure that the process remains on track and that the information being obtained is relevant. So while there is a need for them to be listening, and to be seen to be listening, the facilitator also has to be thinking, for example, about:

- *Relevance*: is this contribution relevant for this study?
- *Timing*: how much time do we have left?
- *Clarity*: am I getting the point this person is making?
- *Detail*: is there sufficient detail here which will be helpful in the analysis?
- *Participation*: is everyone taking part? Are some people dominating?

In short a good facilitator, while actively listening to each participant, also needs to be thinking about these other broader considerations all of the time.

Conclusion

Focus groups can be a very effective way of gathering data about people's views and for generating ideas about future action. In order to work effectively care needs to be taken in being clear about the purposes for which they are being used. There are many other factors that need to be considered in setting up and running groups, including communication, facilitation and analysis. Having a clear process to encourage discussion is important as well as a method that is appropriate to the aims and objectives of the project. A constant factor in all focus groups is the skills of the facilitator. Hopefully this chapter will be of assistance in helping to avoid the sorts of problems described in the first section.

The future of focus groups is fascinating given the advent of social networking media. To date the use of technology for obtaining information from groups has been somewhat limited and uninspiring, e.g. the use of moderated forums and discussion boards. However, an interesting exercise in public engagement is being conducted by the US State Department with the support of the head of that department, Hillary Clinton. It utilizes a new social media technology called Opinion Space, developed by Berkeley's Centre for New Media. Anyone can participate in this exercise. Each person responds to five questions and their results are mapped in relation to everyone else who has participated. In addition, everyone can view these comments, or a sample of the comments, made by others and they can rate each of these. The system then shows the comments that people most agree with. It may be too early to say how successful this approach is, but there can be little doubt that the gathering, sharing and evaluation of qualitative data could be revolutionized by the advent of methods such as this.

Further Reading

For an excellent background to focus groups as well as providing sound practical advice, take a look at one of the following three books: Stewart, Shamdasani and Rook (2007); Morgan (1997); and Kreuger and Casey (2000).

References

Flanagan, J.C. (1954) 'The Critical Incident Techniques', *Psychological Bulletin*, 51: 4.
Kelly, G.A. (1991) *The Psychology of Personal Constructs*. New York: Norton.
Kreuger, R.A. and Casey, M.A. (2000) *Focus Groups: A Practical Guide for Applied Research* (3rd edn). Thousand Oaks, CA: Sage.
Morgan D.L. (1997) *Focus Groups as Qualitative Research* (2nd edn). Thousand Oaks, CA: Sage.
Pearn, M.A and Mulrooney, C. (1995) *Tools for a Learning Organisation*. London: IPD.
Schafer, M. (1990) 'Data collection in the UK and how it differs from the US', *Applied Marketing Research*, Second Quarter, 30: 2.
Stewart, D.W., Shamdasani, P.N. and Rook, D.W. (2007) *Focus Groups: Theory and Practice* (2nd edn). Thousand Oaks, CA: Sage.
Watkins, J.M. and Mohr, B. (2001) *Appreciative Inquiry*. San Francisco, CA: Jossey-Bass/ Pfeiffer.

3 Participant Observation

Matthew J. Brannan and Teresa Oultram

Introduction

Participant observation (PO) is a specific approach to the gaining of knowledge, based upon direct contact between the researcher and the social objects of interest. The *experiential* core of PO means that, to an extent, we are all participant observers, whether consciously or otherwise, as participation is a feature of all social interaction. Thus Hammersley and Atkinson see PO not so much as a particular research technique but rather as a 'mode of being-in-the-world' (1994: 249). From this perspective, unlike many other research techniques and methods, the elementary rules of participation essentially are learned forms of human socialization. At its most basic level, PO works as a mode of inquiry through the direct experience of circumstances and events; the researcher *becomes* the research instrument. Whereas other forms of investigation will produce text, speech and numerical forms of information, PO, in the first instance, produces sensuous bodily experience, which is then encoded into other communicable forms. PO demands that the researcher consciously places him- or herself into the social milieu in which he or she is interested, thus 'getting one's hands dirty' (Hobbs and May, 1993: xviii). This *placing* is both conceptually and practically significant by determining the experience, and thus the inquiry, more generally. Social situations, or research settings, that emerge rather than those that are artificial contrivances are favoured and, in this respect, recurring social rituals such as initiation, celebration and departure are all frequently recurring motifs in PO research.

Closely related to, but not to be confused with, the practice of ethnography (see Yanow, Ybema and van Hulst, in this volume), PO is often the preferred, or chosen, technique in terms of the operationalization of ethnographic study. The distinction between the two is to be found in the way that PO invokes the act of participatory fieldwork itself, rather than a wider research process. Further, if, as is claimed, ethnography consists of two moments (Willis and Trondman, 2000: 5), then PO is often the first moment, or the moment of being, that brings the researcher into contact with the objects of research interest.

This chapter is organized as follows. First we consider variations in the application of PO, a variety of possibilities are noted, and the key themes, issues and challenges for those deploying PO are considered. The chapter in turn seeks to explore some of the problematic features and controversies that are associated with the use of participant observational techniques. In an attempt to illustrate the realities of PO in action, the chapter then presents a dialogue between the authors in the form of an interview, where the use of PO in a specific context is discussed.

Variations in Participation

PO has been deployed in a number of settings and a review of the utilization of PO reveals a range of practice. A useful framework has developed from an influential article by Raymond Gold (1958). Gold identified four idealized PO roles and provided a useful foundational classificatory framework, although some further comments and refinements are necessary here. His approach differentiated between the *degree* of participation of the researcher in the social setting and is, therefore, a researcher-centric mode of classification.

Complete participation (also sometimes known as covert PO): in effect this seeks to disguise the role of observer to the extent that the observational objectives are undisclosed to other research participants. Complete participation gives the researcher sufficient 'cover' to conduct an observation while providing an explanation (the researcher adopts a relevant group membership role) for their location in the social context. However, this is to a large extent dependant upon the maintenance of the narrative and, therefore, the role demands a degree of duplicity.

Participant as observer: this is characterized by the researcher openly adopting *both* the participant and observer roles. While the researcher fully participates in the social situation they also disclose the observational objectives to the other participants, making it known that the development and cultivation of relationships with participants is for the purposes of research. As the adoption of both participant and observer is disclosed, a key challenge for the researcher is to negotiate and establish the specific dimensions of these roles.

Observer as participant: this is characterized by a brief engagement in the research setting, where the role of the researcher is known but they may not have sufficient exposure to develop a full understanding of the meaning and culture of the setting. The title of this category reflects the secondary role of participation and has led some to term this 'quick and dirty' (Hughes et al., 1994) or 'micro' research (Heath and Luff, 1992). In most social situations, full participation, even in elementary forms of social engagement, requires extensive learning and socialization. In the absence of full participation, research of this type is likely to be facilitated by existing full participants allowing or facilitating a partial participation.

Complete observer (disinterested spectator): while classified by Gold as a PO classification, the complete observer does not engage with other participants and therefore it can be questioned whether this style of research belongs within PO. In this mode of engagement, the researcher plays no active role in the social situation, merely observing events as they unfold. It is assumed that the observational role and intent of the observer are communicated to research participants.

Adler and Adler (1987) offer a slightly different typology, focusing on membership roles. This recognizes the extent to which the researcher accepts being and is accepted as a fellow member and, therefore, offers a less researcher-centric classification. Dividing Gold's 'participant as observer' into two categories:

Peripheral membership allows for a close and frequent interaction with the group, with the aim of gaining acceptance as an 'insider' by members, but without taking on a core role within the group. The observational role is seen as the primary role, with participation used as a means to gain a 'better observational point' (Adler and Adler, 1987: 48).

Active membership, in contrast, for Adler and Adler, can fit into either Gold's category of 'participant as observer' or that of 'complete participant', dependent upon whether the researcher adopts an overt or covert position.

Common to both categories, the researcher interacts with participants as a colleague focusing on the group's tasks, with the observational role taking a secondary focus. Finally, they offer a further category, which they claim, goes beyond Gold's 'complete observer' role.

Complete membership allows the researcher to immerse themselves fully in the group and shows a genuine commitment to the group and its goals. For some, this amounts to 'going native' or losing their supposed objectivity, but Adler and Adler believe that the depth of data gathered and the degree of the researcher's own subjective insight make this a valid PO approach.

While these frameworks are useful, it is clear that forms of PO have diversified, that tensions exist between the classifications, and that PO in practice might, in the course of one research project, span several classifications. Renée Fox (2004: 213), for example, claims that at the core of PO is a 'dynamic equilibrium between participation and observation – a continuous balancing and rebalancing of involvement and detachment', and this reminds us that caution is needed when reading PO classifications as ideal types; these act as guides and should not be allowed to become fixed and immutable.

Debates and Controversies in Participant Observation

Having outlined the frameworks for thinking about PO, the next section seeks to explore some of the current major points of debate and controversy in relation to the use of PO. We consider ethical practice, managing field relations and political dimensions to the PO research process.

Ethical practice: the covertness or openness of a PO research

A key decision for researchers in designing and implementing PO is the degree of disclosure they are willing or able to provide in situ. However, irrespective of circumstances and constraints, covert forms of PO, which fail to inform participants of the true intention of the researcher, have been criticized for being unethical, dishonest, failing to respect human rights and potentially putting the participants' interests at risk (Jorgensen, 1989; Hammersley and Atkinson, 1995). Bulmer (1982), for example, questions how covert techniques can be justified when the research relationship should be based on trust and honesty.

Adler and Adler (1987) point out that duplicity is potentially problematic not only for participants but also for researchers. The maintenance of multiple roles for prolonged periods while conducting their research can become confusing and overwhelming. In contrast, Berreman (2007) challenges the idea that the pretence is problematic for the researcher, arguing that social interaction often involves impression management and some form of secrecy. Similarly, Reinharz (1997) points out that we adopt many different identities during fieldwork, and the key to successful research is through reflexive writing practice (see Haynes, in this volume).

Others (Douglas, 1976; Van Maanen, 1988; Ferdinand et al., 2007) have defended the covert approach by arguing that the benefits can outweigh the potential risks. These justifications centre on the minimization of disruption to the field through non-disclosure, which is considered important for the integrity of the observations. Politically it may also be important to document participants acting without any knowledge of the researcher. According to Douglas (1970, as cited in Bulmer, 1982) the use of covert methods is necessary for 'good' research as, he believes, the social order rests on deceitfulness and secrecy and to penetrate this requires researchers, as outsiders, trying to get in by using deception. From this perspective there may be important 'public interest' issues at stake in the pursuit of covert PO and this is especially the case where PO seeks to document social activity which perpetuates division, inequality and repression.

Brewer (2000) challenges the distinction between overt and covert PO, arguing that this may instead be re-conceptualized as a continuum with varying degrees of openness within the types of PO adopted. This is especially significant given that the duration of most PO projects is likely to mean that research aims and objectives change over time. Questions may be raised over the extent of consent, even following full disclosure. It is likely, for example, that consent is given on behalf of group members by a spokesperson or gatekeeper and, although this may be expedient for the researcher, it cannot be assumed that this implicates consent for all participants. In many cases of PO, in fact, permission will not, or could not, be negotiated with every member of the group, where research sites are large or dynamic for example. A further dilemma is that the researcher often does not, or cannot, completely define all research interests to the participants (Fine, 2001; Ferdinand et al., 2007). The dynamic nature of PO implies an iterative process, refining and re-defining its interests and terms of reference. Given this, the completeness of initial disclosure, and therefore consent, is likely to be highly constrained. Hammersley and Atkinson (1995), for example, claim that, unless constantly reminded, participants will quickly forget about the research interests and are likely to make comments they may not wish to have expressed openly.

In summary, therefore, it seems that, although a commonsense consensus emerges for the necessity for PO to be grounded in clear disclosure, for a number of practical and pragmatic reasons it may be impossible for the PO researcher to comply fully with the demands of being an ethical researcher (see Holt, in this volume, for a further discussion of ethics in qualitative research).

The research relationship: understanding the meaning and logic of human cultures

The techniques of PO have arisen out of the wider humanist tradition in the social sciences that seeks to position the researcher 'close' to the research participants in spatial, economic, political, cultural and emotional terms. This proximity fosters a sensitivity to the '*lived experience*' of the social situation in an effort to gain an insight into the 'insiders' world of meaning' (Jorgensen, 1989: 8). Watson (2011), while championing PO, challenges the legitimacy to claims of revealing people's 'lived experience' (see also Jones, 2000). Instead, he claims that the focus should be on 'the connection between the actions and utterances of people in social settings with the culture, discourses, narratives, and social, economic and political structures within which those actions and utterances occur' (Watson, 2011: 213). Seen from this perspective, the focus of PO should be on 'how things work' in field settings (Watson, 2011). PO's purpose thus becomes to understand specific cultures, in particular exploring human experience and relating how participants make sense of their own social situations. PO is therefore often characterized by its sensitivity to the language used by participants as a way of apprehending this point of view. Cultures are considered to have a logic and practice, which makes sense to the participants but may, from the outside, appear illogical, unordered or random. Moreover, culture is learnt and cannot be observed directly (Clifford, 1990; Grills, 1998). PO, and more precisely the researcher's participation in a particular culture, may allow the researcher to experience the culture for him or herself and, through a process of immersion and participation, begin to experience and come to understand the logic and the meanings that lie behind social practice, as these may be tacit or difficult to communicate through verbal interaction or description alone.

Participating in the daily lives of participants allows observation and interaction, by personally experiencing and sharing the daily routines and practices of those being studied (Brewer, 2000: 59). It is through this participation that the researcher may begin to understand the meaning and logic of social practice; thus what was initially experienced as different and alien starts to become more familiar. This has led some writers to claim that PO must involve a level of sustained time commitment (see for example Adler and Adler, 1987; Bate, 1997; Watson, 2011), challenging the validity and rigour of those who have adopted a 'quick and dirty' or 'jet-plane' (Agar, 1980) approach. Nonetheless, the process of familiarization with the strange is a basic human capacity and, in essence, a process of learning. PO, therefore, might usefully be considered as both exposure to the unfamiliar and an inherent process of learning. The articulation of how learning is accomplished through participation (see Lave and Wenger, 1991) is an apt description of the essential mechanics of PO.

The pursuit of objectivity remains a central concern with, for example, calls for researchers to suspend their emotional attachment and maintain an 'objective' detachment, thereby becoming a 'professional stranger' and 'detached participant' to ensure the maintenance of a critical perspective (Malinowski, 1922). In contrast, feminist researchers often argue for a 'total immersion' of the researcher in the field (see Reinharz, 1992), accepting the emotional and subjective nature of research and pointing towards what they see as the politics of the research act. Similarly, postmodernist and poststructuralist writers tend to reject claims that PO can produce an authoritative and objective account, instead favouring a recognition of the privileged position of the researcher and the impact this has upon their always partial account. Work within this tradition draws attention to the fact that all accounts are constructions (Hertz, 1997: viii) and, as such, these reflect the, often implicit, assumptions of the researcher and the social, historical and political circumstances of their production (Agrosion et al., 2000).

The dichotomy of insider/outsider has been challenged as being too crude a polarization (Woodward, 2008). For Naples (1997: 70), for example, 'insiderness' and 'outsiderness' are permeable social locations that are experienced not just by the researcher but also by community members, and are invariably tied into social interactions.

Political nature of PO

Some authors argue that PO has an essentially political nature (Punch, 1994; Fine, 2001), reflecting the privileged position of the researcher in terms of 'doing' the research and disseminating the results (Agrosion et al., 2000). Wray-Bliss (as cited in Ferdinand et al., 2007) asserts that participant observers act within the field in ways that reflect their own personal moral views and behaviours. This opens up important questions in relation to the extent that research can ever be 'value free' and whether researchers can ever remain 'objective and impartial'. Ferdinand et al. (2007) argue that participant observers do not enter into the research field passively; instead, they do so with particular research agendas and questions that they wish to answer.

Alvesson and Deetz (2000), from a critical management perspective, go further here, suggesting researchers have an ethical responsibility to expose unjust or unethical practices observed during fieldwork. Indeed critical theorists enter the field deliberately to seek out and examine the ways in which 'powerful groups oppress and dominate those less powerful' (Rossman and Rallis, 2003) and, in doing so, aim to privilege the voices of those less powerful groups.

Tensions are inherent in the practice of PO in terms of its initial goals and objectives of study and the use to which PO research might be put. Here the historical connection that PO has to forms of anthropology and ethnography cannot be ignored. Seen from this vantage point, critical scholars have noted that the central concern of PO remains an attempt to understand 'the other' and, for a variety of reasons, this might be considered politically problematic. In particular, anthropology has long been associated with political and economic interests, in securing a 'cultural grasp of the "natives"' (Prasad, 2005: 77) in the furtherance of colonization. This debate finds a contemporary articulation in the controversy over the use of anthropological techniques, expertise and knowledge by the United States military during combat operations. McFate (2005: 25), for example, advocates such practice, claiming that 'cultural knowledge' is needed to wage the 'war on terror'. In contrast, González (2007) and Price (2007) question the ethics and academic validity of such actions.

Applying Participant Observation in Practice

In an attempt to highlight some of the challenges of implementing PO in organizational research, we now draw upon an example of the technique in use. In order to do this we use the format of an interview to offer a dialogue between the first and the second authors of this chapter. The interview draws upon the experience of a PO investigation of a call centre located in the West Midlands, United Kingdom, where the first author spent 13 months employed as a customer service representative (CSR).

TO Would you like to give us some background as to why you chose this study?

MB I have always been interested in work and employment issues and understanding how work was changing, which made me want to look at call centres, as they became an increasingly important form of employment.

TO You adopted a PO approach. Had you prior experience of this, how did you know this was the right approach to adopt?

MB I remember reading Paul Thompson and Stephen Ackroyd's 'All Quiet on the Workplace Front' [1995]. This alerted me to the fact that you could take a very detailed single case study as a way of exploring much wider sets of social relations and that there had been a drift away from this kind of detailed empirical work and I started to explore the rich tradition of industrial sociology, including authors like James Ditton [1972; 1977], Huw Beynon [1973], Donald Roy [1958], and Michael Burawoy [1979; 1985]. Shortly after, Sue Fernie and David Metcalf [1997] famously described the call centre as an '*electronic panopticon*' where management surveillance is rendered perfect, foreclosing the possibility of resistance. This set up the basis of my research and, very quickly and clearly, the aim became to get into the call centre and empirically see for myself if the call centre made management control perfect.

TO What were the unique features of PO and why was this the method you adopted?

MB If I wanted to understand workplace resistance, how was it best to do it? I did consider other approaches but I was led by my research question. It seemed counter-intuitive that I would ask management's permission to talk to workers about resisting management. I therefore adopted a dual role – I disclosed my research interest but took a full role as a paid employee, as this seemed to me to be the best way to get close to the action that I wanted to explore. I didn't really think about or theorize this to a massive extent, it just became what I considered to be an effective way for me to experience the social relations of production.

TO What were the limitations or potential dangers of your approach?

MB One of the issues many researchers face is undertaking an extensive fieldwork project when you are intellectually least equipped. So, in my case, I was undertaking fieldwork with no sociological or research methods training – terrifying and exhilarating all at the same time. I was trying to be a call centre worker, while in the evenings and weekends trying to come to terms with sociological concepts and ideas at the same time as writing up my field notes.

TO How concrete were your ideas and concepts before you started your research?

MB I'd read quite a lot of orthodox labour process work, which was like a theoretical backpack that I took into the field with me. But this was quite limited, as I'd gone straight from a degree to a Master's degree to a PhD. I

(Continued)

(Continued)

knew I was looking for empirical examples of how workers thwart managerial ambitions and control strategies and I thought I knew how I could relate this to wider sets of social relations. I also knew that this could take a variety of forms; so I'd read work about pilfering, the re-appropriation of time and more sophisticated ideas around notions of identity.

TO What are your memories and thoughts about actually becoming an employee while still being a researcher and operating this dual role? Having to learn the job while still being a researcher, was this a difficult task?

MB Very challenging, and this was a key research finding. Call centre work at that time was portrayed as being mundane and routine with high levels of labour turnover. In the popular press, for example, I remember call centre workers being presented as battery hens and other animals; and it was considered a job that anyone or 'anything' could do. My first couple of weeks in the call centre were almost a case of shock and awe! Total sensory bombardment, with a cacophony of noise making it really difficult to concentrate on customers' conversations. I also found it difficult to get up to speed with the computer interface and to learn to do this while I was talking to a customer, trying to do what felt like a hundred and one things at once. So, actually, the demands of the job were incredibly high. My difficulty learning the job surprised me and felt like something that needed an explanation in the context of such a negative public perception. That process of just 'becoming', what the call centre managers would refer to as a 'competent CSR', was actually very difficult, so why wasn't this job valued in society?

As a participant observer, the initial entry and shock of the working environment, having not really experienced anything like that before, the sensory feeling of 'overload' and sense of dislocation and confusion, are important in terms of understanding what it means to be a call centre worker and became important sensory data. Making the most of this data is hard, especially when you are trying to learn how to become competent at a particular job and all that this entails. In many ways it's a form of extreme ethnography, and I remember often leaving work with a thumping headache and just having to lie in a dark room with a flannel over my head to recover! You are very much pushed to the limits in terms of your ability to adapt and your capacity to deal with the situation.

TO How did you start to fit into the organization and how did you develop relationships with your colleagues?

MB Like many call centres, the call centre where I worked divided work functionally into teams. A team consisted of between 5 and 12 members of

(Continued)

(Continued)

staff. I went through a period of initial induction of about a month before I was assigned to a team and that became the location for the duration of the fieldwork, so I formed very close bonds with that team. It wasn't unusual, because of the nature of call centre turnover, to have new starters and the group was used to dealing with new employees, having a repertoire of rituals and initiations for new recruits. For example, new team members were referred to in the third person as 'the temp' rather than by name, clearly a status divide which drew attention to the 'newness' of employees and the temporary nature of their employment contracts, despite the fact that not all new employees were temporary. Also, as a recognition I think that the work was quite difficult and tough, not a lot was done to ameliorate this and therefore new employees were very much *temporary* until they proved they were competent to management and also proved their mettle to other CSRs. During that time, as well as taking calls, as 'the temp' I was required to provide 'tea and toast' functions (fetching tea and toast from the canteen for other CSRs). This taught me a lot about PO because it's unlikely that, if I was conducting interviews for example, I would have been asked to make the tea and toast, but this experience gave me the sense of what it is really like to work in the call centre, and more than that, to know the value of what it means to become, or to move beyond, being 'the temp' and to have your colleagues call you by your name, because that suggests that you're actually okay at your job.

TO So would your colleagues and managers have seen you as an employee rather than a researcher who was also employed?

MB Very much so, that was one of the things that struck me. If you were a Foucauldian you might say that there was a dominant discourse about answering calls on time. Other identities really seemed less relevant, you're there to answer calls and, if you are not able to do that, problems arise. But if you are able to do that then you can really be whoever you want to be. It was almost like my secondary identity was as a researcher. It didn't really make sense to the rest of the team, they made fun of my role as a researcher, they saw it as a hobby, but it didn't really matter and they would identify me not as a researcher but as a colleague, someone there to answer the phone. This is also quite similar to the managerial perspective I encountered. When I spoke to the HR manager about my research she quite clearly said, 'I don't mind what you do, as long as it doesn't interfere with you taking calls'.

TO Can you say a little bit about how you gained consent for this research?

MB I started with a top-down approach. I first asked for permission from the HR manager and made clear what I was doing and how I might use my

(Continued)

(Continued)

observations. Soon after I joined my team the call centre manager spoke to the team leader and she was happy also, then it was left to me to frame my research how I wanted with my colleagues. During the period of the fieldwork people came and left the team and I was careful to make sure that I told everyone within the team about my research. But how do you really know when you have consent? I relied on having conversations with those I was working with and talking through what I was doing and what I wanted to achieve. I think the issue of consent is a very vexed and dynamic question for PO. I knew that my colleagues knew about my research because they frequently mocked it – so, for example, when one of the CSRs came in late to work, another colleague stood up with a clipboard and pretended to make a note saying that I should do the same. So quite clearly there was knowledge of what I was doing. On other occasions, however, what I was doing, especially in management circles, would be misinterpreted. My focus on resistance, for instance, became reframed as an interest in knowledge management or performance management. Although I tried to be clear about what I was doing, it struck me that, often, it was almost as if it didn't register, or perhaps those I was working with had different views about what I was doing or what I should be doing. Yet even within these restricted parameters there are limits to consent, thus it was impracticable to prefix every conversation (with customers for example) with a disclosure about my research, or for that matter with the other 400 employees that worked for the call centre but not within my team.

TO What were the practicalities of doing the research? How did you manage a full-time job and conduct your research?

MB I was quite lucky to be on a PhD programme that placed very few demands on me in terms of teaching, so I had quite a lot of liberty to work full time but initially found it difficult to make notes in situ. I ended up making notes on my workstation while at work, and that worked well because it didn't draw unwarranted attention, it wasn't unusual for people to be using the keyboard and making notes. It wasn't that I was being duplicitous but I didn't want to draw massive amounts of attention through note taking.

TO What should PO focus on, key events or the mundane and routine?

MB The beauty and power of PO is its ability to find the extraordinary in the ordinary, and it is going through that process of participation that helps to capture that. Paul Willis talks about the 'dialectics of surprise' and I think that is incredibly important, to try where possible to move away from preconceived ideas, like my focus on resistance, and to be driven by surprise.

(Continued)

(Continued)

Then to try and account for the surprise by, for example, following Burawoy to find and understand events and situations as local manifestations of broader global structures and relations.

TO How did you go about leaving the field?

MB I was really unsure about when I should leave the field and I think that this was an anxiety about having sufficient material for a PhD. I didn't really feel like I had a story to tell and I felt if I hung around more I might find a better story. I always had in my mind that I would do a discrete period of time and then I would leave the field and start a process of analysis. In reality I was constantly evaluating what I came across, and being driven by surprise moves the research focus further on and makes it even more difficult to know when to leave the field.

TO Given your difficulty leaving the field, how much was this an attachment to the call centre and your role there?

MB It took me a while to become known as a competent CSR. I was very aware that I was indebted to my colleagues for helping me through the process – not that that was unusual, new CSRs were helped, although there was a kind of 'tough love' in the call centre. As a competent CSR you know that your presence, not as a researcher, but as a worker, is going to be missed. I felt a loyalty to my team to minimize the impact of my departure and that's quite apart from my anxiety over the value of the research. I also noticed that I had started to come up against what methodologists might call 'theoretical saturation', not really coming across anything new. On reflection, I feel like I misjudged the duration of my fieldwork and stayed too long, probably because I was actually enjoying it!

TO How did you make the transition from PO within the call centre back to researcher?

MB An academic post came up where I could combine my PhD and some tutorial work and this gave me a way out of the field. It seems incredible to me now that I would need an alibi, or reason, to leave the field but I felt that I did and I knew that it would be impossible to combine the PO with the academic role. So I'm lucky the post came when it did or I might still be working within the call centre! I don't recall thinking about an exit strategy before I started my fieldwork, but clearly I should have. I suspect that the portrayal of 'exit' in methodology text books, for example, is rather too straightforward and simplistic, but I think that the practicalities of PO, and certainly my experience, are far more messy and it's very difficult to know when to leave.

TO Did you use any other forms of data collection?

(Continued)

(Continued)

MB I was really keen to conduct follow-up interviews, to test my ideas on colleagues and to see what they thought about what I found. I thought this would give me the chance to reflect on my time in the call centre and ask some pretty direct questions. I think it's a sign of the strength of the research that management was willing to let me come back to the call centre to conduct interviews and, more importantly, that people would be let off the phones to come and talk to me because that was incredibly unusual.

TO Do you think there was a different relationship during the follow-up interviews?

MB Looking at the text of the interviews reveals a formality in the way that my former colleagues were talking to me, which is, I think, interesting. The interviews were conducted between four and six months after I had left the field but with people that I'd worked with for a year, and yet it was like they didn't know me at all. I asked for permission to record the interviews and that became a symbol, it was remarked on and interviewees became coy about talking to me where, in contrast, they were enthusiastic and effusive during the fieldwork. In talking about resistance, for example, things that we had engaged in together became a discussion that was off limits; at least as far as a tape recorded interview was concerned. Very clearly there was a different relationship at play and this is incredible when thinking about the start of this conversation, where I said that it seemed counter-intuitive to interview on a subject like resistance where I would need managerial consent to hold the interviews. If, having spent a year with these workers, they were still coy about talking on tape – can you imagine what sort of response I would have received, what sort of dynamics would be at play if I had only conducted interviews? The strangeness and awkwardness of these interviews really told me something interesting about PO and its strengths as a research method.

TO What would your advice be to someone who is considering PO and other techniques?

MB PO needs to be designed in from the research question stage. I think, as researchers, we always face a set of limitations and compromises but what is crucial to PO is the sensuousness of the experience of putting yourself on the line. Feeling what it is like to be in a given situation transforms the way in which you interpret other people's actions in that same situation. But this is incredibly difficult to achieve, the maintenance of relationships, together with physical, emotional and intellectual work, all place a huge burden on the researcher. I also think it has become more difficult to conduct PO more generally; institutional pressures to publish, the impact

(Continued)

> *(Continued)*
>
> agenda and trends in research ethics have all moved in directions which I think makes PO more difficult. PO makes high demands and it's difficult to take a full role in any in-group and meaningfully inhabit other worlds at the same time. In the workplace, for example, the work that is done *matters* – in the call centre the amount of calls that you take, and the way that you take them, *matter.* If you are not pulling your weight this has real implications for those around you. You can very quickly find yourself having to choose between participation and observation and I certainly went through periods where I wasn't taking notes because I was solely concentrating on trying to 'cut it' on the call centre floor. But this, in itself, is a research finding that tells us something very important and dramatic about 'what it means to be a call centre worker.'

Conclusion

This chapter provides a brief introduction to the practice and theory of PO, as characterized as a process of sustained contact between the researcher and research participant. The chapter highlights the experiential core of PO as a mode of being in the world and this is illustrated with the example drawn from call centre research. The *placing* of the researcher, and the collection of data through a bodily sensuous experience, as seen in the example discussed, are a defining characteristic of the approach and present unique potentials and equally pose many problematic issues. The strength of PO is its ability to place the researcher close to the issues of interest: in the case above this was working within the call centre to gain a sense of the dynamics of employment within the organization first hand. Participation allows the exploration of domains of human experience, such as informal, emotional or cultural aspects of life, which may not be revealed through other more distant methods. Yet these strengths are also problematic features of PO, as they place significant burdens on the researcher in a broad sense and raise complex and difficult issues in relation to ethical research practice. The chapter highlights the problematic nature of conducting ethical PO, the issues that start with, rather than are resolved by, informed consent. Moreover, the management of the research relationship, especially where field relations are fostered for the purpose of research, provides an inherently political dimension to PO research. Yet despite these difficulties, and an institutional context that seems increasingly hostile to long duration PO work, the interest in and development of PO remains healthy. The depth and sophistication of understanding that PO potentially fosters are likely to ensure that this long remains the case.

Further Reading

For more details on participant observation, we suggest you read Spradley (1980), Jorgensen (1989) and DeWalt (2010), which provide comprehensive guides to conducting PO. Czarniawska (1998) offers insights into the experiences of being a PO researcher, focusing, in particular, on narrative and the identity of the researcher. More details on the case study featured in this chapter can be found in Brannan (2005a; 2005b; and 2007), Brannan and Hawkins (2007) and Brannan and Priola (2010).

References

Adler, P. and Adler, P.A. (1987) *Membership Roles in Field Research*. Newbury Park, CA: Sage.

Agar, M. (1980) *The Professional Stranger: An Informal Introduction to Ethnography*. New York: Academic Press.

Agrosion, M., Perez, A. and Mays, K. (2000) 'Rethinking observation: from method to context,' in N.K. Denzin and Y.S. Lincoln (eds), *Handbook of Qualitative Research* (2nd edn). Thousand Oaks, CA: Sage, pp. 673–702.

Alvesson, M. and Deetz, S. (2000) *Doing Critical Management Research*. London: Sage.

Bate, S.P. (1997) 'Whatever happened to organizational anthropology? A review of the field of organizational ethnography and anthropological studies', *Human Relations*, 50 (9): 1147–1174.

Becker, H. and Geer, G. (1957) 'Participant observation and interviewing: a comparison', *Human Organization*, 16 (3): 28–32.

Berreman, G. (2007) 'Behind many masks: ethnography and impression management', in A. Robben and J. Stuka (eds), *Ethnographic Fieldwork: An Anthropological Reader*. Oxford: Wiley-Blackwell, pp. 135–158.

Beynon, H. (1973) *Working For Ford*. London: Penguin.

Brannan, M.J. (2005a) 'Workplace resistance in a call centre environment', unpublished PhD thesis, University of Wolverhampton.

Brannan, M.J. (2005b) '"Once more with feeling": ethnographic reflections on the mediation of tension in a small team of call centre workers', *Gender, Work and Organization*, 12 (5): 420–439.

Brannan, M. J. (2007) 'Sexuality, gender and legitimate peripheral participation: an ethnographic study of a call centre', in J. Hughes, N. Jewson and L. Unwin (eds), *Communities of Practice: Critical Perspectives*. London: Routledge, pp. 120–130.

Brannan, M.J. and Hawkins, B. (2007) '"London calling": selection as pre-emptive strategy for cultural control', *Employee Relations*, 29 (2): 178–191.

Brannan, M.J. and Priola, V. (2010) '"Girls who do boys like they're girls'? Exploring the role of gender in the junior management of contemporary service work', *Gender, Work and Organization*. DOI: 10.1111/j.1468-0432.2009.00493.x.

Brewer, J.D. (2000) *Ethnography*. Buckingham: Open University Press.

Bulmer, M. (1982) 'Merits and demerits of covert observation', in M. Bulmer (ed.), *Social Research Ethics*. New York: Homes and Meier Publishers Inc., pp. 217–251.

Burawoy, M. (1979) *Manufacturing Consent*. London: University of Chicago Press.

Burawoy, M. (1985) *The Politics of Production: Factory Regimes under Capitalism and Socialism*. London: Verso.

Clifford, J. (1990) 'Notes on (field)notes', in R. Sanjek (ed.), *Fieldnotes: The Makings of Anthropology*. New York: Cornell University Press.

Czarniawska, B. (1998) 'A narrative approach to organization studies', *Qualitative Research Methods, Volume 43*. Thousand Oaks, CA: Sage.

DeWalt, K. (2010) *Participant Observation: A Guide for Fieldworkers*. California: Altamira Press.

Ditton, J. (1972) 'Absent at work: how to manage monotony', *New Society*, 21: 697–681.

Ditton, J. (1977) *Part-time Crime: An Ethnography of Fiddling and Pilferage*. London: Macmillan.

Douglas, J. (1976) *Investigative Social Research: Individual and Team Field Research*. Beverly Hills, CA: Sage.

Ferdinand, J., Pearson, G., Rowe, M. and Worthington, F. (2007) 'A different kind of ethics', *Ethnography*, 8 (4): 519–543.

Fernie, S. and Metcalf, D. (1997) '(Not) hanging on the telephone: payment systems in the new sweatshops', *Centre for Economic Performance, Discussion Paper No. 390*. London: London School of Economics.

Fine, G.A. (2001) 'Ten lies of ethnography: moral dilemmas of field research', in A. Bryman (ed.), *Ethnography, Volume III*. London: Sage, pp. 370–383.

Fox, R. (2004) 'Observations and reflections of a perpetual fieldworker', *The Annals of the American Academy of Political and Social Science*, 595 (1): 309–326.

Gold, R. (1958) 'Roles in sociological field observation', *Social Forces*, 36: 217–233.

González, R. (2007) 'Towards mercenary anthropology?', *Anthropology Today*, 23 (3): 14–28.

Grills, S. (1998) 'An invitation to the field: fieldwork and the pragmatist's lesson' in S. Grills (ed.), *Doing Ethnography: Fieldwork Settings*. Thousand Oaks, CA: Sage.

Hammersley, M. and Atkinson, P. (1994) 'Ethnography and participant observation', in N.K. and Y.S. Lincoln (eds), *Handbook of Qualitative Research*. Thousand Oaks, CA: Sage, pp. 88–98.

Hammersley, M. and Atkinson, P. (1995) *Ethnography: Principles in Practice*. London: Routledge.

Heath, D. and Luff, P. (1992) 'Collaboration and control: crisis management and multimedia technology in London Undergound line control rooms', *CSCW*, 1 (1): 69–94.
Hertz, R. (1997) 'Introduction: reflexivity and voice', in R. Hertz (ed.), *Reflexivity & Voice*. London: Sage, pp. vii–xviii.
Hobbs, D. and May, T. (1993) *Interpreting the Field: Accounts of Ethnography*. Oxford: Clarendon Press.
Hughes, J., King, V., Rodden, T. and Andersen, H. (1994) 'Moving out from the control room: ethnography in system design', *CSCW '94 Proceedings of the 1994 ACM Conference on Computer Supported Cooperative Work*, pp. 429–439.
Jones, T.E. (2000) 'Ethnography, belief ascription, and epistemological barriers', *Human Relations*, 53 (1): 117–152.
Jorgensen, D.L. (1989) *Participant Observation*. London: Sage.
Lave, J. and Wenger, E. (1991) *Situated Learning – Legitimate Peripheral Participation*. Cambridge: Cambridge University Press.
Malinowski, B. (1922) *Argonauts of the Western Pacific*. London: Routledge.
McFate, M. (2005) 'Anthropology and counterinsurgency: the strange story of their curious relationship', *Military Review*, March–April: 24–38.
Naples, N.A. (1997) 'A feminist revisiting of the insider/outsider debate: the "outsider phenomenon" in rural Iowa,' in R. Hertz (ed.), *Reflexivity & Voice*. London: Sage, 70–9
Prasad, P. (2005) *Crafting Qualitative Research: Working in the Postpositivist Traditions*. New York: M.E. Sharpe.
Price, D. (2007) 'Buying a piece of anthropology?', *Anthropology Today*, 23 (3): 8–13.
Punch, M. (1994) 'Politics and ethics in qualitative research,' in N.K. Denzin and Y.S. Lincoln (eds), *Handbook of Qualitative Research*. Thousand Oaks, CA: Sage, pp. 88–98.
Reinharz, S. (1992) *Feminist Methods in Social Research*. New York: Oxford University Press.
Reinharz, S. (1997) 'Who am I? The need for a variety of selves in the field', in R. Hertz (ed.), *Reflexivity & Voice*. London: Sage, pp. 3–20.
Rossman, G. and Rallis, S. (2003) *Learning in the Field: An Introduction to Qualitative Research* (2nd edn). Thousand Oaks, CA: Sage.
Roy, D. (1958) '"Banana time": job satisfaction and informal interaction', *Human Organization*, 18: 58–68.
Spradley, J. (1980) *Participant Observation*. New York: Rinehart and Wilson.
Thompson, P. and Ackroyd, S. (1995) 'All quiet on the workplace front? A critique of recent trends in British industrial sociology', *Sociology*, 29 (4): 610–633.
Van Maanen, J. (1988) *Tales of the Field*. Chicago: University of Chicago Press.
Watson, T.J. (2011) 'Ethnography, reality, and truth: the vital need for studies of "how things work"', *Journal of Management Studies*, 48 (1): 202–217.
Willis, P. and Trondman, M. (2000) 'Manifesto for ethnography', *Ethnography*, 1 (1): 5–15.
Woodward, K. (2008) 'Hanging out and hanging about: insider/outsider research in the sport of boxing', *Ethnography*, 9 (4): 536–560.

4 Practising Organizational Ethnography

Dvora Yanow, Sierk Ybema, and Merlijn van Hulst

On Ethnography and Organizational Ethnography: An Overview

'Ethnography' is typically used to mean three things. Its literal meaning, from the Greek, refers to a particular kind of writing: a written account (*graphein*) of a people (*ethnos*). This meaning has been eclipsed by two others, especially as ethnography has been taken up in some disciplines outside of anthropology. Its second and more common usage refers to a set of methods or a research strategy, also called field research or fieldwork: some combination of observation, with whatever degree of participation (see Brannan and Oultram, in this volume); talking to people (often called 'interviewing' when the formalities of setting up appointments are involved; see Alvesson and Ashcraft, in this volume); and the study of material artefacts, to understand their meanings for situational actors. In organizational settings, material artefacts will typically include research question-relevant texts (e.g. annual reports, correspondence, internal memos, cartoons/jokes/photos on office doors and bulletin boards, webpages, etc.; see Lee, in this volume). In a third sense of the term, methodologists are increasingly pointing to ethnography's distinctive 'sensibility': an orientation towards the social world – actors, (inter-)actions, settings – and the material objects in it, which focuses on the centrality of meaning and meaning-making to research practices (see also Pader, 2006).

In our view, ethnography entails all three of these: a research process involving *fieldwork methods* engaging the extraordinary-in-the-ordinary with a particular sensibility towards often more hidden or concealed meaning-making processes, reported in *a particular form of writing* that places both author and reader at the scene, in the thick of things, through actor-centred and context-sensitive analysis and theorizing grounded in layered data (Ybema et al., 2009, Chapter 1). As its purpose is to give readers a sense of what 'life' is like in the setting under study, ethnography commonly rests on an in-dwelling in that place, typically in a situation-specific role. This usually requires prolonged observation over time (and perhaps over different spatial locations; discussed below). Such in-dwelling requires ethnographers to be *there*, in the setting, long enough to be able to understand the common sense, everyday, unwritten and unspoken, tacitly known 'rules of engagement' used by situational 'natives', moving from being more of a stranger to that setting to being more of a 'familiar' in and with it (while rendering it 'strange' again in the writing). Much as 'being there' in everyday life involves engaging with those one encounters (family members, co-workers, bus drivers, shopkeepers, etc.), ethnography itself is more than a set of interviews, entailing a degree of 'living with and living like those who are studied' (Van Maanen, 1988: 2). Ethnographic fieldwork can be done in a variety of ways and with differing intensities (we therefore see little use in specifying a minimal field period), but it typically involves more than flying in and out of the field for a brief, tourist-like visit. Hence, we would join with Bate (1997) in decrying the use of 'airplane' (quick, short-duration) ethnography, whether by consultants or by academics (see also Brannan and Oultram, in this volume). Ethnographic 'being there' becomes a characteristic not only of the field research but also of the writing as well: layered descriptions of objects, events, actors and interactions help to create a non-fictional (albeit necessarily fabricated) account of organizational life, which places both author and reader at the scene.

Methodologically speaking, ethnographic research can be informed by either realist-objectivist or constructivist-interpretivist approaches (see Duberley, Johnson and Cassell, in this volume). Ethnographers can seek to discover 'how things are really done' or 'what really happened' in a particular organizational situation, in an ontologically realist fashion, seeing themselves as objective observers and sensemakers. Or they can proceed from the perspective that social realities are intersubjectively constructed, seeing themselves as co-constructors and co-interpreters of the meaning(s) of organizational events along with situational members, reflecting on their own roles in shaping those interpretations.

Lastly, although ethnography is thought by many to have originated in anthropology, an historical account of its academic origins shows that they lie in administrative practices, specifically in empires' need to manage far-flung and distant outposts. Hence, it might be 'better to regard academic anthropology as a specific instance of ethnographic practice than the other way around' (Salemink, 2003: 9). Those organizational ethnographers not trained in anthropology departments who are anxious about their methods training manqué and bona fides can, then, relinquish these concerns and get to work on developing and articulating what *organizational* ethnography is or should be, drawing on a rich heritage of organizational ethnographic research, ranging from government bureaucracies to schools, from hospitals to coal mines.

In what follows we discuss the uses of ethnography in organizational research, after which we present three examples of ethnographic research to illustrate the particular problematics of organizational ethnography. These examples inform our subsequent discussion of the multi-sited, reflexive and relational character of ethnographic research.

Uses in Organizational Research: Historical to the Present

Organizational ethnography enjoys a long heritage, across a wide range of organizational types and disciplinary homes. Elton Mayo's 1920s–1930s Hawthorne studies are a case in point (e.g. Mayo, 1933), as are the classic, late 1940s to early 1960s in-depth analyses of the 'informal organization', such as Whyte (1948), Selznick (1949), Gouldner (1954), Blau (1955), Dalton (1959), Goffman (1959), Kaufman (1960), Roy (1960) and Crozier (1964). These detailed accounts of organizational life based on field research communicate the sense of 'being there' amid the social aspects of organizations, their backstage politics, power games and other unintended, non-rational and at times dysfunctional consequences. These studies, as organizational ethnography *avant la lettre*, upended the purportedly 'rational' organizing that Max Weber's ideal type bureaucracy theories, depicting formal organizations as efficiently functioning machines, had led researchers to expect.

The development from the 1950s onwards of mainframe computers, survey research, statistical science and behaviouralist theories eclipsed ethnographic approaches, as research aiming to measure organizational structures, contingencies and behaviours by quantitative means came to dominate organizational studies. Towards the end of the 1970s, a growing unease with such quantification and the concomitant neglect of social actors' everyday practices, lived experiences and processes of meaning-making generated a renewed interest in qualitative methods. Theoretical developments across the social sciences, among them the interpretive and linguistic turns (e.g., Geertz, 1973; Rabinow and Sullivan, 1979/1985), also drove these methodological changes. Notable among the theorists leading this 'methodological renewal' in organizational studies is John Van Maanen (e.g. 1979; 1988; 1995), whose empirical and methodological work both demonstrated and theorized the place of *organizational* ethnography.

First manifested in studies of organizational symbolism and culture, the renewed attention to ethnography also invigorated older fields of study, from strategy to leadership, organizational design and change to workplace practices, cross-cultural communication to ethics and normative behaviour (see, e.g. Barley, 1983; Dubinskas, 1988; Kondo, 1990; Collinson, 1992; Ingersoll and Adams, 1992; Watson, 1994; Orr, 1996; Yanow, 1996; Delbridge, 1998; Rosen, 2000). Ethnographic (and other qualitative) research strategies have increasingly been coming back into organizational studies, in various theoretical contexts (see, e.g. Morey and Luthans, 1987; Schwartzman, 1993; Bate, 1997; and more recently, Prasad and Prasad, 2002; Neyland, 2008; Fine et al., 2009; Ybema et al., 2009). Ethnographies of public sector organizations are also returning, joining the earlier bureaucracy and public administration work of Blau, Crozier, Kaufman and Selznick cited above (e.g. Stein, 2004; Dubois, 2010), along with others in educational studies, healthcare studies and other fields.

The intertwining of ethnographic methods with a growing interpretive methodological awareness might be seen as having moved the study of particular organizational studies topics toward more 'collective', meaning-focused perspectives, among them organizational culture, identity formation and organizational learning (e.g. Kunda, 1992; Cook and Yanow, 2006 [1993] ; Nicolini et al., 2003; Brown and Humphreys, 2006), arenas erstwhile dominated by more positivist psychological and social-psychological approaches. From there, it was not a big leap to narrative or discursive approaches (e.g. Ybema, 2010) or to the practice studies (e.g. Orr, 1996; Miettinen et al., 2009) that join activity theory and actor-network theory, both drawing on ethnographic methods. Apart from its ability to depict the liveliness of organizational life, organizational ethnography promises to elucidate two aspects for which other methods, such as surveys, are less suitable: (1) its 'hidden' dimensions, and (2) its actor-context relations.

Sensitivity to hidden dimensions of organizational life

In drawing close to subjects and situations, organizational ethnographers can potentially make explicit often overlooked, tacitly known and/or concealed dimensions of meaning-making, among them emotional and political aspects. In noting the relative power of organizational actors, their interests and their strategies, ethnographies can have a direct, critical, even shocking quality, laying bare otherwise hidden and even harsh social realities and exposing the entanglements of culture with power. For organizational members, such explicit descriptions of routine, taken-for-granted ways of thinking and acting can be both familiar and surprising as they see themselves through the ethnographer's eyes. In revealing these aspects of organizational life, such ethnographies may at times challenge what organizational actors would like to hear or read about themselves and their organizations. While offering a much needed critical voice, such ethnographies also, however, require ethnographers to consider their own position, their positionality (discussed below) and the ethical implications of their work.

Sensitivity to the interplay between actors and context

Secondly, organizational ethnography can contribute to current structure-agency debates in the social sciences that continue to carve up organizational studies (Reed, 2006), as it combines an orientation towards subjective experience and individual agency with a sensitivity to the broader social settings and the historical and institutional dynamics in which these are embedded. Alternating close-ups of actors, situations and interactions with broader views that sketch wider social and historical contexts, power relations and meta-discourses, ethnography 'sees the world in a grain of sand' (slightly paraphrasing William Blake), exploring and exemplifying the general through the local and the particular. The combination of contextual analysis with an actor-centred approach promises to remedy the 'ahistorical, acontextual and aprocessual' qualities of much of organizational studies (Pettigrew, quoted in Bate, 1997: 1155).

Ethnography's research techniques take on a particular form in meeting the specific demands of management and other organizational settings. For one, researchers cannot count on walking in on an executive unannounced, and so ethnographic 'talk' often includes formal interviews. Mintzberg's (1970) 'structured observation', an alternative to the diary studies used at the time, added direct observation to the study of managers. Wolcott's (2003 [1973]) 'shadowing' (of a school principal) is yet another way to observe organizational leaders ethnographically.

The variety of ethnographic studies of organizations and organizing is reflected in our own fieldwork. We draw on three examples, conducted in different periods and in different contexts, to illustrate the attributes of organizational ethnography discussed above, its range and its sensitivity to the hidden dimensions of organizational life as well as to the interplay between contexts and actors. These studies also lay the empirical groundwork for our subsequent discussion of three current issues relevant to organizational ethnography: (1) multi-sited research in which fieldworkers follow actions, actors and artefacts; (2) highly reflexive research with respect to knowledge claims; and (3) highly relational research that treats participants as co-researchers.

Three Examples

Collective identity formation among newspaper editors (Sierk Ybema)

The very first day of my 1997 and 1998 fieldwork in the editorial rooms of two Dutch national newspapers started with the daily meeting of *Trouw*'s editorial staff at the end of the morning (Ybema, 2003). Later, I learned that these meetings usually took less than 30 minutes and were frequented by no more than 10 editors. This time, however, the room was stuffed, all 25 seats taken, at least another 25 editors sitting on tables on the sides or leaning against the walls. A prolonged debate ensued about a front-page article in that morning's newspaper that had outraged a large number of editors. If I was truly interested in identity I had found my bread buttered on both sides, the editors assured me afterwards. Following these discussions gave me a beeline right into the middle of the newspaper's internal debates about its identity and thus into the more or less concealed power- and emotion-ridden dimensions of meaning-making. Detailed descriptions of ritual gatherings in organizational settings, such as Christmas celebrations (Rosen, 2000) or informational meetings (Alvesson, 1996; see also Schwartzman, 1993), were in the back of my mind when I decided to focus my research on the heated discussion in this editorial meeting and, subsequently, to follow the forming of opinion on that day's opening article in conversations, on the intranet and in formal and informal get-togethers.

Processes of de-ideologization in Dutch society, along with the professionalization of journalism, from the 1960s onwards and the slow but gradual decrease of newspaper readership in the 1990s had created a problem of identity and image for those newspapers that had drawn inspiration from their religious or political roots. This ideological and 'reputational' crisis challenged editors of the originally Protestant newspaper *Trouw* and the politically left-wing *de Volkskrant* to rethink their overall direction, refashion the papers' profiles and thereby fundamentally reconsider the organizational identity of each. I was interested in this intense process of renewed meaning-making, asking how that collective identity came to be represented in the everyday discourse of newspaper editors now that these institutions had been cut loose from their ideological moorings.

Throughout the research I 'followed' particular issues, events, persons and texts. Shadowing the Day Chief and, subsequently, the Night Chief in the early weeks of my fieldwork, for instance, provided an excellent, 16-hour-long introduction to the editorial process and the time-pressures, groups of professionals and content demands it involved. Identity discourse was commonly present in everyday discussions about actual practices and newspaper contents, and I closely followed debates about particular identity-sensitive (and heavily discussed) issues, such as that front-page article at *Trouw* or the journalistic 'profile' of the new weekly *Volkskrant-magazine*. Using the discursive interactions over these issues as *tableaux vivant* in my writing and treating them as a 'total social fact' (Mauss, 1990 [1925]) – a comprehensive social event that opens up windows on a range of related micro-events and broader contingencies – allowed me to trace the different threads – professional, political, ideological, commercial – of the process of identity formation knotted together in these issues or incidents. Following issues, events, persons and texts on the move allowed me in my research narrative to provide a view of 'the inside' or, more accurately, the multiple insides of identity formation processes, while simultaneously sketching the wider contexts in which these 'insides' were embedded (the second aspect of organizational ethnography described above). In Sergio Leone filmic fashion, I alternated 'extreme close-ups' that 'zoomed in' on persons-in-(inter)action, with their detailed facial expressions, gestures, talk and intonation, with 'wide-angle' or 'long shots' that 'zoomed out' and showed panoramic views of institutional contexts, historical backgrounds, power relations and societal discourses (see also Nicolini, 2009).

Influenced by the 'linguistic turn' in the social sciences and organizational studies' growing interest in identity issues, I adopted a discourse analytical approach (see also Oswick, in this volume). Having read literature that theorizes social, ethnic and organizational identities in terms of continuity, distinctiveness and cohesion, including describing organizational members' firm positioning of a shared and stable collective self vis-à-vis competitors or clients, I was surprised to notice that editors did not try to restore or shore up their precarious, non-cohesive, collective selves. Instead, they claimed that neither the ideological content of their newspaper nor the symbolic boundaries between different newspapers could define their collective identity in a clear, unifying, historically consistent way. Rather than impress an outside world of competitors, readers or the general public by making self-praising comparisons with 'others' (as is usually described in the identity literature), the editors emphasized historical discontinuities, the increasing *in*distinctiveness of the newspaper vis-à-vis its competitors and the looming danger of losing the competition to those 'others'. A condensed explanation for why the editors engaged in this unexpected rhetoric rests on their felt need to stress the drama of the situation, to express their hopes and fears and to sell a change process or to resist it (Ybema, 2010).

Sensemaking in local government (Merlijn van Hulst)

Between the end of 2003 and the beginning of 2006, I conducted ethnographic fieldwork in two Dutch municipalities (van Hulst, 2008a). I had no formal position in the local governments under study, but my research role and work were supported by the administrators and announced in a letter to municipal employees and council members. Each municipality provided a desk and access to almost all meetings and archives. After a while I began to sit in on the weekly meetings of each board of aldermen with their respective mayors. This gave me, on the one hand, an overview of things happening in each place and, on the other, a sort of fieldwork rhythm. In each municipality I decided to zoom in on two political and administrative processes that people I spoke to regarded as highly relevant to that municipality.

Although the fieldwork was hosted by formal organizations, the local bureaucracies of the two towns, my focus on sensemaking processes took me beyond the boundaries of these organizations. I observed meetings of the municipalities' management teams, most of the town council meetings and many meetings of the various council committees. In addition to those taking place within the town halls, I became interested in presentations of plans to members of the public outside of them. I also visited the meetings of political parties, sounding boards and a neighbourhood committee to find out how different groups and individuals made their own interpretations of events.

Being in the field opened doors to all kinds of data and data sources that would otherwise have been hard to access. These included meetings that were closed to the general public, informal documents, such as leaflets or handwritten speeches, and unplanned casual conversations at the photocopy machine. In both municipalities I obtained copies of a large number and variety of documents: agendas and minutes of meetings, policy documents, politicians' speeches, local and regional newspaper articles, texts on municipality webpages, materials on political parties' websites, political pamphlets and political programmes. In addition, I had many conversations with actors involved in or knowledgeable about the issues under study. The character, duration, time and location of these conversations differed. Most typical were the short chats in the hallways of the town halls before or after meetings and during breaks, longer conversations during lunches and dinners, and formal, open-ended interviews in offices and at people's homes. Requiring many hours in the field, ethnographic fieldwork places demands on the researcher's social and improvisational skills. Overall, ethnographic fieldwork offered the possibility of personally experiencing the events taking place and processes unfolding (see also van Hulst, 2008b), and observation made it possible to generate data that would have been impossible to find in documents and hard to gather through interviewing alone.

On a theoretical level, the fieldwork enabled me to move from 'culture' to 'narrative'. My initial research puzzle had concerned culture in local government. When I studied organizational anthropology in the second half of the 1990s, the concept of culture as something shared and stable was no longer the only view in organizational studies. However, explaining this to public administration researchers and political scientists especially was not always easy, due to their disciplines' different orientations. Following organizational scientists such as Linda Smircich (1983), I defined organizational culture as a process of sensemaking. While writing about the issues I studied in the first town, however, I stumbled upon a concept that was even more helpful in 'seeing' what was going on there: storytelling. As I entered my second fieldwork period, that concept helped me understand more clearly how the experiences I encountered during various forms of observation, conversation and reading connected people in the field to each other, as well as connecting myself as a researcher to the field.

Implementing public policies through organizations (Dvora Yanow)

Between 1972 and 1975 I worked in a series of roles in two community centres, as part of a government corporation in Israel, in two different towns, returning in 1980–1981 for six months' follow-up observation, interviewing and document analysis from a base adjacent to the national headquarters (Yanow, 1996). Both towns were immigrant towns remote from urban centres, and the agency's raison d'être was to provide non-formal educational and cultural activities – language, cooking and photography courses, folkdancing, tennis, etc. – leading to residents' integration into the state and the adoption of its national cultural ethos. As a Community Organizer, my first role, a position funded by the Housing Ministry, my supervisor in each centre had me map each town and its neighbourhoods, noting the type and condition of housing and infrastructure (poor lighting, bad sewerage, uncollected garbage), the locations of services (the town hall and its departments; banks, grocery stores, markets, synagogues; youth, sports, union and other kinds of clubs and social halls; and so on), and residents' demographic characteristics (year of immigration, ethnic group, family size, ages, etc.). At one point I became Acting Director of the second centre, subsequently becoming the Director of two departments. I also became a member of the corporation's national advisory group, giving me an overview of the larger operation. When I returned for the follow-up study, it was as a non-participating observer.

My research question grew out of the initial experience: why was it so difficult for my community organizer colleagues and myself to accomplish in the field what we thought we had a clear national mandate for? My undergraduate background in political science led me to frame my research as a policy implementation study, as the community centres were implementing national public policy. To understand this implementation, I needed to know something about organizations, the entities charged with putting policy into practice. Yet existing implementation and organizational theories, emphasizing rational-technical decision-making and instrumental goal-setting, did not help me understand my own lived experience. US social sciences were then opening up to science studies, hermeneutics and phenomenology, and what came to be called 'the interpretive turn', and these readings (e.g. Kuhn, 1970 [1962]; Berger and Luckmann, 1966; Geertz, 1973) led me to others in symbolic-cultural anthropology and the philosophy of (social) science. I came to see the events and circumstances I was studying as entailing the communication of policy and organizational meanings through language (especially the organization's name and an organizational metaphor), material objects (the centres' buildings and their design and programmes) and acts (organizational rituals and their myth-like components). Implementation, I saw, was enabled or confounded by overlaps or differences between policy and organizational founders' and leaders' intended meanings, embedded in and communicated through those elements, and town residents' and others' own 'readings' of those elements and their meanings.

Given the research focus on meaning, I cannot imagine conducting the study in any other way. My theorizing grew out of the observations, experiences, readings and conversations that I had on site, informed by knowledge of the organization's history and sociopolitical context and by the theoretical literature's debates. Experience in two centres added a comparative angle. Without 'being there', experiencing the organization, the towns, their physical layout and problems, and their residents' ways of life, I would not have understood the founder's statement that the 'community centre would be a functional supermarket' – I needed to know what 'supermarket' meant to people there at that time to understand its meaning in community centre terms. As I was interested in present-day problems, historical-archival analysis, while engaging, would have been insufficient, even with interviews; nor would a survey have enabled me to explore the meaning-focused questions I was interested in.

The disadvantages were personal, rather than methods-related in the narrow sense. Being on location in remote settings, let alone 'foreign' ones, for extended periods of time, separated from family and friends and one's familiar way of living, is not easy. The literature has not spoken much of the emotional strain of prolonged field research (but see Ortbals and Rincker, 2009), let alone of the sexual and other physical aspects that can pose challenges – relationships between researchers and researched; harassment of female researchers; being 'out' in the field (see Lewin and Leap, 1996); mobility and other problems of 'wheelchairedness' (Mike Duijn, personal communication, 2009); the aging field researcher; and other bodily, emotional, mental or social limitations (Schwartz-Shea and Yanow, 2011).

Contemporary Issues in Organizational Ethnography: Multi-sited, Reflexive and Relational

These research examples illuminate three issues on the methodological table today: ethnography's 'multi-sitedness'; reflexivity (see also Haynes, in this volume), including on the researcher's positionality; and the intrinsically relational character of ethnographic fieldwork.

Multi-sited ethnography

The settings of traditional ethnography had a distinctive character: the locations were relatively bounded – or appeared that way. More recently, anthropologists have started speaking of 'multi-sited' ethnography, its marking underscoring the difference in this conceptualization. Our examples suggest, however, that in organizational ethnography, multi-sitedness is the norm; it may even be one of its distinctive characteristics, as organizational ethnographers typically follow actors, actions, artefacts and the ideas they embody and reflect. Following these travelling ideas, persons and so forth leads researchers to different organization-related sites, especially when conceiving of organizations as loosely coupled systems, inter-organizational fields or networks. We see this in Ybema's following of the newspaper editors' work, decisions, rituals, rumours, discussions and the report, new logo, front page, product, etc.; in van Hulst's following of actors and acts both inside and outside of the town halls; and in Yanow's trailing of self-contained centres and the parent organization, as well as of oversight ministries, funding agencies and overseas donors and ideas. Orr (1996), in another example, followed copier technicians visiting clients and meeting colleagues in multiple locations far from the corporation's central office. Indeed, such 'following' can make the research process seem to meander, challenging the researcher to travel with or trail issues, persons and/or texts to various locations. Even if one remains within the walls of a single organization, 'mapping' across its departments and hierarchical levels, one is perforce engaged in a multi-sited study.

Reflexivity and positionality

Reflexivity, including on the researcher's positionality, is increasingly central to ethnographic research, in particular that which is informed by a constructivist-interpretivist methodology in which researcher objectivity is not (assumed to be) present. This casts in heightened relief the matter of 'truth claims' and what positivist-informed research calls their 'validity' and 'reliability'. As those terms encapsulate the notion that research can mirror the world being observed, they are less appropriate for assessing research that proceeds from a constructivist-interpretivist perspective. Rather than seeing data as existing independent of the researcher, waiting in 'the field' to be discovered, interpretive ethnographers look at how happenstance shaped their access to various organizational parts, persons, documents, etc. The truth claims question pivots on how both data and analyses were generated and developed, requiring reflective transparency on researchers' positionality in two senses: their 'geographic' location within the organization and their demographic characteristics, either of which might shape access and sight, enabling some things while limiting others. Rather than seeing themselves as objective, uninvolved discoverers of pre-existing data, interpretive ethnographers see themselves as actively involved in the (co-)construction of those data, and they also see their narratives as constructing the organizational 'realities' they report. While reflecting on these matters could certainly be part of the field research itself, such reflexivity is primarily marshalled on the written page.

Location-based positionality is a matter of particular concern in organizational ethnography, given the links between hierarchy, knowledge and power. Researchers who immerse themselves in 'being there' make themselves more likely to be associated with or drawn into a particular perspective. The community centre study's second phase illustrates one dimension of this problematic: perceiving Yanow as 'coming from agency headquarters' because she was located nearby, local centre staff at times treated the research visit as an opportunity to put a particular spin on what was said and shown, thinking it a way to convey messages to the CEO (despite the fact that she had no such access to him). In the newspaper case, positionality was interpreted in professional terms: some journalists seemed highly suspicious that Ybema would want to make headlines with his research, in a journalistic fashion. To overcome this, he positioned himself as someone who was not interested in headlines and scoops, whose (academic) book would not be out for at least another year (which made them more cooperative, albeit puzzled at the value of such 'outdated' data). For van Hulst, a kind of locational positionality emerged in one board meeting when civil servants were asked to leave the room so that board members could have a private conversation. As he packed his ethnographer's gear to leave too, one of the board members announced: 'Researcher-of-the-administration stays'. While experiencing this as both a surprise and honour, van Hulst noted the trickiness of such a positioning, which might affect his ability to take a critical stance towards those in power. Geographic positionality can also be a matter of the (in-)sight afforded by different locations, as Pachirat (2011) documents with his promotion from slaughterhouse floor to Quality Control.

In its demographic sense, positionality entails the gender, race-ethnic, class, age, sexuality and other characteristics that can affect a researcher's access to certain situations and/or (categories of) persons, others' sensemaking of the researcher and the researcher's ability to understand others' experiences. Shehata (2006), for instance, documents how his birthplace, educational attainment, socio-economic background, gender and religious affiliation shaped how he was perceived on the shopfloor, what he was allowed to do and kept from doing, and the kinds of settings he could and could not enter. Interpretive ethnographers are increasingly expected to provide greater transparency concerning their methods and their positionality, in all senses of the term, as a way of supporting the truth claims they advance.

'But I thought we were friends?!' and other issues in the relational character of research

Explicit recognition of the relational character of fieldwork is increasing, and along with it both the ethical and methodological implications. To begin with, ethnographers must negotiate 'access' to their research sites; but whereas this traditionally was seen as a kind of 'knocking on the administrative and/or chief's door', today it is increasingly seen as a matter of establishing and sustaining relationships over time. This makes access more than a one-shot permissional activity, as the essays in Feldman et al. (2003) make clear. Moreover, fieldwork 'friendships' require care, including making decisions about how instrumentally to treat those whom researchers encounter or seek out in the conduct of the research: there is a difference between conceiving of situational actors as properties of the researcher ('my' informants) and treating them in a Buberian 'I-Thou' fashion. What will happen to fieldwork relationships when the researcher concludes his/her time in the field? And what slights or betrayals might bring a situational member to exclaim, in anger and/or anguish, 'But I thought we were friends?!' (Beech et al., 2009).

A second aspect of the relational character of ethnographic research links to epistemological concerns: the researcher's need to become as familiar as possible with the local culture in order to understand its workings, while maintaining enough epistemological 'stranger-ness' that a recognition of the common sense, the everyday, the unspoken/unwritten and the tacit retains its analytic purchase (see, e.g. Ybema and Kamsteeg, 2009). The ways of knowing and kinds of knowledge entailed in this balancing have been called emic/etic (see Headland et al., 1990), insider/outsider (e.g. Bartunek and Louis, 1996), experience-near/experience-distant (Geertz, 1973). For Ybema, for instance, working to remain a relative 'outsider' to the newspaper and to preserve some of the initial surprise was as important as working to become an 'insider' and to achieve immersion. The long time it took him to understand the implications of his observations was frustrating, but it was only through taking seriously his own bewilderment that new insights emerged.

Some confusion has developed, however, particularly in organizational studies, concerning what it means as a researcher to be an 'insider'. Is the aim truly to lose one's 'outsider' status? Is that even conceivable? The ontological possibility of organizational 'outsiders' becoming 'insiders' as they seek to add local, emic knowledge to theory-rooted etic knowledge is far more fraught than has been acknowledged to date. Insider/outsider objectifies local 'informants', treating them as a means toward the researcher's ends in ways that nullify the relational character of field research. On the epistemological side of things, emic/etic reifies the notion that 'local' knowledge and 'theoretical' knowledge are separate kinds. In interaction, the two term pairs negate the hermeneutic-phenomenological notion that knowledge, or understanding, is co-created in the interaction between researchers and their situational partners, neither of whom can become the other (with the possible exception of 'native anthropologists'; see Narayan, 1993; see Nencel and Yanow, 2008). On this, further theorizing is called for.

Why Organizational Ethnography?

To conclude, we must engage with the matter of what might lead an organizational researcher to undertake an ethnographic study. Current methodological debates often stipulate that the choice of method should be driven by the research question, rather than vice versa. Although in sympathy with this argument, we think it shortchanges the matter by implying that methods are chosen in an entirely rational fashion. Our own research and teaching experiences suggest, instead, that research questions and methods are much more mutually constituted – and at times are so intricately bound up with each other as to be inseparable. Our sense of this links strongly to the third understanding of ethnography named in the opening section.

An ethnographic sensibility is not something that a researcher just sets aside; neither is it something that one picks up as one would select a method from a 'toolbox', a common metaphor in methods textbooks. At least one of us would want to say that her question-methods packet chose her, rather than vice versa – meaning that their development was intertwined, as well as being linked to, her (unspoken) proclivities. For another of us, training in survey research and statistical analyses had provided little knowledge of other research traditions; still, he was strongly drawn to processes of meaning-making and organizational power games, believing these notions would help him understand what was 'actually' going on in the organization he was studying. This predilection for meaning-focused research and qualitative methods was also inspired by opportunity (good access to inner decision-making circles) and situation (strong disagreements surfacing in the field, which were hard to ignore).

Although this position may be in keeping with a hermeneutic-phenomenological stance, it is driven not by our philosophical presuppositions but by our lived experiences, as both researchers and teachers, in which we have seen people, ourselves included, drawn towards framing research questions in particular ways that will call on particular methods because of ways of seeing and knowing that preceded the research project, reflecting something much deeper than the rational-instrumental choosing of a tool.

Ethnographic research is a complex practice. Although reading about organizational ethnography as well as reading well-written organizational ethnographies can definitely help researchers become good ethnographers, its practice is largely learned through the doing – in the field – as one experiences and develops a certain sensibility for organizational ethnography itself. This suggests that a discussion of ethnography's advantages and disadvantages is misplaced to the extent that it rests on those very rational considerations and choices that we think do not well describe the research experience. Organizational and other scholars need, instead, to know what ethnographic methods do well and less well and perhaps to focus more on enabling students and colleagues to recognize their own personal strengths and limitations and how these might play out in the conduct of ethnographic research.

Further Reading

Interest in organizational ethnography has recently taken off, garnering attention through workshops, conferences, journal special issues and methods-focused books, leading us to anticipate a surge in monographs. Kunda (1992) and Orr (1996) remain the most cited as leading exemplars of the genre. For introductions to organizational ethnographic methods and methodological concerns, see Neyland (2008), Kostera (2007) and Ybema et al. (2009). The first two of these focus more on methods, conveying something of the 'how to' of ethnographic research, with introductory chapters on culture, ethnography and organizations (Kostera) and treatments of the whole research process illustrated by various organizational ethnographies (Neyland). The third is more methodological in orientation; it both introduces and critically discusses various practices in organizational ethnography, tackling the key challenges and methodological, analytical, (re)presentational, ethical and social problematics that arise in the doing and writing of organizational ethnography. For an overview of ethnography's past and potential contributions to organizational studies, see Fine et al. (2009). And while not specific to organizational studies, Atkinson et al. (2001) offer an outstanding collection of essays on methodological issues of concern to organizational ethnographers.

References

Alvesson, M. (1996) *Communication, Power and Organization.* Berlin: De Gruyter.

Atkinson, P., Coffey, A., Delamont, S., Lofland, J. and Lofland, L. (eds) (2001) *Handbook of Ethnography.* London: Sage.

Barley, S. (1983) 'Semiotics and the study of occupational and organizational cultures', *Administrative Science Quarterly*, 28 (3): 393–413.

Bartunek, J.M. and Louis, M.R. (1996) *Insider/Outsider Team Research.* Thousand Oaks, CA: Sage.

Bate, S.P. (1997) 'Whatever happened to organizational anthropology?', *Human Relations*, 50 (9): 1147–1171.

Beech, N., Hibbert, P., MacIntosh, R. and McInnes, P. (2009) 'But I thought we were friends?', in S. Ybema, D. Yanow, H. Wels and F. Kamsteeg (eds), *Organizational Ethnography.* London: Sage, pp. 196–214.

Berger, P.L. and Luckmann, T. (1966) *The Social Construction of Reality.* New York: Anchor Books.

Blau, P. (1955) *The Dynamics of Bureaucracy.* Chicago: University of Chicago Press.

Brown, A.D. and Humphreys, M. (2006) 'Epic and tragic tales: making sense of change', *Journal of Applied Behavioral Science*, 39 (22): 121–144.

Collinson, D.L. (1992) *Managing the Shopfloor.* Berlin: De Gruyter.

Cook, S.D. and Yanow, D. (2006 [1993]) 'Culture and organizational learning', in B. Czarniawska (ed.), *Organization Theory*, vol. 1. Cheltenham: Edward Elgar, pp. 259–276.

Crozier, M. (1964) *The Bureaucratic Phenomenon.* Chicago: University of Chicago Press.

Dalton, M. (1959) *Men who Manage*. New York: Wiley.

Delbridge, R. (1998) *Life on the Line in Contemporary Manufacturing*. Oxford: Oxford University Press.

Dubinskas, F.A. (ed.) (1988) *Making Time: Ethnographies of High Technology Organizations*. Philadelphia, PA: Temple University Press.

Dubois, V. (2010) *The Bureaucrat and the Poor*. Aldershot: Ashgate.

Feldman, M.S., Bell, J. and Berger, M.T. (eds) (2003) *Gaining Access*. Walnut Creek, CA: Altamira.

Fine, G.A., Morrill, C. and Surianarain, S. (2009) 'Ethnography in organizational settings', in D.A. Buchanan and A. Bryman (eds), *The Sage Handbook of Organizational Research Methods*. London: Sage, pp. 602–619.

Geertz, C. (1973) *The Interpretation of Cultures*. New York: Basic Books.

Goffman, E. (1959) *The Presentation of Self in Everyday Life*. Garden City, NY: Anchor Books.

Gouldner, A.W. (1954) *Patterns of Industrial Bureaucracy*. New York: Free Press.

Headland, T.N., Pike, K.L. and Harris, M. (eds) (1990) *Emics and Etics: The Insider/Outsider Debate*. Newbury Park, CA: Sage.

Ingersoll, V.H. and Adams, G. (1992) *The Tacit Organization*. Greenwich, CT: JAI Press.

Kaufman, H. (1960) *The Forest Ranger*. Baltimore, MD: Johns Hopkins Press.

Kondo, D. (1990) *Crafting Selves*. Chicago, IL: University of Chicago Press.

Kostera, M. (2007) *Organisational Ethnography*. Lund: Studentlitteratur AB.

Kuhn, T. (1970 [1962]) *The Structure of Scientific Revolutions* (2nd edn). Chicago: University of Chicago Press.

Kunda, G. (1992) *Engineering Culture*. Philadelphia, PA: Temple University Press.

Lewin, E. and Leap, W.L. (eds) (1996) *Out in the Field*. Urbana: University of Illinois Press.

Mauss, M. (1990 [1925]) *The Gift*. London: Routledge.

Mayo, E. (1933) *The Human Problems of Industrial Civilization*. New York: Macmillan.

Miettinen, R., Samra-Fredericks, D. and Yanow, D. (2009) 'Re-turn to practice', *Organization Studies*, 30 (12): 1309–1327.

Mintzberg, H. (1970) 'Structured observation as a method to study managerial work', *Journal of Management Studies*, 7 (1): 87–104.

Morey, N.C. and Luthans, F. (1987) 'Anthropology: the forgotten behavioral science in management history', in F. Hoy (ed.), *Best Papers Proceedings of the 47th Annual Meeting of the Academy of Management*. Athens, GA: University of Georgia, pp. 128–132.

Narayan, K. (1993) 'How native is a "native" anthropologist?', *American Anthropologist*, 95: 671–686.

Nencel, L. and Yanow, D. (2008) 'On methodological relics: reconsidering etic outsiders, emic insiders, and fieldwork relationships', paper presented at the European Association of Social Anthropologists, Ljubljana (26–30 August).

Neyland, D. (2008) *Organizational Ethnography*. London: Sage.

Nicolini, D. (2009) 'Zooming in and zooming out: a package of method and theory to study work practices', in S. Ybema, D. Yanow, H. Wels and F. Kamsteeg (eds), *Organizational Ethnography*. London: Sage, pp. 120–138.

Nicolini, D., Gherardi, S. and Yanow, D. (2003) 'Toward a practice-based view of knowing and learning in organizations', in D. Nicolini, S. Gherardi and D. Yanow (eds), *Knowing in Organizations: A Practice-based Approach*. Armonk, NY: M.E. Sharpe, pp. 3–31.

Orr, J. (1996) *Talking about Machines*. New York: Cornell University Press.

Ortbals, C.D. and Rincker, M.E. (eds) (2009) 'Fieldwork, identities, and intersectionality: a symposium', *PS: Political Science & Politics*, 42 (2): 287–385.

Pachirat, T. (2011) 'The *political* in political ethnography: reflections from an industrialized slaughterhouse on perspective, power, and sight', in E. Schatz (ed.), *Political Ethnography: What Immersion Contributes to the Study of Power*. Chicago: University of Chicago Press, pp. 143–162.

Pader, E. (2006) 'Seeing with an ethnographic sensibility', in D. Yanow and P. Schwartz-Shea (eds), *Interpretation and Method: Empirical Research Methods and the Interpretive Turn*. Armonk, NY: M.E. Sharpe, pp. 161–175.

Prasad, A. and Prasad, P. (2002) 'The coming of age of interpretive organizational research', *Organizational Research Methods*, 5 (1): 4–11.

Rabinow, P. and Sullivan, W.M. (eds) (1979, 1985) *Interpretive Social Science* (1st and 2nd edns). Berkeley: University of California Press.

Reed, M. (2006) 'Organizational theorizing', in S.R. Clegg, C. Hardy, T.B. Lawrence and W.R. Nord (eds), *The Sage Handbook of Organization Studies* (2nd edn). London: Sage, pp. 19–54.

Rosen, M. (2000) *Turning Words, Spinning Worlds*. Amsterdam: Harwood.

Roy, D. (1960) 'Banana time', *Human Organization*, 18: 156–68.

Salemink, O. (2003) 'Ethnography, anthropology and colonial discourse', in *The Ethnography of Vietnam's Central Highlanders*. London: Routledge Curzon, pp. 1–39.

Schwartzman, H.B. (1993) *Ethnography in Organizations*. Newbury Park, CA: Sage.

Selznick, P. (1949) *TVA and the Grass Roots*. Berkeley: University of California Press.

Shehata, S. (2006) 'Ethnography, identity, and the production of knowledge', in D. Yanow and P. Schwartz-Shea (eds), *Interpretation and Method: Empirical Research Methods and the Interpretive Turn*. Armonk, NY: M.E. Sharpe, pp. 244–263.

Smircich, L. (1983) 'Studying organizations as cultures', in G. Morgan (ed.), *Beyond Method*. London: Sage, pp. 160–172.

Stein, S.J. (2004) *The Culture of Education Policy*. New York: Teachers College Press.

van Hulst, M.J. (2008a) *Town Hall Tales*. Delft: Eburon.

van Hulst, M.J. (2008b) 'Quite an experience: using ethnography to study local government', *Critical Policy Analysis*, 2 (2): 143–159.

Van Maanen, J. (1979) 'The fact of fiction in organizational ethnography', *Administrative Science Quarterly*, 24: 539–550.

Van Maanen, J. (1988) *Tales of the Field*. Chicago: University of Chicago Press.

Van Maanen, J. (1995) 'An end to innocence: the ethnography of ethnography', in J. Van Maanen (ed.), *Representation in Ethnography*. Thousand Oaks, CA: Sage, pp. 1–35.

Watson, T. (1994) *In Search of Management*. London: Routledge.

Whyte, W.F. (1948) *Human Relations in the Restaurant Industry.* New York: McGraw-Hill.

Wolcott, H.F. (2003 [1973]) *The Man in the Principal's Office: An Ethnography.* Walnut Creek, CA: AltaMira Press.

Yanow, D. (1996) *How Does a Policy Mean?* Washington, DC: Georgetown University Press.

Ybema, S. (2003) *De Koers van de Krant: Vertogen over Identiteit bij Trouw en de Volkskrant [Discourses on Tradition and Transition: Conflict about the Newspaper's Identity among Editors of Trouw and de Volkskrant].* Amsterdam: VU University Amsterdam.

Ybema, S. (2010) 'Talk of change', *Organization Studies,* 31 (4): 481–503.

Ybema, S. and Kamsteeg, F. (2009) 'Making the familiar strange', in S. Ybema et al. (eds), *Organizational Ethnography.* London: Sage, pp. 101–119.

Ybema, S., Yanow, D., Wels, H. and Kamsteeg, F. (2009) 'Studying everyday organizational life', in S. Ybema et al. (eds), *Organizational Ethnography.* London: Sage, pp. 1–20.

5 Action Research

Julie Wolfram Cox

Introduction

In this chapter action research (AR) is presented as an endeavour that is both liminal and hybrid in nature. It is liminal in the sense that it exists in the interstices between research, consulting, social action and reflection. It is hybrid in the sense that new forms of AR combine and supplement earlier approaches (e.g. Stebbins and Shani, 2009). The associated variety and popularity of AR in organizational studies has been the subject of much discussion and several attempts have been made to compare and contrast different emphases among AR approaches (Cassell and Johnson, 2006; Gill and Johnson, 2010). Given this variety it is important that the prospective action researcher takes time to situate AR practice within the field of study and consider carefully the nature and assumptions underlying his or her work. While such considerations are, of course, relevant to all research (Crotty, 1998), they remain of particular importance for AR given (much contested) concerns with its rigour, its heralded death (Sanford, 2005 [1970]) and even its more recent hubris (Wolfram Cox and Cooke, 2007).

This chapter aims to assist the action researcher to gain (more) familiarity with such discussions. After presenting some widely used definitions of AR, a brief introduction to its development is presented in an effort to display the sources of variety among AR approaches. Next comes a consideration of what AR is *not*. Issues to consider are highlighted, as are the author's own reflections on navigating and re-negotiating relationships over the term of a project on governance and accountability in policing.[1] Emphasis is placed on AR in organizational settings and recent reflexive efforts to display rather than sanitize or evaluate AR in absolute terms are applauded.

What is Action Research?

As defined by French and Bell (1999: 130), AR is:

> the process of systematically collecting research data about an ongoing system relative to some objective, goal, or need of that system; feeding these data back into the system; taking actions by altering selected variables within the system based both on data and on hypotheses; and evaluating the results of actions by collecting more data.

In recent times Reason and Bradbury's broader (2001: 1) definition has also gained currency. They saw AR as 'a participatory, democratic process concerned with developing practical knowing in the pursuit of worthwhile human purposes … and more generally the flourishing of individual persons and their communities'.

In recognition of the variety of perspectives on AR, some have claimed that there is neither a simple guide nor a single definition for AR (Robinson, [1993] 2005). Indeed, it has been argued that AR is best represented as a 'family' of approaches (Reason and Bradbury, 2001; Stebbins and Shani, 2009; Bradbury Huang, 2010) or perhaps a food of many flavours (Chandler and Torbert, 2003).

Within this diversity some common threads remain. Gill and Johnson (2010: 99) suggest that most action researchers (still) 'tend to follow Lewin' and use 'an iterative cycle of problem identification, diagnosis, planning, intervention and evaluation of the results of action in order to learn from experience and as a prelude to further diagnostic activity and the planning of subsequent interventions'. In many representations this process appears as a spiral (Sykes and Treleaven, 2009). Whatever the specific approach, Gill and Johnson (2010: 103) have stressed the collaborative nature of the AR relationship and the notion that 'action research is not done *upon* people, rather it is research that is done *with* those people'.

[1]The research discussed here was funded by an Australian Research Council Linkage Project Grant and by Victoria Police, for whose continued support I am most grateful. I would also like to thank Georgina Caillard for her assistance with and comments on this draft.

Development and Differentiation[2]

Sources and streams of action research

In an early commentary on the derivations of AR, Rapoport (2005 [1970]: 26) distinguished four 'streams of development': the Tavistock stream of experience in the United Kingdom during and after World War II, an operational research stream that also developed out of the war, a group dynamics stream attributed to Kurt Lewin and his followers in the United States and an applied anthropology stream. While Rapoport's derivation may be readily contested (e.g., Curle, 2005 [1949]; Fals-Borda, 2005 [1984]; Cooke, 2005 [2003]) it remains useful in tracing particular emphases in the practice of AR and for allowing a consideration of influences other than those of Lewin and Tavistock (e.g. Maurer and Githens, 2010).

Scope of action research

The emphasis of early AR work was on material changes assessable in the short term and usually conducted by an outside professional consultant (e.g. Lippitt, 2005 [1959]; Whyte, 2005 [1961]). In contrast, more recent models of AR practice include the use of internal researcher/consultants who lose the remoteness and the impartiality of the unfamiliar, detached 'expert' (e.g. Coghlan, 2005 [2001]; Coghlan and Brannick, 2009).

Also contrasting with the local and material locus of early AR researchers were those who depicted its purpose as broader social change. As early as 1945 Lewin supported an extension of the reach of AR on the basis that its focus on the *how* of social interventions obscured the bigger *why* questions of their purpose and legitimacy (Lewin, 2005 [1945]: 20). This interest in large societal issues is also evident in Lewin's (2005 [1946]) account, *Research on Minority Problems*, where he argued for AR's potential both for solving social problems and for extending the principles of experimental science (Greenwood and Levin, 1998; see also Cassell and Johnson, 2006).

Participation and action

After several other early papers on AR also addressed issues of racism and ethnicity, AR's social change imperative started to gather momentum. What

[2]Developed from Wolfram Cox and Cooke (2007).

became known as participatory research was seen to be concerned more with conflict than consensus social theory and to place more emphasis on promoting system transformation and the problems of equity, self-reliance and oppression than on promoting reform and the problems of efficiency and growth within a client system (Brown and Tandon, 2005 [1983]). Departing from Lewin, and arguing that both AR and participatory research 'explicitly reject the irrelevance [*sic*] of more traditional conceptions of social science research', Brown and Tandon ([1983] 2005: 32) examined the prospects for beneficial, but inevitably problematic interactions between the traditions.

Participatory research was also termed 'participatory action research (PAR)', a conflation itself subject to variations of meaning (see Brown, 2005 [1993]). For example, Orlando Fals-Borda (2005 [1984]; 2005 [1987]), the foremost developer and advocate of PAR, aimed to use action-research-type techniques for progressive social change. His approach to PAR can be compared with that of W.F. Whyte (Whyte et al., 2005 [1989]; Argyris and Schön, 2005 [1989]). In Whyte's version, PAR is explained as an applied research strategy, unusual in its recognition of the value and legitimacy of labour unions and affinity with traditions of industrial democracy.

Whyte and his co-authors also connected PAR to wider understandings of the nature of science in society. Lacking the societal praxis of Fals-Borda and associated more with organizational or corporate settings (Cassell and Johnson, 2006), Whyte's PAR is hard to distinguish from 'normal' AR when participation is a defining feature. By 1983, Brown and Tandon (2005 [1983]) framed this comparison as one between First World AR and the tradition of participatory research that had emerged in the Third World. They stated that the First World tradition focused on individual and group levels of analysis while that of the Third World was concerned with societal change.

Negotiating (and re-negotiating) participatory action research: an example from the field

Such categorizations assume that the nature and intent of an AR project will remain fairly static throughout its duration, a stability that is ironic given the iterative nature of the AR process and assumes that a shared concept of the research can be both attained and maintained over time. A project with which I have been involved over the last four years highlights that such stability is not always the case.

The project concerned governance and accountability with Victoria Police (VP) in the state of Victoria, Australia. The original plan was to use action research to investigate, analyse, evaluate and facilitate a shift from command and control-based governance to more collaborative and even collegiate (professional, egalitarian) structures and processes. The project was set up along traditional (First World) PAR lines: as a working collaboration between an external research team from two universities and an internal VP steering committee as the client. An assessment of the effectiveness of police research networks had called for the greater use of such participatory action research due to its emphasis on equal partnership and dialogue among participants and researchers and in this sense the methodology for the research to be undertaken for this project was to be congruent with its focus, for this collaboration was to be modelled through the research process as well as being the subject of the research. Based on a joint consultation, the original research design incorporated joint VP and research team participation ranging from the refining of the research questions and methodology through to the data collection, analysis, implementation and assessment of interventions.

The initial encouragement for what became our project had been given by an advisor (now retired) to the then Chief Commissioner of Police, Christine Nixon. Ms Nixon had introduced several changes to the structures and emphases of Victoria Police and her advisor was keen for our work to take the form of an AR project, 'so that it would not sit on the shelf'. Together we applied for additional funding from the Australian Research Council. Such funding applications are encouraged both within Australian universities, where they hold much prestige, and within Victoria Police, which has developed a good reputation as a major supporter of publicly funded collaborative research, including the involvement of police officers in data collection and analysis. After two tries and various adjustments in personnel and content to strengthen its theoretical contribution, the application was successful. While much research into the organization had been initiated during Ms Nixon's term, ours was the first such project to involve work with police management as its subject.

The news of the application's success finally arrived about seven months after its submission and the start of the project was further delayed due to the need to set up research contracts and to arrange ethics clearances across two universities and Victoria Police. Within this period (roughly a further year), an initial steering committee was formed and some internal 're-selling' of the project was required as senior personnel had changed. Soon afterwards, and in the first of several re-negotiations, I was asked to meet with VP's then Organization Development Steering Committee and to respond to suggestions about the project's emphasis. Over time the membership of our project steering committee was subject to some further changes due to the promotion and retirement of several staff, meaning that we again needed to re-negotiate the nature of what had originally been a project identified as needed from within Victoria Police, to explain the collaborative intent behind the research process and to justify our interest in qualitative research to officers and managers who were more familiar and more at ease with large quantitative data sets.

Thus the very basis for and ownership of the project was subject to several shifts. Its form also changed, for in developing the funding proposal the written project outline had had to be translated into a form that was acceptable for academic peer review and then had to be re-translated for the steering committee. Over the period since our initial meetings, organizational priorities had changed and the steering committee suggested some specific emphases for our studies based on a change in leadership at VP and an assessment of some existing experimentation in governance arrangements.

We requested union representation on the steering committee but this was declined. We were required to attend steering committee meetings every three months, much of which were devoted to meeting formal project management requirements including the submission of progress documents and a discussion of the project risks. Over time the length of the steering committee meetings was reduced and the researcher membership of all such committees was also reduced to include only the chief investigators for each project, meaning that our research assistants were unable to attend most meetings. After two such steering committee meetings we received two formal letters outlining changes to the scope of the project, including one that precluded us from continuing our ongoing observation of particular committees when all such observations (for all projects involving external researchers) were stopped in response to a senior management request.

This process of negotiation and re-negotiation meant that we needed to re-start the project several times, which also involved several re-drafts of our suggested methodology. In the meantime a series of organizational changes was already underway and the emphasis of the project moved away from implementation and towards evaluation and feedback. However, and to some extent despite formal requirements from VP, the universities, their lawyers and administrators, much goodwill remained. The formal management processes did not stifle the collaboration itself, our ability to interview far and wide or to present our findings with reference to the full diversity of opinions represented in our research and more general implications for public management. As argued by Sykes and Treleaven (2009: 226), 'effective engagement of participants require[s] a sensitive consideration of organizational contexts and power relationships'.

Action research and science

In addition to the importance of the politics of organizational collaboration, other challenges to the potential of AR reflect larger concerns about the very nature of social science. For example, while not naming AR as such, Selltiz and Cook (2005 [1948]) set out the case for AR to be brought to a wider audience. They described the need to bridge a gap between 'pure' research aimed at identifying general social principles and 'applied' research so narrowly designed as to have no relevance other than to the often artificially constructed scenarios it investigates. Required instead, they argued, was research that addresses real and immediate social problems but uses the traditional scientific method and produces actual social change. Adding to this, Rapoport (2005 [1970]: 25) wrote that: 'Action research aims to contribute both to the practical concerns of people in an immediate problematic situation and to the goals of social science by joint collaboration within a mutually acceptable ethical framework'.

Taking a more pessimistic perspective toward AR at the time, Sanford (2005 [1970]) adopted the tone of a premature and indeed mistaken obituary in his comparison of AR of the 1940s and 1950s with that of the late 1960s, by which time he argued that there had been little emphasis on the study of actions and that the separation of action from research had meant that AR had had little influence in the social sciences, except in education, his chosen context. His preference was for 'research-action' with the aim of promoting liberation and growth through the processes of research.

Such a reference – and deference – to science has proved common even from the early days (see Chein et al., 2005 [1948]) and, as suggested by Cooke (2006), scientism was embedded by Lippitt (2005 [1950]) into his constructions of the AR-derived 'change agent' identity. While the notion, tacit and explicit, of the action researcher as change agent still prevails, and some forms of AR retain a positivist epistemology and commonality with the scientific method (Aguinis, 2005 [1993]), most do not (Chandler and Torbert, 2003; Ellis and Kiely, 2005 [2000]). Action researchers have moved from the somewhat defensive claim that AR 'transcends the sterile specialization of the social sciences' (Blum, 2005 [1955]: 316) to a careful differentiation of themselves *from* positivist scientism, albeit through such (scientific) terms as validity (Ellis and Kiely, 2005 [2000]), generalization and rigour (Melrose, 2005 [2001]; see also Cassell and Johnson, 2006).

For example, Susman and Evered (2005 [1978]) located the action researcher within a 'different' science, one that also requires different criteria and methods; namely, understanding rather than explanation, making things happen rather than prediction, conjectures rather than deduction or induction, engagement rather than detachment, and action rather than contemplation. More specifically, McTaggart (2005 [1998]) put forward the view that the discourse of validity has been colonized by positivist thought and argued for validation to become, instead, a social and political process concerned with making commitments transparent to participants through appropriate communicative structures (see also Checkland and Howell, 2005 [1998]). He argued that PAR was not valid unless it met the criteria of defensibility, educative value, political efficacy and moral appropriateness. In terms of external validity, in particular, Schön (2005 [1995]) placed discussions of rigour and of relevance within the institutional context of the research university and in relation to the new scholarship advocated by Boyer, with its emphasis on integration and application. Schön argued for the need to legitimize a new type of generalization: that of 'reflective transfer', where actionable knowledge can be carried over to new practice situations through the use of models or prototypes.

Thus, points of reference and distinction have moved from the development of varieties of AR within the span of activity that bridges organizational consultation and science towards some effort to breach that span altogether and to establish broader criteria for the assessment of action. For example, and like Third World PAR, Reason's (1994; 2005 [1999]) development of the related notion of co-operative inquiry aimed for democratization and emancipation through research. It also problematized 'the positivist view of the action researcher as a detached expert who exercises a legitimate role as architect of change' (Cassell and Johnson, 2006: 800).

Action science, action inquiry and action learning

Thus, comparisons among the varieties of AR are important as they help us to understand both the scope and the type of science relevant to AR in organizations (see Bain, 2005 [1951]; Shumsky, 2005 [1958]). In a much-cited paper, Argyris and Schön (2005 [1989]) sought to locate AR by comparing it with PAR

(Whyte's version) and action science, with the latter two being 'members of the same action research family' (Argyris and Schön, 2005 [1989]: 139). As described by Cassell and Johnson (2006: 794), action science interventions are based on 'the researcher's interpretive understanding of organizational participants' practical reasoning as "theories-in-use" that occupy organizational back stages and are hidden by the evasions constituted through "espoused theories"'. Argyris and Schön (2005 [1989]) drew attention to tacit practitioner theories-in-use that serve to distort and undermine AR findings and interventions if they are not surfaced. Doing so through action science was seen to allow for learning about tacit theories-in-use through which feelings of embarrassment and threat develop.

As argued by Gustavsen, such a combination of theory and practice has long been evident in AR, even if there have been shifts in emphasis over the years: from analytic-descriptive with a strong element of systems thinking, to a theoretical foregrounding of local constructivism, and on to a renewed emphasis on theoretical generalizing from local organizational patterns to 'make a number of (initially) local projects interact with each other to constitute broader waves of change' (Gustavsen, 2008: 432). Further, Reason (1994: 49) distinguished action science from Torbert's action inquiry:

> Action *science* focuses on the ways practitioners construe their behavior, their implicit cognitive models, and their actual behavior. Action *inquiry*, while addressing these, in addition addresses outcomes ... and the quality of one's attention ... Further, action inquiry addresses the question of how to transform organizations and communities into collaborative, self-reflective communities of inquiry.

Raelin (2005 [1989]) has argued that action science goes deeper in such surfacing than does action learning, although both show the same 'action' perspective. Action learning, also called 'work-based learning' (Raelin, 2000; 2006) has a fairly narrow focus and usually takes place within facilitated learning sets that meet on a regular basis and reflect on members' actions in negotiating real-time work problems. (For a useful summary see Ellis and Kiely (2005 [2000]) who compare AR with PAR, action learning and action science in terms of ideology, procedure and validity criteria.)

Thus, the various and changing identities of AR and of action researchers have been represented through a series of differentiation and comparison processes, with the divisions within these showing an increasing specification while remaining highly normative.

Appreciative inquiry and transformative AR

The normative nature of AR is perhaps most evident in the now popular form of appreciative inquiry (e.g. Cooperrider and Srivastva, 2005 [1987]), which moves away from a problem-centred approach to AR on the basis that a resolution of problems can, at best, assist a system to return to the status quo rather than to progress and develop. Avoiding social frames of reference to distinguish their contributions, these authors drew instead on metaphysics, ancient inspirational archetypes (Cooperrider and Srivastva, 2005 [1987]) and ecology (see Reason and Torbert, 2005 [2001]) to argue the importance of their works. In their widely cited paper, Cooperrider and Srivastva (2005 [1987]) argued for the replacement of value-free science with the more active, invested, appreciative and transformative emphasis of 'socio-rational' science, stating their 'conviction that action-research has the potential to be to the postindustrial era what "scientific management" was to the industrial' (2005 [1987]: 52).

Like Cooperrider and Srivastva, and taking a broader perspective than Friedman and Rogers (2009), Maurer and Githens (2010: 269) have also aimed to move beyond problem-solving approaches to consider AR as a 'worldview', suggesting that 'the potential of AR lies in the creation of mutual understanding and learning in and through dialogue, critical reflection, and action'. They distinguished conventional, critical and dialogical AR, noting that these categories overlapped but also stressing the potential of dialogical AR, which encourages critical reflection on practices, for surfacing values and for a subtle exploration of critical issues. They concluded by suggesting an inquiry into the possibilities for such (democratic) dialogue even in strict hierarchical and authoritarian organizations.

Also aiming for a transformational social science, although not in a radical sense, Reason and Torbert (2005 [2001]) argued a case for the importance of practical knowledge and for 'critical inquiry in action' (2005 [2001]: 234). In contrast to the linguistic turn where the emphasis is on the role of language in constructing reality, they stated that the action turn gives an emphasis to enquiry that contributes directly to the flourishing of human persons, their communities and the ecosystems of which they are part.

In many ways, such grand statements about AR are quite understandable, for they represent one response to its provisionality and somewhat secondary status in relation to positivist science. They are certainly not new, for Shumsky (2005 [1958]) presented a manifesto in which he suggested the need for an AR 'movement'. However, such efforts are arguably conservative in the interests that they serve. For example, the paper by Cooperrider and Srivastva (2005 [1987]) accepts social arrangements as arising from agreement (unlike Rahman, 2005 [1982]; Fals-Borda, 2005 [1984]) and is exclusively organizational/managerial when it comes to intervention. Similarly, Reason and Torbert (2005 [2001]) have argued that good theory is not just descriptive, inductive or deductive, universalizable and analytic, but also normative, analogical, timely and implementable so as to sustain personal, social and community development.

What Action Research is Not

In terms of form, both Cooperrider and Srivastva (2005 [1987]) and Reason (2005 [2003]) made liberal use of antimonies in their carving out of potential futures for AR, supplementing these with persuasive illustrations to drive home their arguments. Differentiating what AR was *not* was also evident in Schein's (2005 [1995]) attempt to clarify what he saw as confusion among notions of process consultation, AR and clinical inquiry in terms of researcher and client needs and interests; joint ownership of interventions; and the recognition that entry into a diagnostic relationship is itself a major intervention. While Schein viewed both process consultation and clinical inquiry as client-centred, AR may be more consultant-driven, unlikely to surface valid data, and may even cause damage to the client. In all these narratives, though, there are at least two processes in hand – of differentiation and specification, of what is and is not required of the authentic practitioner.

In the face of such complexity, Bradbury Huang (2010) has suggested that it is still possible to articulate what AR is *not*: interacting only with formal powers and with researcher-only ownership of research data; offering insights alone; and poorly conducting conventional research. To this may be added Gill's earlier (1986) comparison of (problem-based traditional) AR with consultancy and basic research and Gill and Johnson's (2010) comparison of such AR with both true experiments and quasi-experiments.

However, in recent times the growing complexity of approaches to AR has made such clear differentiations difficult. For example, in one recent article Stebbins and Shani (2009) presented a framework of collaborative research orientations. Reflective design theory is described as a collaborative framework (Docherty et al., 2008) for large and complicated organizations; a hybrid that 'incorporates aspects of clinical inquiry, AR, appreciative inquiry, collaborative management research, sociotechnical systems, and self-design theory' (Stebbins and Shani, 2009: 60). As noted by Dick (2011: 123), '[l]abels for participative, action-oriented research methods continue to multiply'.

Conclusion

Wilson's (2005 [1947]) call for a meaningful self-awareness on the part of the action researcher launched what has become a recent emphasis in, if not type of, AR: reflexive AR. While action researchers are, by and large, no longer required to undergo psychoanalysis, as was the case for those who worked for the Tavistock Institute in its early days (Trist and Murray, 1990), the framing of reflexivity primarily as a personal and individualistic concern remains. For example, like McTaggart (2005 [1998]) and Checkland and Holwell (2005 [1998]), Regehr outlined some means by which researchers can allow greater scrutiny of their value position.

Both Regehr (2005 [2000]) and Greenwood (2005 [2002]) called for action researchers to show greater courage in these endeavours. Such courage is evident in the recent flood of reflexive writing on the limits of collaboration (Cunningham, 2008; Arieli et al., 2009; Galuppo et al., 2011) and, in particular, on PAR (David, 2005 [2002]; Smith et al. 2010), including accounts of partial successes and failures (Williams et al., 2005 [2003]) and of compromises such as within our VP project, as described above. This reflexivity is perhaps most evident in recent feminist PAR (Gatenby and Humphries, 2005 [2000]; Katila and Meriläinen, 2005 [2002]).

In combination such works present dilemmas faced by the authors as action researchers while also addressing the precarious identity of AR, an identity which is perhaps most evident in what Cassell and Johnson (2006: 805) have termed 'deconstructive AR' practices that may 'question the familiar and taken-for-granted'. Cassell and Johnson raise the possibility that a postmodern stance may inform 'interventions that unsettle hegemonic discourses, and give voice to alternatives so as to encourage heteroglossia, rather than directing substantive organizational change' (Cassell and Johnson, 2006: 804). Examples included were Barry's (1997) discussion of interventions designed to unsettle dominant organizational narratives and Treleaven's (2001) discussion of the processes and effects of destabilizing gender narratives developed by female participants in a collaborative enquiry group.

Returning to our own example, shifts in the focus of the organization and the researcher/client relationships and priorities over the course of our VP project have meant that the nature of research analysis and 'intervention' also became deconstructive and dialogical in nature. Rather than intervene in the organization's decision-making and accountability structures and processes (as we had originally planned), the focus of our work to date has shifted towards a joint articulation and dialogue about discourses of professionalism, tradition, collaboration, community responsibility and gender within the organization and their effects on the breadth and depth of organizational change. Originally aimed at reviewing what had been heralded as a most progressive, if controversial, period within Victoria Police's history, we found that the more palatable 'good news stories' were complicated by other perspectives that were sometimes discounted or individualized as unrepresentative of the (current) organization as a whole. Our challenge was to work with the steering committee over time so that these views were heard, at least in part; a process that has involved the joint planning of research and some joint analysis of data and has now developed towards the co-authorship of a paper on the doing of collaborative research. At the boundary between action and more traditional research in terms of the extent of the intervention, the building of relationships has allowed for candid exchanges and facilitated the ongoing development of a project that could have otherwise been dismissed as lacking contemporary relevance due to changes in both the internal organizational and external political environment of the organization since its initiation.

In this context it is notable that Treleaven's more recent work includes a discussion of the links between critical AR and organizational ethnography and the application of critical discourse analysis 'in order to identify and understand the production and operation of the powerful discourses driving competing political agendas within organizations' (Sykes and Treleaven, 2009: 220). This includes not only the 'possibility for the discussion of multiple interpretations, representations and discourses' but also for 'engaging with people toward participant-led change and action' (2009: 224), perhaps heralding a further research-led turn in the story of AR.

Further Reading

Many original and important review works appear in the edited collection *Fundamentals of Action Research* (Cooke and Wolfram Cox, 2005) and Gill and

Johnson (2010) have presented a comprehensive review of suggested readings. Regular updates on contemporary AR literature have been provided by Dick (2004; 2006; 2009; 2011).

References

Aguinis, H. (2005 [1993]) 'Action research and scientific method: presumed discrepancies and actual similarities', in B. Cooke and J. Wolfram Cox (eds), *Fundamentals of Action Research*, vol. 3. London: Sage, pp. 347–367.

Argyris, C. and Schön, D. A. (2005 [1989]) 'Participatory action research and action science compared: a commentary', in B. Cooke and J. Wolfram Cox (eds), *Fundamentals of Action Research*, vol. 2. London: Sage, pp. 137–147.

Arieli, D., Friedman, V. J. and Agbaria, K. (2009) 'The paradox of participation in action research', *Action Research*, 7 (3): 263–290.

Bain, R. ([1951] 2005) 'Action research and group dynamics', in B. Cooke and J. Wolfram Cox (eds), *Fundamentals of Action Research*, vol. 1. London: Sage, pp. 319–366.

Barry, D. (1997) 'Telling changes: from narrative family therapy to organizational change and development', *Journal of Organizational Change Management*, 10 (1): 30–46.

Blum, F. ([1955] 2005) 'Action research – a scientific approach?', in B. Cooke and J. Wolfram Cox (eds), *Fundamentals of Action Research*, vol. 3. London: Sage, pp. 309–317.

Bradbury Huang, H. (2010) 'What is good action research'? *Action Research*, 8 (1): 93–109.

Brown, L.D. (2005 [1993]) 'Social change through collective reflection with Asian nongovernmental development organizations', in B. Cooke and J. Wolfram Cox (eds), *Fundamentals of Action Research*, vol. 3. London: Sage, pp. 57–83.

Brown, L.D. and Tandon, R. (2005 [1983]) 'Ideology and political economy in inquiry: action research and participatory research', in B. Cooke and J. Wolfram Cox (eds), *Fundamentals of Action Research*, vol. 2. London: Sage, pp. 25–49.

Cassell, C. and Johnson, P. (2006) 'Action research: explaining the diversity', *Human Relations*, 59 (6): 783–814.

Chandler, D. and Torbert, B. (2003) 'Transforming inquiry and action: interweaving 27 flavors of action research', *Action Research*, 1 (2): 133–152.

Checkland, P. and Howell, S. (2005 [1998]) 'Action research: its nature and validity', in B. Cooke and J. Wolfram Cox (eds), *Fundamentals of Action Research*, vol. 3, London: Sage, pp. 423–437.

Chein, I., Cook, S. and Harding, J. (2005 [1948]) 'The field of action research', in B. Cooke and J. Wolfram Cox (eds), *Fundamentals of Action Research*, vol. 1. London: Sage, pp. 151–164.

Coghlan, D. (2005 [2001]) 'Insider action research projects: implications for practising managers', in B. Cooke and J. Wolfram Cox (eds), *Fundamentals of Action Research*, vol. 3. London: Sage, pp. 229–244.

Coghlan, D. and Brannick, T. (2009) *Doing Action Research in your own Organization* (3rd edn). London: Sage.

Cooke, B. (2005 [2003]) 'A new continuity with colonial administration: participation in development management', in B. Cooke and J. Wolfram Cox (eds), *Fundamentals of Action Research*, vol. 4. London: Sage, pp. 207–225.

Cooke, B. (2006) 'The Cold War origin of action research as managerial cooptation', *Human Relations*, 59 (5): 655–693.

Cooke, B. and Wolfram Cox, J. (eds) (2005) *Fundamentals of Action Research*. London: Sage.

Cooperrider, D. and Srivastva, S. (2005 [1987]) 'Appreciative inquiry in organizational life', in B. Cooke and J. Wolfram Cox (eds), *Fundamentals of Action Research*, vol. 2. London: Sage, pp. 51–97.

Crotty, M. (1998) *The Foundations of Social Research: Meaning and Perspective in the Research Process*. St. Leonards, Australia: Allen and Unwin.

Cunningham, W. S. (2008) 'Voices from the field', *Action Research*, 6 (4): 373–390.

Curle, A. (2005 [1949]) 'A theoretical approach to action research', in B. Cooke and J. Wolfram Cox (eds), *Fundamentals of Action Research*, vol. 1. London: Sage, pp. 263–277.

David, M. (2005 [2002]) 'Problems of participation: the limits of action research', in B. Cooke and J. Wolfram Cox (eds), *Fundamentals of Action Research*, vol. 4. London: Sage, pp. 107–205.

Dick, B. (2004) 'Action research literature: themes and trends', *Action Research*, 2 (4): 425–444.

Dick, B. (2006) 'Action research literature 2004–2006', *Action Research*, 4 (4): 439–458.

Dick, B. (2009) 'Action research literature 2006–2008', *Action Research*, 7 (4): 423–441.

Dick, B. (2011) 'Action research literature 2008–2010: themes and trends', *Action Research*, 9 (2): 122–143.

Docherty, P., Kira, M, and Shani, A.B. (eds) (2008) *Creating Sustainable Work Systems: Emerging Perspectives and Practice* (2nd edn). London: Routledge.

Ellis, J. and Kiely, J. (2005 [2000]) 'Action inquiry strategies: taking stock and moving forward', in B. Cooke and J. Wolfram Cox (eds), *Fundamentals of Action Research*, vol. 4. London: Sage, pp. 85–119.

Fals-Borda, O. (2005 [1984]) 'Participatory action research', in B. Cooke and J. Wolfram Cox (eds), *Fundamentals of Action Research*, vol. 2. London: Sage, pp. 3–24.

Fals-Borda, O. (2005 [1987]) 'The application of participatory action-research in Latin America, in B. Cooke and J. Wolfram Cox (eds), *Fundamentals of Action Research*, vol. 3. London: Sage, pp. 33–55.

French, W.L. and Bell, C.H. (1999) *Organization Development* (6th edn). Upper Saddle River, NJ: Prentice-Hall.

Friedman, V.J. and Rogers, T. (2009) 'There is nothing so theoretical as good action research', *Action Research*, 7 (1): pp. 31–47.

Galuppo, L., Gorli, M. and Ripamonti, S. (2011) 'Playing dissymmetry in action research: the role of power and differences in promoting participative knowledge and change', *Systemic Practice and Action Research*, 24 (2): 147–164.

Gatenby, B. and Humphries, M. (2005 [2000]) 'Feminist participatory action research: methodological and ethical issues', in B. Cooke and J. Wolfram Cox (eds), *Fundamentals of Action Research*, vol. 2. London: Sage, pp. 261–288.

Gill, J. (1986) 'Research as action: an experiment utilising the social sciences', in F. Heller (ed.), *The Use and Abuse of Social Science*. London: Sage.

Gill, J. and Johnson, P. (2010) *Research Methods for Managers* (4th edn). Los Angeles, CA: Sage.

Greenwood, D.J. (2005 [2002]) 'Action research: unfulfilled promises and unmet challenges', in B. Cooke and J. Wolfram Cox (eds), *Fundamentals of Action Research*, vol. 4. London: Sage, pp. 173–195.

Greenwood, D.J. and Levin, M. (1998) *Introduction to Action Research: Social Research for Social Change*. Thousand Oaks, CA: Sage.

Gustavsen, B. (2008) 'Action research, practical challenges and the formation of theory', *Action Research*, 6 (4): 421–437.

Katila, S. and Meriläinen, S. ([2002] 2005) 'Metamorphosis: from "nice girls" to "nice bitches": resisting patriarchal articulations of professional identity', in B. Cooke and J. Wolfram Cox (eds), *Fundamentals of Action Research*, vol. 4. London: Sage, pp. 275–296.

Lewin, K. (2005 [1945]) 'Action research and minority problems', in B. Cooke and J. Wolfram Cox (eds), *Fundamentals of Action Research*, vol. 1. London: Sage, pp. 19–31.

Lewin, K. (2005 [1946]) 'Research on minority problems', in B. Cooke and J. Wolfram Cox (eds), *Fundamentals of Action Research*, vol. 1. London: Sage, pp. 32–42.

Lippitt, R. (2005 [1950]) 'Action-research and the values of the social scientist', in B. Cooke and J. Wolfram Cox (eds), *Fundamentals of Action Research*, vol. 3. London: Sage, pp. 301–307.

Lippitt, R. (2005 [1959]) 'Dimensions of the consultant's job', in B. Cooke and J. Wolfram Cox (eds), *Fundamentals of Action Research*, vol. 3. London: Sage, pp. 191–199.

Maurer, M. and Githens, R. P. (2010) 'Toward a reframing of action research for human resource and organization development: moving beyond problem solving and toward dialogue', *Action Research*, 8 (3): 267–292.

McTaggart, R. (2005 [1998]) 'Is validity really an issue for participatory action research?', in B. Cooke and J. Wolfram Cox (eds), *Fundamentals of Action Research*, vol. 3. London: Sage, pp. 395–421.

Melrose, M.J. (2005 [2001]) 'Maximizing the rigor of action research: why would you want to? How could you?', in B. Cooke and J. Wolfram Cox (eds), *Fundamentals of Action Research*, vol. 3. London: Sage, pp. 439–461.

Raelin, J.A. (2005 [1989]) 'Action learning and action science: are they different?', in B Cooke and J. Wolfram Cox (eds), *Fundamentals of Action Research*, vol. 2. London: Sage, pp. 159–180.

Raelin, J.A. (2000) *Work-based Learning: The New Frontier of Management Development*. Upper Saddle, NJ: Prentice-Hall.

Raelin, J.A. (2006) 'Does action learning promote collaborative leadership?', *Academy of Management Learning and Education*, 5 (2): 152–168.

Rahman, M.A. (2005 [1982]) 'The theory and practice of participatory action research', in B. Cooke and J. Wolfram Cox (eds), *Fundamentals of Action Research*, vol. 2. London: Sage, pp. 11–24.

Rapoport, R.N. (2005 [1970]) 'Three dilemmas in action research with special reference to the Tavistock experience', in B. Cooke and J. Wolfram Cox (eds), *Fundamentals of Action Research*, vol. 4. London: Sage, pp. 25–44.

Reason, P. (1994) 'Human inquiry as discipline and practice', in P. Reason (ed.), *Participation in Human Inquiry*. London: Sage, pp. 40–56.

Reason, P. (2005 [1999]) 'Integrating action and reflection through co-operative inquiry', in B. Cooke and J. Wolfram Cox (eds), *Fundamentals of Action Research*, vol. 2. London: Sage, pp. 235–259.

Reason, P. (2005 [2003]) 'Pragmatist philosophy and action research: readings and conversation with Richard Rorty', in B. Cooke and J. Wolfram Cox (eds), *Fundamentals of Action Research*, vol. 4. London: Sage, pp. 297–319.

Reason, P. and Bradbury, H. (eds) (2001) 'Introduction: inquiry and participation in search of a world worthy of human aspiration', *Handbook of Action Research*. London: Sage, pp. 1–14.

Reason, P. and Torbert, W. (2005 [2001]) 'The action turn: towards a transformational social science', in B. Cooke and J. Wolfram Cox (eds), *Fundamentals of Action Research*, vol. 4. London: Sage, pp. 229–266.

Regehr, A. (2005 [2000]) 'Action research: underlying or undermining the cause?', in B. Cooke and J. Wolfram Cox (eds), *Fundamentals of Action Research*, vol. 4. London: Sage, pp. 157–172.

Robinson, V.M.J. (2005 [1993]) 'Current controversies in action research', in B. Cooke and J. Wolfram Cox (eds), *Fundamentals of Action Research*, vol. 4. London: Sage, pp. 59–84.

Sanford, N. (2005 [1970]) 'Whatever happened to action research?', in B. Cooke and J. Wolfram Cox (eds), *Fundamentals of Action Research*, vol. 4. London: Sage, pp. 3–23.

Schein, E.H. (2005 [1995]) 'Process consultation, action research and clinical inquiry: are they the same?', in B. Cooke and J. Wolfram Cox (eds), *Fundamentals of Action Research*, vol. 2. London: Sage, pp. 149–158.

Schön, D. (2005 [1995]) 'Knowing-in-action: the new scholarship requires a new epistemology' in B. Cooke and J. Wolfram Cox (eds), *Fundamentals of Action Research*, vol. 3. London: Sage, pp. 377–394.

Selltiz, C. and Cook, S.W. (2005 [1948]) 'Can research in social science be both socially useful and scientifically meaningful?', in B. Cooke and J. Wolfram Cox (eds), *Fundamentals of Action Research*, vol. 1. London: Sage, pp. 165–173.

Shumsky, A. (2005 [1958]) 'Action research and modern man', in B. Cooke and J. Wolfram Cox (eds), *Fundamentals of Action Research*, vol. 3. London: Sage, pp. 3–13.

Smith, L., Bratini, L., Chambers, D.-A., Jensen, R. V. and Romero, L. (2010) 'Between idealism and reality: meeting the challenges of participatory action research', *Action Research*, 8 (4): 407–425.

Stebbins, M. W. and Shani, A.B. (2009) 'Clinical inquiry and reflective design in a secrecy-based organization', *Journal of Applied Behavioral Science*, 45 (1): 59–89.

Susman, G., and Evered, R. (2005 [1978]) 'An assessment of the scientific merits of action research', in B. Cooke and J. Wolfram Cox (eds), *Fundamentals of Action Research*, vol. 3. London: Sage, pp. 319–345.

Sykes, C. and Treleaven, L. (2009) Critical action research and organizational ethnography', in S. Ybema, D. Yanow, H. Wels and F. Kamsteeg (eds), *Organizational Ethnography: Studying the Complexities of Everyday Life*. Los Angeles, CA: Sage, pp. 215–230.

Treleaven, L. (2001) 'The turn to action and the linguistic turn: towards an integrated methodology', in P. Reason and H. Bradbury (eds), *Handbook of Action Research: Participative Inquiry and Practice*. London: Sage, pp. 261–272.

Trist, E. and Murray, H. (1990) 'Historical overview: the foundation and development of the Tavistock Institute to 1989', in E. Trist and H. Murray (eds), *The Social Engagement of Social Science, A Tavistock Anthology*, vol. 1: *The Socio-Psychological Perspective*. Philadelphia: University of Pennsylvania Press, pp. 1–34.

Whyte, W. F. (2005 [1961]) 'An action research program for the personnel man', in B. Cooke and J. Wolfram Cox (eds), *Fundamentals of Action Research*, vol. 2. London: Sage, pp. 291–315.

Whyte, W. F., Greenwood, D. and Lazes, P. (2005 [1989]) 'Participatory action research: through practice to science in social research', in B. Cooke and J. Wolfram Cox (eds), *Fundamentals of Action Research*, vol. 2. London: Sage, pp. 99–136.

Williams, G., Srivastava, M., Corbridge, S. and Véron, R. (2005 [2003]) 'Enhancing pro-poor governance in eastern India: participation, politics and action research', in B. Cooke and J. Wolfram Cox (eds), *Fundamentals of Action Research*, vol. 3. London: Sage, pp. 321–346.

Wilson, A.T.M. (2005 [1947]) 'Some implications of medical practice and social casework for action research', in B. Cooke and J. Wolfram Cox (eds), *Fundamentals of Action Research*, vol. 1. London: Sage, pp. 131–149.

Wolfram Cox, J. and Cooke, B. (2007) 'Action research and identity', in A. Pullen, N. Beech and D. Sims, *Exploring Identity: Concepts and Methods*. Houndmills: Palgrave, pp. 221–236.

6 Combining Qualitative Methods

Katrina Pritchard

Introduction

In this chapter I explore the practice of combining qualitative methods, drawing specifically on my own experience in organizational research. I aim to deal with both the pragmatic issues of combining qualitative methods across different types and stages of research practice, while also unpacking broader methodological concerns. This is particularly pertinent since typically discussions of methodological combination focus on quantitative-qualitative ('quan-qual') blends, often under the heading of 'multi-method' or 'mixed-methods' research (Creswell, 2003; Tashakkori and Teddlie, 2003). In contrast, despite the representation of qualitative research as 'bricolage' (Kincheloe, 2005), the actual practice of working with qualitative-qualitative ('qual-qual') combinations receives much less attention within the literature and can remain inaccessible, particularly to new researchers (Hesse-Biber, 2010).

This lack of focus on 'qual-qual' combinations may in part be due to the increasing 'brand identity' of individual methods which, along with the usual chapter per method structure of many textbooks, gives an impression of separation and incompatibility. Indeed, researchers may feel the need to adopt a clear and specific label for their research so as to secure legitimacy and credibility with reviewers or examiners. However, such labels are not necessarily indicative of a definitive methodological commitment or of the specific way in which methods have been applied. For example, Broadfoot et al. (2004: 200) observe in respect to Critical Discourse Analysis (CDA) that 'there are as many kinds of CDA as there are analysts' (see also Oswick, in this volume).

At the same time, there is a shared and somewhat generic language of qualitative research (for example, of coding frameworks and themes), which hints at common concerns across methods. Indeed, informal discussions with other qualitative researchers suggest that many do experiment with different approaches and ideas during the course of a research project but that these practices may not be reflected in the final published accounts (Bryman, 2008).

However, there is a broader methodological perspective at stake here. That is to say, methodological decisions often entail more than the simplistic selection of a means by which data are collected, analysed and reported. Rather, such decisions imply overarching (and hence potentially incompatible) ontological and epistemological commitments (Bryman, 1984). Qualitative researchers cannot side step such issues when investigating the potential to combine different approaches, but there is little within the broader 'quan-qual' mixed-methods literature to guide us through such debates. Further, engaging in debates regarding the ontological and epistemological foundations of qualitative research, both more broadly and when considered in respect to individual approaches, might be a potentially paralysing process since, as Shotter and Lannamann (2002: 578) suggest, 'the possibilities for continued disagreement seem endless'. Therefore an important consideration for the researcher exploring the potential of combining qualitative methods is the extent to which they can tolerate the resulting ontological insecurity (Giddens, 1990) and engage in productive ontological oscillation (Weick, 1995) when required. There is unfortunately no 'one size fits all' solution to this challenge, but a key requirement is a strong sense of reflexive engagement throughout the research process.

My aim here is not to catalogue every potential combination of methods but rather I explore three examples from my own research to illustrate different approaches to (and challenges of) combining qualitative methods:

- *An instrumental approach:* using a twenty statements test (TST) as a primer for qualitative research interviews.
- *An integrative approach:* using a tracer study within the preliminary fieldwork stage of an ethnographic project.
- *A dialogic approach:* using ethnography and discourse analysis together across all stages of a research project.

The above labelling is not intended as a definitive classification of a methodological combination (Denzin, 2010) but rather is a purposive categorization proposed to highlight the range of approaches that may be considered. In the instrumental combination, a second method is used to facilitate the first (here as an interview primer) but remains marginal in the broader research process. An integrative approach sees an increased methodological and practical combination, with a closer interaction between the research methods (here, a tracer study and the preliminary fieldwork phase of ethnography) as they are implemented. The dialogic approach represents a more complex means of combining qualitative methods in which the researcher engages in a dialogue with emerging methodological and practical tensions (here between discursive and ethnographic approaches) in order to facilitate a reflexive research process. In the examples presented later, there are elements of both a pre-planned and more opportunistic combination, though all are more characteristic of simultaneous rather than sequential approaches to mixed-methods research.

The Broader Context of Mixed-Methods Research

As highlighted above, the notion of methodological combination and the associated term mixed-methods research is most commonly used when referring to a combination of qualitative and quantitative methodologies within a single research project (Creswell, 2003; Tashakkori and Teddlie, 2003). Methods may be applied in parallel (simultaneously) or sequentially and include different forms of 'mixing' such that data may be converted to a single (usually quantitative) form before analysis, applied to different levels of research question or used as a means of triangulation around a single research question (Lewis and Grimes, 1999; Cox and Hassard, 2005).

There are many resources concerned with the different applications and combinations of mixed-methods (including in the *Journal of Mixed Methods Research* and in a recent special issue of *Qualitative Inquiry*). However, much of this debate glosses over both the potential for, and challenges of, 'qual-qual' combinations (Burke Johnson et al., 2007; Morse, 2010), focusing instead on the more visible divide assumed in 'quan-qual' approaches. Moreover, as Greene and Caracelli (2003: 107) comment, there is a broader concern that 'mixed-methods inquirers are insufficiently reflective and their practice is insufficiently problematized'. Certainly it appears that the challenges discussed within the existing literature focus on technical research topics related to the time and manner in which methods are to be 'mixed'. Here, even in the relatively rare discussions of qualitative method combinations, there is primarily attention being paid to the research design (as a period of planning) and to analysis (as the point at which the methods are 'mixed') (Waddington, 2005; Frost et al., 2010; Morse, 2010). But even in respect to those areas that do receive attention in the literature, there is still much more work to be done: 'the key idea that mixed methods research requires some form of integration is clear; still however additional research is needed to further explicate this process' (Burke Johnson et al., 2007: 125). Indeed Bryman's (2008) content analysis of mixed-methods articles suggests that it is often difficult to detect why and in what ways methods have been combined, since the actual research practices remain hidden from view (Hesse-Biber, 2010).

Further, the focus on differences between quantitative and qualitative perspectives results in insufficient attention being given to the 'paradigm soup' (Buchanan and Bryman, 2007: 486) of qualitative research itself. Moreover, the researcher is largely absent from accounts of mixed-methods research or appears to move easily and silently between methods, selecting from a menu of combinations and 'mixing' only when desired. There is little attention paid to the impact of adopting a mixed-methods research approach across the life-cycle of the research process which, as qualitative researchers, we would expect to see reflexively unpacked (Pritchard and Symon, 2009). Some, however, might suggest that in itself this is not a bad thing and that the qualitative researchers' tendency for navel gazing also often stems more from a broader concern with (ontological and epistemological) inadequacy than a genuine concern for openness (Finlay, 2002; Knights, 2006). Yet for the researcher wishing to combine qualitative methods, a lack of detailed accounts and guidelines might be frustrating. Overall then, while the mixed-methods literature provides a useful backdrop for qualitative researchers to examine when considering the issues associated with combining qualitative methods, the discussions do not address directly those areas of most concern (Hesse-Biber, 2010).

Combining Qualitative Methods: Examples of Instrumental, Integrative and Dialogic Approaches

Based on the discussion above it is clear that we need to unpack what 'combining qualitative methods' might imply by considering both the notion of 'combining' and that of 'method'. It is also important to consider what prompts a researcher to utilize different methods or methodologies in a particular research project (Kincheloe, 2005). For example, are there strong influences within the field of research, the academic institution or the site of investigation? Further, we should attend to how (when and with whom) the decision was made. For example, was it a planned approach or adopted in response to a problem encountered during the research process? Finally, we need to think about the degree of combination that results, and the different issues that arise depending on the degree of methodological *vs* technical combination attempted. The approach taken to examining these issues below is a broadly confessional account based on my own research practice. In developing this, I have drawn on official accounts of my own research practice (e.g. in conference papers and my PhD thesis), reflexive research diaries and logs maintained during these undertakings, and various communications with others researchers (including emails and seminar presentations). These sources are inevitably partial and incomplete, but have proved useful in prompting the recall of, and reflection on, these research projects. Such accounts, developed either solely by a single researcher or jointly by co-researchers and potentially even participants, are not only useful in a retrospective summary such as this chapter but also may prove invaluable in working through the many and varied challenges of combining qualitative methods during the various times and places of the research undertaking (Richards, 2009). The examples discussed below have been deliberately selected to highlight different modes of combination and represent a chronological development of my own research exploring different aspects of the professional identity of HR (Human Resources) practitioners.

Instrumental approach: using a twenty statements test (TST) as a primer for qualitative research interviews

In this study, my focus was on the role of HR practitioners and their perception of professional knowledge (Pritchard et al., 2004). Initially, following a standard process, I identified specific research questions, which I used to develop a semi-structured interview protocol. However, at this point I encountered two key challenges. Firstly, I wanted to unpack participants' own understandings and constructions of professional knowledge, rather than impose my own definitions. Secondly, I was keen to avoid any sense of assessment within the interview.

Rather than extend the length of the interview, I developed a 'primer' for participants to complete in advance, which would then form the basis for the topics explored during the interview discussion. I considered a range of options (including a pre-interview questionnaire and the use of visual methods) but determined that the TST would provide a useful and practical (from the perspective of both participants and researchers) primer. Further, the original application of the TST, to look at relationships between self-concept and role, fitted with the broader aims of my own research (Rees and Nicholson, 1994) in respect of concerns with professional identity. After pilot testing several options, the statement set for the test was 'I believe an HR professional should be …' and this was given to individuals along with 20 blank lines on which to write their responses. This was described as 'a form to collect some initial views' in the accompanying email sent to participants.

The resulting TSTs were used in the interviews as a spring-board to explore participants' views and perceptions regarding to the areas of key interest to my research questions. The TST responses were not analysed in and of their own right, rather they were used only as an interview primer in this study. This priming, however, worked both collectively and individually. Looking at the TST statements collected provided prompts both generically across all interviews as well as with the individual who provided the response. Further, it provided some insight into specific issues within the organization that I had not previously been aware of, again enabling me to consider in advance how to approach certain topics. At an individual level the TST not only acted as a primer from a topic perspective but also as an ice-breaker at an interpersonal level, particularly when participants provided unexpected or witty responses (e.g. one participant's response to the question 'I believe an HR professional should be' was 'paid a fortune'). However, it does raise the issue that the TST (here removed from a specific theoretical consideration of the self-concept) also acted to prime my perceptions of the participant, which in turn shaped the interaction that took place. As a researcher it is therefore important to be aware that different methods (and different combinations of methods) will influence the construction of researcher and participant subjectivities (Cassell, 2005). While the primary use of the TST in this instance was as an interview primer, looking back through my notes I am reminded that I also completed the TST myself. Initially, I used the same prompt question as the participants just to test the process, but subsequently revised and revisited these lists to reflect on my personal construction of the research topic, particularly considering how my assumptions and perceptions had changed over time. This was a particularly useful aid to reflexivity when positioned alongside my use of template analysis (see King, in this volume) to interpret the interview transcripts.

In this example there was an instrumental combination of data collection methods, with the TST facilitating the interview process rather than featuring as an independent methodological component of the research project. The combination was both relatively straightforward and successful. It also highlights the benefit of a broader consideration of the data collection process beyond an assumption, particularly by novice researchers, that a researcher-led interview is the default option.

Integrative approach: using a tracer study within the preliminary fieldwork stage of an ethnography

In this second example, combining qualitative methods emerged as a response to a challenge experienced during the research process, rather than as a planned strategy developed during the research design phase. I had planned to conduct an ethnographic study and obtained access for an initial phase of preliminary fieldwork. However, on arrival I found it difficult to understand how the organization operated or to make contact with different teams who were spread across a number of locations. Initial attempts to set up meetings and interviews in order to facilitate further access proved problematic, since the dates offered were usually after the preliminary fieldwork was scheduled to finish.

While the distinctive characteristic of ethnography is some form of participant observation, ethnographers will often utilize a wide range of data collection methods, which in turn may shape and direct the understanding of the research site (Brewer, 2004; see also Yanow, Ybema and van Hulst, in this volume). I reflected on the nature of the research site and my research project and investigated the potential of using a tracer study approach to facilitate further access. In a tracer study a specific organizational process is identified and followed via the use of 'tags', which provide the basis for identifying participants and then discussing the nature of their involvement in the activity under investigation (Hornby and Symon, 1994). There is a specific focus on the active tracking of a process through and across the research site, which may set up tensions with broader (traditional) observationalist approaches to ethnography (Brewer, 2004).

Despite these concerns, introducing the idea of a tracer study to the organization prompted a very positive response from the participants. I wrote in my field notes that the organization seemed to regard this as a more tangible research activity than 'participant observation' and it was an activity that they seemed to be able to relate to more clearly. Indeed, the participants became actively involved in the tracer study and as a result process flow diagrams were produced for the organization. This prompted a further reflexive consideration of the ways in which undertaking the tracer study had changed the nature of 'participant observation' within the broader ethnographic study; specifically that it had increased the organizational participation in the research activity and that this subsequently acted to increase my participation in the organization later on. In this respect, combining these particular methods became more than a technical issue and prompted a broader methodological consideration of both my own and the organization's construction of this research project.

In this particular tracer study the 'tags' were HR activities, the progress of which was logged and monitored on a newly implemented work management system. Different types of activities were selected including an expatriate assignment, a creativity workshop, the launch of a diversity networking group and the development of a local HR plan. For each activity, I interviewed the individual with overall responsibility and then (using activity reports generated from the work management system) followed the process both forwards and backwards, talking to the others involved and collecting related documentation. In addition to conducting these data collection interviews under the heading of the tracer study, I continued to keep detailed field logs of my research activities, and thus more broadly integrated the tracer study within an ethnographic frame. Analysis of the interviews and documents produced an annotated map or chart summarizing the activities and highlighting any issues or problems identified by participants. In parallel, I wrote ethnographic accounts that adopted a broader, descriptive perspective on the local understandings of the organization generated via the tracer study.

From this perspective, the tracer study could be viewed as an act of 'participant observation' in and of its own right. Certainly it could be seen as fitting within the broad range of activities undertaken by ethnographers, who are often depicted as adopting a 'suck it and see' approach (Bate, 1997: 1152). However, it is important to reflect that the tracer study was actively constructed (by myself) as a specific research initiative, in part in reaction to the difficulties faced during this preliminary fieldwork project. It was important not only as an act of research in its own right but also as a means of generating enhanced organizational access and support for a longer-term ethnographic study. In this respect, while this example is labelled integrative, it retains some characteristics of an instrumental combination. Combining qualitative research methods should therefore not be considered as a generic or uniform practice, but viewed from the perspective of the context within which it is conducted. It is worth noting that in the subsequent analysis and academic write-up of this research, the tracer study faded into the background in respect to the broader ethnographic study (Pritchard, 2010). As identified earlier, it perhaps does not have the 'brand identity' which qualitative researchers assume may assist with the review and publication process.

In contrast to the first example then, what emerges here is a more complex picture of combining qualitative methods, which highlights the active role of the researcher at all stages of the research process. Moreover, the ways in which methods are combined may emerge and develop during the research process rather than being clearly defined during the research design stage.

Dialogic approach: using ethnography and discourse analysis

The overall research design of this study into the construction of professional knowledge and identity by HR practitioners was planned as a combination of ethnographic and discursive approaches. This project was undertaken while in pursuit of my PhD (Pritchard, 2007), which is a particular genre of research with a specific academic framing. Indeed, given that the notion of 'originality' is central to the judgement of a PhD thesis, this perhaps acts as a direct prompt to methodological inventiveness. Certainly there was a feeling that the PhD provided both space and time to engage in methodological issues; space and time which (as I have subsequently discovered) may be harder to find in shorter, budget restricted research undertakings.

Many writers on ethnography have highlighted 'discourse' as a valid research interest (Bate, 1997; Fine et al., 2008). Further, the combination of ethnographic and discursive analysis is often suggested as a useful 'mix' within organization studies. For example, this combination has the potential to address the criticism that discourse analysis removes texts from their original, organizational context (Alvesson and Karreman, 2000). Further, Fairclough (2003) suggests that CDA offers a reflexive framing for ethnography while Hansen and colleagues (Barry et al., 2006; Hansen, 2006) suggest a 'diatextual' reading (Barry et al., 2006: 1107) in which each approach is used by different researchers who will then come together to debate their findings.

However, in common with the broader mixed-methods research literature, these suggestions tend to place one or other approach in a dominant position, with the other providing a supplementary view (Creswell et al., 2003). The focus is placed on a specific aspect of research or phase rather than looking across the whole research process. In short, there is relatively little to guide the researcher as to how discourse analysis and ethnography may be combined or what challenges may be faced along the way.

In the remainder of this section I shall therefore set out some of the challenges faced during the different stages of my research project and explain how these have shaped my understanding of combining qualitative methods. Three different phases of research are examined:

- *Research design*: as the researcher attempts to map out both a philosophical and practical path to informing a research area.
- *During fieldwork*: as the researcher is removed from the academic environment and is both actively and passively constructing data.
- *Subsequent analysis*: as the researcher returns from the field and (re)constructs the story to be told.

The approach adopted here was one of engaging in a reflexive dialogue with and between these different research approaches. As will be seen, sometimes this dialogue builds on the similarities between approaches, while at other times it will be prompted by the argument or debate caused by tensions between them. In this way the researcher engages in an ongoing (self) negotiation as the approaches are used together within a single research project.

Research design

As outlined above, at the outset of the research project I was conceptually engaging with the ideas of both ethnography and discourse analysis (see Yanow, Ybema and van Hulst, and Oswick, in this volume), although at this stage they remained somewhat separated. Issues of discourse were conceptual and theoretical, entangled with my research questions and literature review. Ontological and epistemological concerns were themselves discursive, and I was unclear as to how they related to my role as a researcher. On the other hand, issues of ethnography seemed much more practical and directly related to my role as a researcher during this time, particularly in terms of securing access to a research site. There seemed to be less need to theorize and more emphasis on experiencing.

From this perspective then, the engagement with ethnography provided a framework that allowed me to defer decisions regarding my approach to discourse analysis and enabled me to move forward with the research. At the same time adopting an ethnographic perspective encouraged me to actively engage with the research context and the individuals within it. The process of obtaining access and negotiating my role and identity as a researcher within the organization was part of the research project, not preliminary to it. In contrast, my engagement with discourse analysis prompted a consideration of the researcher's role and identity as positioned within a broader discursive frame (e.g. that of academic research), which offered alternative ways of viewing both my own and others' construction of research. My experience has been that debating these two approaches and exploring alternate means of seeing the research process aided my reflexive understanding of the project, my role and participant relationships.

During fieldwork

It was at this stage that the different timeframes of the two methodological approaches came more sharply into focus. Being there and spending time is a central part of the ethnographic approach. In contrast, accounts from discourse analysts tend to focus on identifying and obtaining the 'right' texts, sometimes to the extent of giving the impression of the researcher as a 'ram raider'; namely getting what they need and then making a quick getaway. In contrast, despite the label 'participant observation', ethnographic research may be portrayed as an almost passive approach, during which the researcher somehow obtains information through a process of osmosis. Further, there is potential tension as a result of discourse analysts' interest in 'bodies of texts' (Phillips et al., 2004: 636) in contrast to ethnographers' interest in other sorts of bodies (i.e. the research participants themselves or material objects).

However, I found this tension constructive rather than destructive. Moving from one perspective to the other (and looking at the space in-between) prompts the researcher to debate the assumptions about research practice. Shifting between the consideration of 'researcher' and 'participant' roles and relationships from both a discursive and ethnographic perspective enabled a richer, more textured understanding of these to emerge during the course of the research project. For example, I considered my own field notes as texts to be analysed rather than simply as descriptions of events. Indeed, a regular discursive consideration of my field notes provided a useful prompt to reflect on the construction of research processes throughout the fieldwork. Moreover, there is a concern here that the ethnographer may go native and lose the benefit of an outsider's perspective. In this respect, I found that having a parallel focus on discourse was particularly useful; in a sense this provided the means to get close to the individual participants and still remain detached when looking at organizational texts. I was also able to reflect on my research relationships and experience these through a discursive lens. This provided a useful prompt to reflexivity by means of engaging in questions such as: how is my position as a researcher constructed? How is the process of research constructed? What means are used to construct these and what is being ignored?

At the same time, accounts of discourse analysis concentrate on analysing various types of organizational documents, yet the processes and relationships essential to obtaining these documents may be glossed over, potentially ignoring the issue that the researcher has a relationship with the text other than via analysis. In contrast, the ethnographer's focus on participant relationships helps maintain a contextual sensitivity. Furthermore, the discourse analyst may treat collected documents as fixed or static but combining discursive and ethnographic approaches offers the opportunity to adopt a more dynamic perspective, for example following the drafting of an organizational text through its various stages of production and consumption.

However, there is also a broader concern that researchers may end up flitting between these methods in a random or haphazard manner and/or executing both approaches poorly. Combining qualitative methods requires a disciplined approach to data collection activities, ensuring that this will later enable a productive viewing of the research context through different lenses. In this research project this was managed by keeping detailed field notes along with detailed logs of the organizational texts collected and created (e.g. interview transcripts). NVivo (a qualitative data analysis software package) was also used to track the links between individuals, events and texts, with the aim of recording information that would enable rather than constrain the later analysis phase.

This is not to say, however, that combining these approaches will be trouble free. There were times when the broader tensions between deconstructive and critical tendencies of discourse analysis and a more descriptive interpretative orientation to ethnography proved to be more challenging. At these points I attempted to write down my debates about working through these issues. The aim during the fieldwork was not to resolve these tensions but rather to acknowledge and record them as a resource for later analysis (Richards, 2009).

Analysis

Various authors have written about the difficulties that ethnographers can face at this stage of the research process, commenting that the process of leaving the field is as complex as arriving (Brewer, 2004). Once again ethnography offers a useful lens by which to view the researcher's role and acts as a prompt for ongoing reflexivity; which can sometimes be lost at the boundaries between stages in the research process. The issues of combining methods also come sharply into focus here. Authors discussing both ethnography and discourse analysis have plenty to say about the processes of analysis and writing. In practical terms, this combining of methods involved a mid-range approach that requires the researcher to move backwards and forwards between a detailed consideration of the textual data and a broader awareness of both the proximal and distal context (Wetherell et al., 2001). This approach offered the best 'fit' in terms of my research questions and offered a means of working with both ethnographic and discursive perspectives.

The approach adopted continued the principle of using a single approach to reflect back on the other, and of debating the emerging tensions. For example, in the early stages of analysis I wrote specific ethnographic accounts that focused on the different groups within the organization in which the research was being conducted. This process allowed me to work through different themes and issues and to highlight where to concentrate my efforts in terms of the more detailed discursive analysis of specific organizational texts. Subsequently, at regular intervals I was then able to step back from the discourse analytic process and look at the analysis developing alongside these accounts, particularly focusing on areas of confusion or complexity where different stories might be unfolding. This process allows the researcher to play with different analytical stories, to develop different threads and then step back and see what is emerging. I did not attempt to produce an overall integrative account but rather sought to understand the range of stories (both ethnographic and discursive) that could be told.

Obviously it is not possible to say that all researchers would experience the creative tension I have outlined here in the same way; however, I suggest that combining qualitative research methods offers the opportunity to enhance the researcher's understanding of the phenomenon under investigation.

Conclusion

In this chapter I have examined the practice of combining qualitative methods within the broader context of mixed-methods research and then explored three examples (described as instrumental, integrative and dialogic) from my own research experience. Taken together, these highlight the importance of reflexivity (Alvesson and Sköldberg, 2000; see also Haynes, in this volume) and an increasing emphasis on the temporal dimensions of research practice (Cunliffe et al., 2004).

However, we can also see that notions of 'combining' and 'mixing' warrant more attention to be paid in the methodological literature. In some cases, more obviously here in the first two examples explored, the combinations may be relatively straightforward but can still exert a critical influence on the construction of the research process. In other cases, particularly where there are more significant methodological tensions between the approaches, we can see that 'combining' is an active process that continues through all the stages of the research project. It becomes a key aspect of the researchers' role and may involve a process of continual adjustment and readjustment as the project unfolds.

And yet there are risks as well. While the accounts above examine the way in which the researcher can move between different methods, this needs to be a considered and careful undertaking rather than a constant switching that could prove confusing and counterproductive. In all the examples discussed, I have noted that the practice of reflexively documenting the research process provides an essential means of examining how the practice of combining methods is unfolding. This practice, along with paying considerable attention to data management throughout, is a critical aspect of the research process. I would also recommend opening up your research practice to others, for example to participants and/or academic peers, in order to generate discussion.

I am not suggesting that we try to develop new 'super-methods' as a result of such a combination nor that we simply increase a project's method count for effect. However, I do offer the view that working through and between theoretical and practical tensions when combining qualitative methods provides opportunities to enrich both the research process and the findings that emerge. Moreover, I hope to encourage other researchers to share their experiences of 'qual-qual' mixed-methods approaches, so we can further develop and enhance our qualitative research practice.

Further Reading

Please see other relevant chapters in this book for further information regarding the individual qualitative methodologies and methods discussed.

For a critical examination of mixed-methods practice see Bryman (2008). For a comprehensive overview of the methodological and method issues encountered within a wide range of mixed-methods research contexts see Tashakkori and Teddlie (eds) (2003).

For a consideration of mixed-methods practice from a qualitative perspective see the recent special issue in *Qualitative Inquiry* (2010, volume 16, issue 6), which includes the Denzin, Morse and Hesse-Biber articles cited in this chapter.

Acknowledgements

Aspects of this chapter were first presented at the European Association of Management (EURAM) conference (with Gillian Symon, May 2009). I would like to thank all those present, and Cathy Cassell and Bill Lee in particular, for their support in developing this line of enquiry.

Funding

Aspects of this research were supported by the Economic and Social Research Council (Grant Number PTA-0302004-00095).

References

Alvesson, M. and Karreman, D. (2000) 'Varieties of discourse: on the study of organizations through discourse analysis', *Human Relations*, 53 (9): 1125–1149.

Alvesson, M. and Sköldberg, K. (2000) *Reflexive Methodology: New Vistas for Qualitative Research*. London: Sage.

Barry, D., Carroll, B. and Hansen, H. (2006) 'To text or context? Endotextual, exotextual and multi-textual approaches to narrative and discourse', *Organization Studies*, 27 (8): 1091–1110.

Bate, S.P. (1997) 'Whatever happened to organizational anthropology? A review of the field of organizational ethnography and anthropological studies', *Human Relations*, 50 (9): 1147–1175.

Brewer, J.D. (2004) 'Ethnography', in C. Cassell and G. Symon (eds), *Essential Guide to Qualitative Methods in Organizational Research*. London: Sage, pp. 312–322.

Broadfoot, K., Deetz, S. and Anderson, D. (2004) 'Multi-levelled, multi-method approaches to organizational discourse', in D. Grant, C. Hardy, C. Oswick and L. Putnam (eds), *The Sage Handbook of Organizational Discourse*. London: Sage, pp. 193–212.

Bryman, A. (1984) 'The debate about quantitative and qualitative research: a question of method or epistemology', *The British Journal of Sociology*, 35 (1): 75–92.

Bryman, A. (2008) 'Of methods and methodology', *Qualitative Research in Organizations and Management*, 3 (2): 159–168.

Buchanan, D.A. and Bryman, A. (2007) 'Contextualising methods choice in organizational research', *Organizational Research Methods*, 10 (3): 483–501.

Burke Johnson, R., Onwuegbuzie, A.J. and Turner, L.A. (2007) 'Towards a definition of mixed methods research', *Journal of Mixed Methods Research*, 1 (2): 112–133.

Cassell, C. (2005) 'Creating the interviewer: identity work in the management research process', *Qualitative Research*, 5(2): 167–179.

Cox, J. and Hassard, J. (2005) 'Triangulation in organizational research: a re-presentation', *Organization*, 12 (1): 109–133.

Creswell, J.W. (2003) *Research Design: Qualitative; Quantitative and Mixed Method Approaches* (2nd edn). London: Sage.

Creswell, J.W., Plano Clark, V.L., Gutman, M.L. and Hanson, W.E. (2003) 'Advanced mixed methods research design', in A. Tashakkori and C. Teddlie (eds), *Handbook of Mixed Methods in Social and Behavioral Research*. London: Sage, pp. 209–240.

Cunliffe, A.L., Luhman, J. and Boje, D.M. (2004) 'Narrative temporality: implications for organizational research', *Organization Studies*, 25 (2): 261–286.

Denzin, N. (2010) 'Moments, mixed methods and paradigm dialogs', *Qualitative Inquiry*, 16 (6): 419–427.

Fairclough, N. (2003) *Analyzing Discourse: Textual Analysis for Social Research*. London: Routledge.

Fine, G.A., Morrill, C. and Surianarain, S. (2008) 'Ethnography in organizational settings', in D.A. Buchanan and A. Bryman (eds), *Handbook of Organizational Research Methods*. London: Sage.

Finlay, L. (2002) 'Negotiating the swamp: the opportunity and challenge of reflexivity in research practice', *Qualitative Research*, 2 (2): 209–230.

Frost, N., Nolas, S.-M., Brooks-Gordon, B., Esin, C., Holt, A., Mehdizadeh, L. and Shinebourne, P. (2010) 'Pluralism in qualitative research: the impact of different researchers and qualitative approaches on the analysis of qualitative data', *Qualitative Research*, 10 (4): 441–460.

Giddens, A. (1990) *The Consequences of Modernity*. Cambridge: Cambridge University Press.

Greene, J.C. and Caracelli, V.J. (2003) 'Making paradigmatic sense of mixed methods', in A. Tashakkori and C. Teddlie (eds), *Handbook of Mixed Methods in Social and Behavioral Research*. London: Sage, pp. 91–110.

Hansen, H. (2006) 'The ethnonarrative approach', *Human Relations*, 59 (8): 1049–1075.

Hesse-Biber, S. (2010) 'Emerging methodologies and methods practices in the field of mixed methods research' (Introduction to the special issue), *Qualitative Inquiry*, 16 (6): 415–418.

Hornby, P. and Symon, G. (1994) 'Tracer studies', in C. Cassell and G. Symon (eds), *Qualitative Methods in Organizational Research: A Practical Guide*. London: Sage, pp. 167–188.

Kincheloe, J.L. (2005) 'On to the next level: continuing the conceptualization of the bricolage', *Qualitative Inquiry*, 11 (3): 323–350.

Knights, D. (2006) 'Authority at work: reflections and recollections', *Organization Studies*, 27 (5): 699–720.

Lewis, M. and Grimes, A. (1999) 'Metatriangulation: building theory from multiple paradigms', *Academy of Management Review*, 24 (4): 672–690.
Morse, J. (2010) 'Simultaneous and sequential qualitative mixed methods designs', *Qualitative Inquiry*, 16 (6): 483–491.
Phillips, N., Nelson, B.J., Lawerence, K.A., Thomas, B. and Hardy, C. (2004) 'Discourse and institutions', *Academy of Management Review*, 29 (4): 635–652.
Pritchard, K. (2007) 'Knowledge at work: a study of HR professionals'. Unpublished PhD Thesis, Birkbeck College, University of London, London.
Pritchard, K. (2010) 'Becoming an HR strategic partner: tales of transition', *Human Resource Management Journal*, 20 (2): 175–188.
Pritchard, K., Briner, R.B. and Symon, G. (2004) 'Talking about knowledge with human resource practitioners', paper presented at the 5th European Conference on Organizational Knowledge Learning and Capabilities, Innsbruck, April.
Pritchard, K. and Symon, G. (2009) '"Going between": insights gained from combining qualitative methods in organisational research', paper presented at the 9th EURAM Annual Conference, Liverpool, May.
Rees, A. and Nicholson, N. (1994) 'The twenty statements test', in C. Cassell and G. Symon (eds), *Qualitative Methods in Organizational Research*. London: Sage, pp. 37–54.
Richards, L. (2009) *Handling Qualitative Data: A Practical Guide* (2nd edn). London: Sage.
Shotter, J. and Lannamann, J. W. (2002) 'The situation of social constructionism: its "imprisonment" within the ritual of theory-criticism-and-debate', *Theory and Psychology*, 12 (5): 577–609.
Tashakkori, A. and Teddlie, C. (eds) (2003) *Handbook of Mixed Methods in Social and Behavioural Research*. London: Sage.
Waddington, K. (2005) 'Using diaries to explore the characteristics of work-related gossip: methodological considerations from exploratory multimethod research', *Journal of Occupational and Organizational Psychology*, 78 (2): 221–236.
Weick, K.E. (1995) *Sensemaking in Organizations*. London: Sage.
Wetherell, M., Taylor, S. and Yates, S. (2001) *Discourse as Data: A Guide for Analysis*. London: Sage.

7 Doing Template Analysis

Nigel King

What is Template Analysis?

One common feature of the many different types of qualitative research described in this and other books is that it produces extensive and complex textual data (and occasionally also visual data: see Vince and Warren, in this volume). How the researcher moves on from this to produce an understanding of the experiences captured in the texts depends on their choice of data analytical techniques. In this chapter, I will describe one such technique: template analysis (TA). I will outline the principles behind it and consider the circumstances in which it might be preferred to other well-known forms of qualitative data analysis. Through the use of an extended example from a real research project I will go through the key steps required to utilize the technique.

Template analysis is a style of thematic analysis that balances a relatively high degree of structure in the process of analysing textual data with the flexibility to adapt it to the needs of a particular study. It has mostly been used to analyse data from individual interviews (see Alvesson and Ashcraft, in this volume, for more on qualitative interviewing), but it can be applied to other forms too. The example used in this chapter employed focus group interviews (see also Kandola, in this volume), while Kent (2000) used it to analyse free response items on a questionnaire, and it could certainly be applied to data from diaries or to observational field notes (see Yanow, Ybema and van Hulst on ethnography and Brennan on participant observation, in this volume). Central to the technique is the development of a coding template, usually on the basis of a subset of the data, which is then applied to further data, revised and reapplied. The approach is very flexible regarding the style and format of the template that is produced and unlike some other thematic approaches does not suggest in advance a set sequence of coding levels.

Template analysis revisited

The first version of this chapter appeared more than ten years ago (Symon and Cassell, 1998). Since then, the number of publications describing studies that have used TA has grown considerably. An ongoing literature review I am compiling with Jane Melvin has identified well over 200 such articles. In terms of broad area, organizational research (including business and management) is clearly the largest (e.g. Kenny and Briner, 2010), followed by health (Howard et al., 2008). Beyond these, TA is used in a wide range of other settings, including education (Au, 2007), clinical psychology/psychotherapy (Stratton et al., 2006) and sports science (Nash and Sproule, 2009). TA studies vary considerably in size, from a single autobiographical case (King, 2008) to studies that in qualitative terms may be considered very large (Donnelly, 2008, for instance included 81 interviews).

Definitional and epistemological issues

Template analysis is not a complete and distinct methodology, but rather is a technique that may be used within a range of epistemological positions (see Duberley, Johnson and Cassell, in this volume). On the one hand, it can be employed in the kind of realist qualitative work that accepts much of the conventional positivistic position of mainstream quantitative social science. By this I mean research that is concerned with 'discovering' the underlying causes of human action and which seeks to achieve researcher objectivity and to demonstrate coding reliability (Kidd, 2008). On the other hand, template analysis can be used within what Madill et al. (2000) call a 'contextual constructivist' position. Here, the researcher assumes that there are always multiple interpretations to be made of any phenomenon, which will depend upon the position of the researcher and the context of the research. Concern with coding reliability is therefore irrelevant; instead the emphasis is on the reflexivity of the researcher (see Haynes, in this volume), the attempt to approach the topic from differing perspectives and the richness of the description produced (Wimalasiri et al., 2008). Phenomenological, interactionist and some narrative approaches (see Maitlis, in this volume) fall within this category.

Template analysis is generally not used in methodologies that take a radical relativist approach to examining how language is used in interaction to construct versions of our world – as in various forms of discourse and conversation analysis (see Oswick, and Greatbatch and Clark respectively, in this volume). There are, however, examples of social constructionist studies that are concerned with broad patterns of discourse use rather than the close analysis of interactions, and that have used a thematic style of analysis (e.g. Taylor and Ussher, 2001). In principle, such studies could use a template style for their thematic analysis.

Why use template analysis?

Why should anyone about to embark on a qualitative research project choose to use template analysis? In particular, why should they choose it over other approaches that resemble it, such as grounded theory (for example, Corbin and Strauss, 2008, and see Kenealy, in this volume), interpretative phenomenological analysis (IPA; for example, Smith et al., 2009) or more generic forms of thematic analysis (e.g. Braun and Clarke, 2006)? In this section I will consider the advantages that template analysis may offer in relation to these alternatives.

Focusing first on grounded theory, for some researchers a preference for template analysis may be based on their philosophical position. Since its inception by Glaser and Strauss in *The Discovery of Grounded Theory* (1967), grounded theory has developed in a number of different directions, including a divergence between the original authors (Strauss and Corbin, 1990; Glaser, 1992) and a social constructionist version proposed by Charmaz (1995). The Strauss and Corbin approach is probably the best known and most widely used, and both it and Glaser's version retain a realist orientation. That is to say, its users have mostly claimed to be discovering the 'real' beliefs, attitudes, values and so on of the participants in their research. Those qualitative researchers taking a contextual constructivist stance that is sceptical of the existence of 'real' internal states to be discovered through empirical research may therefore feel that template analysis is more conducive to their position.

Template analysis may also be preferred by those who are not inimical to the assumptions of grounded theory but find it too prescriptive (especially in the Strauss and Corbin version), in that it specifies procedures for data gathering and analysis that *must* be followed (Corbin and Strauss, 2008). By contrast, template analysis is, on the whole, a more flexible technique with fewer specified procedures, permitting researchers to tailor it to match their own requirements.

When employed within a broadly phenomenological approach, template analysis is in practice very similar to IPA. The main differences between approaches are the use of a priori codes in template analysis and the balance between, within and across case analysis. IPA tends to analyse individual cases in greater depth before attempting any integration of a full set of cases. The net effect of these differences is that template analysis is generally somewhat less time-consuming than IPA and can handle rather larger data sets more comfortably. IPA studies are commonly based on samples of 10 or fewer; template analysis studies usually have rather more participants, with 15 to 30 being common.

Some writers – notably Braun and Clarke (2006) – argue for the use of a generic form of thematic analysis, one that is not wedded to a particular methodological and theoretical position. This is in effect the same position that I would take in stating that template analysis is a technique rather than a methodology, which can be used from varying philosophical positions. It is worthwhile considering why one might choose template analysis rather than the kind of thematic analysis Braun and Clarke describe. I would suggest that there are three features that vary between the techniques and that might influence a researcher's choice: the flexibility of the coding structure, the use of a priori themes, and use of the initial template.

Flexibility of the coding structure

Some approaches specify in advance how the coding should be structured, typically moving from descriptive themes that are close to the data, to feeding into a smaller number of interpretive themes and then in turn into a few major (or 'overarching') themes (see Langdridge, 2004; King and Horrocks, 2010). By requiring a step-by-step move from the more concrete and data-grounded to the more abstract and interpretive, such techniques can be useful in discouraging inexperienced qualitative researchers from rushing to impose strong interpretations on the data at an early stage. However, it is debatable whether there is ever such a clear distinction between descriptive and interpretive coding. Furthermore, the norm of a three-level hierarchy may restrict analysts from exploring the richest aspects of the data in any real depth. Template analysis does not insist on a fixed number of levels of coding hierarchy – instead it encourages the analyst to develop themes more extensively where the richest data (in relation to the research question) are found. Equally, template analysis does not insist on an explicit distinction between descriptive and interpretive themes, nor on a particular position for each type in the structure.

Use of a priori themes

Types of thematic analysis can be considered in terms of the extent to which they take a 'bottom up' or 'top down' approach. In the former, existing theoretical or practical commitments are actively avoided, to allow themes to be developed inductively from the data. This is the case in the thematic analysis used in IPA and grounded theory. By contrast, top down approaches seek to define and apply themes that are informed by theory or practice ('practice' here could mean, for example, basing the coding structure around evaluation criteria). Matrix analysis (Nadin and Cassell, 2004) and framework analysis (Pope et al., 2000) generally adopt this kind of approach. Template analysis can be positioned in the middle ground between top down and bottom up styles of analysis. It allows the researcher to define some themes in advance (a priori themes), but usually only a limited number that correspond to key concepts or perspectives for the study. It also insists that these are used tentatively, with the possibility always considered that any a priori theme may need to be redefined or discarded.

Use of the initial template

Most thematic approaches will require the researcher to carry out each step of the analysis on each transcript (or other piece of textual data). In template analysis, the use of an initial template based on a sub-set of the data changes the process. Following the construction of the initial template, the researcher does not need to begin with preliminary coding for the next and subsequent transcripts. As will be seen in the example later in this chapter, analysis progresses instead through an iterative process of applying, modifying and re-applying the initial template. This style of analysis can be more efficient than those that require all the steps to be carried out on all the data. Crucially, using the initial template does not, in my experience, seriously risk reducing the depth of the analysis if this is carried out properly.

Key Features of Template Analysis

Defining themes and codes

Themes in qualitative analysis may be defined as the recurrent and distinctive features of participants' accounts (in interviews, diaries, blogs and so on) that characterize perceptions and/or experiences, seen by the researcher as relevant to the research question of a particular study. The issues involved in defining the concept of 'theme' are explored further in Braun and Clarke (2006) and King and Horrocks (2010). For the purposes of the present chapter, there are three points related to this definition that require some comment:

1 The term 'theme' implies repetition. It should not be applied to a single isolated instance where a view is expressed or an experience described. While themes are usually identified across several cases, something important that is identified several times within a single case could still be defined as a theme.

2 Themes are not independent of the researcher who defines them. They do not lie waiting to be discovered, like a fossil in a rock. Even the most realist-oriented qualitative research recognizes that themes are not objective 'facts'.

3 To be useful, themes must be relatively distinct from each other. Some overlap is inevitable, but an extensive blurring of boundaries between themes is to be avoided.

Coding is the process of attaching a label (code) to a section of text to index it as relating to a theme. Within a template there may also be some codes that strictly speaking do not index themes but rather serve as 'placeholders' (Gibbs, 2002) to help organize associated themes. For instance, in a study of staff views on a new IT system, we might use staff groups as placeholder codes under which themes relating to each group are organized.

Hierarchical coding

A key feature of template analysis is the hierarchical organization of codes, with groups of similar codes clustered together to produce more general higher order codes. Hierarchical coding allows the researcher to analyse texts at varying levels of specificity and there can be as many levels of themes as the researcher finds useful. Importantly, the extent to which main (i.e. top level) themes are elaborated – in terms of the number and levels of sub-themes – should reflect how rich they prove to be in terms of offering insights into the topic area of a particular study. It is worth bearing in mind, though, that too many levels can be counter productive to the goal of attaining clarity in organizing and interpreting the data.

As well as being organized hierarchically, the template can present lateral links between themes. This may be in the form of a small number of integrative themes that cut across many of the main themes or it may involve more complex links between individual themes. Using and depicting such lateral links on the template is discussed below.

Parallel coding

Template analysis usually permits a parallel coding of segments of text, whereby the same segment is classified within two (or more) different codes at the same level. Parallel coding is only likely to be problematic in research that is located strongly towards the positivist end of the qualitative research spectrum, where researchers may wish to combine template analysis with elements of quantitative content analysis.

Integrative themes

Sometimes as the template develops it will become clear that there are certain themes that seem to pervade much of the data, cross-cutting many or all of the other thematic clusters. For example, in a study of experiences of diabetic renal disease (King et al., 2002), we found that 'uncertainty' permeated much of the data. To have simply treated this as a top-level theme in itself would not have drawn sufficient attention to the way it related to all the other thematic clusters. Equally, adding 'uncertainty' as a sub-theme to each top-level theme would not in our view have made its importance apparent enough. We therefore identified it as an integrative theme, shown on the template as connecting the other themes laterally.

One way to conceptualize integrative themes is as undercurrents running through participants' accounts; often, perhaps, not addressed explicitly but very apparent to the careful reader. In the diabetic renal disease study we identified a second integrative theme of 'stoicism' to indicate the typical stance towards their illness taken by almost all participants. They did not explicitly describe themselves as 'stoical' but demonstrated it in many different aspects of their accounts of their illness experience. The integrative theme of 'stoicism' was of interest because it appeared to contradict claims in the literature that people no longer felt the need to maintain a 'stiff upper-lip' towards personal suffering.

Displaying the template: lists and mind-maps

The template itself has an important communicative function; it is therefore worthwhile to think carefully about how best to present it. There are two main styles that can be used. First, themes can be presented in a list, with levels indicated by indentation, typography (e.g. font size and style) and/or a numbering system. Second, themes can be laid out in a format similar to a 'mind-map', which might also use typographic details as well as connecting arrows to indicate hierarchical levels. The mind-map version allows lateral links between thematic clusters to be shown more clearly than in the list style. It is, however, more complex and for the full template would take up considerably more space in its display than the list version. Although most published studies using template analysis present the template in list form, it is useful to think about using the mind-map style when the lateral links between thematic clusters are important. It is always possible to convert this to a list format if that works better in a written account of the study.

Quality checks

The issue of quality in qualitative research is dealt with in detail by Symon and Cassell in this volume. Here I will highlight specific points relating to template analysis. Some of the commonly used strategies for enhancing the quality of data analysis include: independent coding and critical comparison among researchers and by expert panels; respondent feedback; and the provision of audit trails. All of these are assisted by the systematic nature of template analysis and the possibility it offers to document emerging thinking through the modification of the template. The compiling of an audit trail, in particular, fits very well with this approach. An audit trail in qualitative research is a record of the steps the researcher has gone through in carrying out an analysis and the way his or her thinking has developed. I would always recommend that a full record is kept of how the template develops over the course of the analysis, numbering and dating successive versions and keeping notes as to the reasons for any major changes made to it.

Developing the Template: An Example

Having described the approach in general terms, I will present here the steps involved in using it for the analysis of data from a quite recent study carried out by members of my team at the University of Huddersfield. Some background to the project is necessary here in order to understand the material that we were working with.

Background: the community group participation study

As part of their wider health strategy (Department of Health, 1999) from 2002 the UK government set up 350 Health Living Centres (HLCs) . These served as a focus for community-based initiatives and activities to improve health and wellbeing in areas of significant deprivation. The Centre for Applied Psychological Research (CAPR) at the University of Huddersfield was commissioned to carry out a series of evaluation studies for an HLC in a deprived urban area in northern England, which I will refer to as the Broomville Health Partnership (BHP). The project team of myself, Emma Kirkby-Geddes and Alison Bravington carried out focus groups (see Kandola, in this volume) with members of three community groups supported by the BHP. Details of the groups are given in Table 24.1 below.

Table 24.1 Focus group participants

Group	Number of participants	Characteristics of participants
Coffee Morning	4 (+ leader)	1 female, 3 male Approx. age range: 58–82 All white
Craft Group	10 (+ leader) Volunteer helpers: 1 Carers: 1	8 female, 2 male Approx. age range 42–86 8 white, 2 SE Asian
Exercise Group	6 (+ leader)	5 female, 1 male: Approx. age range: 68–88 All white

The focus groups were audio-recorded, transcribed verbatim and analysed using template analysis. The stages of this analytical process are described below. The transcripts were laid out double spaced with wide margins, and line numbered, to facilitate analysis – especially in the early stages.

The overall aim of this part of the evaluation programme was:

- To examine how those participating in group activities supported by BHP experience their involvement with the Healthy Living Partnership, in the context of their views of Broomville as a community.

By 'involvement' we meant both participation in their own group and their wider engagement with the BHP and the activities and facilities it supported.

A priori themes and preliminary coding

Before beginning preliminary coding, it is essential to read through the transcripts for familiarization and to check for any possible errors in transcription.

The first transcript should be taken and every section of text that seems to offer something of relevance to answering the research question marked, noting in the margin a preliminary code title that sums up what is of interest here. If using a priori themes, it is best to have a sheet beside the transcript listing and defining these; should a section of text emerge that can be encompassed by one of the a priori themes, make a note of this in the margin. At this stage if there is doubt as to whether a particular issue is relevant, it is best to err on the side of inclusivity and code it. It can always be set aside later if it transpires that it does not add to the interpretation.

In the BHP community group participation study we began our analysis with the focus groups, listening to the recordings and then focusing particularly on the Coffee Morning group transcript. Before commencing preliminary coding we identified six a priori themes, based on the BHP's evaluation priorities and on our initial reading and discussion of the transcripts. These are described in Table 24.2.

Next we each independently read through the selected transcript and added preliminary codes in the margins and/or above the text wherever any section of the discussion appeared to relate to matters relevant to the study aims. If such sections could be encapsulated by one of the a priori themes we noted this on the transcript too.

Initial template

A key decision in template analysis is when to begin to develop an initial template. As noted above, this is normally based on a sub-set of the data, but there can be no fixed rule as to how soon it should be attempted. In general, the

Table 24.2 A priori themes in the community group participation study

A priori theme	Description
Perception of self	Includes: physical insecurity, social isolation, personal effects of ageing
Quality of group	Includes: atmosphere, values of the group
Practicalities	Includes: practical aspects of the groups, such as rooming, scheduling sessions
Who we are as a group	Includes: issues of group identity and how these relate to personal identity
Perceptions of Broomville	Includes: physical space and resources, local people
World gone down the plughole	Includes: all references to a general sense of quality of life and values deteriorating over time

more diverse the accounts provided by participants within a study, the more transcripts will need to be analysed to produce a workable initial template.

Developing the initial template begins with the clustering of preliminary codes, to bring them into meaningful groups within which hierarchical and lateral relations between themes can be defined. This should be a very fluid and exploratory process, in which many different ways of organizing themes are attempted. In the clustering process, it should not be assumed that a priori themes are necessarily going to be at the top levels of clusters; they can be moved around anywhere in the emerging structure until a place is found where they seem to function best.

In our study we produced an initial version of the template on the basis of the preliminary coding of the first focus group. We began by looking at each other's coding, discussing the similarities and differences and agreeing on a provisional set of themes to organize. We wrote each potential theme on a Post-it note and placed the notes on large sheets of paper in what seemed to be meaningful clusters. The advantage of using Post-its is that they can easily be moved around to explore alternative ways of organizing the template, but of course other methods could be used. After a lengthy process of trying out different versions of the structure we agreed on the initial template shown in Figure 24.1.

Two of the a priori themes were not included in the initial template – Perception of Self and Practicalities. In both cases, we found there was little that would 'fit' under the a priori theme title that did not also fit elsewhere on the template. Further, Perception of Self seemed overly individualistic when the data showed that issues such as ageing and physical insecurity were almost always raised in the context of relationships in the group, the community and society more widely. There were also a number of preliminary themes that we could not include comfortably on the template. At this stage we simply left these as Uncategorized.

The initial template included one integrative theme: Shrinkage. This captured the way that many participants seemed to describe a sense of their world shrinking – personally through such things as the effects of ageing and collectively through the loss of local amenities and facilities.

Modifying the template

Once an initial template is constructed, the researcher must work systematically through the full set of transcripts, identifying those sections of text that are relevant to the project's aims and marking them with one or more appropriate code(s). In the

1. WHO WE ARE AS GROUP

1.1 Our purpose as a group
1.1.1 Doing specific activities
1.1.2 Vehicle for activity *vs* End in itself
1.1.3 Being a presence in Broomville (Church)

1.2 Inward *vs* outward looking
1.2.1 Exclusivity

1.2.1.1 Not too much growth
1.2.1.2 Existing relationships

1.2.2 Inclusivity

1.2.2.1 Seeking growth

1.2.3 Fundraising
1.2.4 Connection with other church activities

2. QUALITY OF GROUP

2.1 Caring for each other
2.1.1 Practical help
2.1.2 Ethos of caring
2.1.3 Christian fellowship

2.2 Intra-group dynamics
2.2.1 Leader telling group what they (should) think
2.2.2 Resisting leader

2.2.2.1 Re. faith/ethnic diversity
2.2.2.2 Re. children = vibrancy

2.2.3 Humour
2.2.4 Reassurance

3. PERCEPTIONS OF BROOMVILLE

3.1 Physical geography of Broomville
3.1.1 Proximity of Village Hall

3.2 Diversity
3.2.1 +ve re diversity of people
3.2.2 Diversity of worship
3.2.3 Diversity of activities

3.2.3.1 Plenty
3.2.3.2 Not enough

3.3 Green environment
3.3.1 Improvements to environment
3.3.2 Better than other similar (multi-cultural) areas
3.3.3 Ownership of environmental improvements (children)

(Continued)

(Continued)

3.4 'Broomville don't care'
3.4.1 Involvement from outside Broomville
3.4.2 People won't get involved
3.4.3 Excuses (or not) for lack of involvement

3.5 Intergenerational issues
3.5.1 Children as constructive
- 3.5.1.1 In organized contexts
- 3.5.1.2 Schools' involvement in community
  - 3.5.1.2.1 Flower beds
  - 3.5.1.2.2 Pensioner dinners

3.5.2 Children as destructive
- 3.5.2.1 Wild
- 3.5.2.2 Environmental damage
- 3.5.2.3 Litter

3.5.3 Children as future/sign of life
3.5.4 General negativity (nothing to like about Broomville)

3.6 World down plughole
3.6.1 Night-time dangerous

A. SHRINKAGE
(INTEGRATIVE THEME)
A1 Churches going/moving to fringes
A2 People not going out at night

[Uncategorized]
Activities outside the group
Involvement in/understanding of wider PPH activities
Finding out about PPH activities
Getting older
Impact of lottery funding

Figure 24.1 Initial template from the community group participation study

course of this, inadequacies in the initial template will be revealed, requiring changes of various kinds. It is through these that the template develops to its final form.

Having developed the initial template in the community group participation study, we again went through the first focus group transcript to check that it had succeeded in capturing everything we felt to be important in the data in relation to our research aims. As a result we made several changes:

- We added a new top-level theme: Understanding and Perception of BHP.
- We added a new integrative theme: Getting Older.
- We divided the top-level theme Perceptions of Broomville into two second-level themes: People and Physical Space and Facilities.

We then applied this revised initial template to the remaining two focus groups, noting where relevant material in these could not be readily covered by any theme on the template and where necessary revising the template accordingly. Finally we read through the individual interview transcripts to identify any further revisions needed. This resulted in the final version of the template shown in Figure 24.2.

Throughout this process we reorganized the template in various ways. Examples of these are given below.

Insertion

After producing the initial template we added a new third-level theme of Inter-racial Issues, under Perceptions of Broomville/People. While some issues relating to ethnicity did appear on the first version of the initial template, and more were added subsequently, it was only at this point that we recognized that the importance of the area in general was best reflected by pulling together such a theme. The theme included both an explicit discussion of 'race' (mostly regarding the South Asian community) in the Coffee Morning Group and more implicit allusions in the other two groups.

> I've lived with Asians, they've been there 10 to 12 years, and they, it's taken that long for them to start speaking to you. They just ignore you, and even now, they'll turn their nose up at you and look the other way when they walk past you. (Roger, Coffee Morning Group)
>
> Well, if you can speak the truth and speak out, we were pushed out [of our usual room] for the Asian ladies; if I shouldn't have said that, I don't know, but we were – so. (Joyce, Exercise Group)
>
> [Member next to Joyce makes exaggerated gesture of holding her head in her hands; others look embarrassed.]

1. US AS A GROUP

1.1 Looking inward
1.1.1 Exclusivity
- 1.1.1.1 Restricting growth
- 1.1.1.2 Existing relationships

1.1.2 Ethos of group
- 1.1.2.1 Caring
- 1.1.2.2 Practical help
- 1.1.2.3 Christian fellowship

1.1.3 Intra-group dynamics
- 1.1.3.1 Leader telling group what they (should) think
- 1.1.3.2 Resisting dominant voice
  - 1.1.3.2.1 Re. faith/ethnic diversity
  - 1.1.3.2.1 Re. children = vibrancy
  - 1.1.3.2.2 Re. takeaways
- 1.1.3.3 Humour
- 1.1.3.4 Leader supporting members

1.1.4 Value of activity
- 1.1.4.1 Activity as ends or means
- 1.1.4.2 Sharing food/drink
- 1.1.4.3 Importance of talk/sociability
- 1.1.4.4 An excuse to get out
- 1.1.4.5 Direct health benefits
- 1.1.4.6 Meanings related to specific activities

1.2 Looking outward
1.2.1 Seeking growth
1.2.2 Taking group activity home
1.2.3 Spreading/sharing the ethos
- 1.2.3.1 Being a presence in Broomville
- 1.2.3.2 Wider Christian/faith activities
- 1.2.3.3 Fundraising for charities

2. PERCEPTIONS OF BROOMVILLE

2.1 People
2.1.1 Intergenerational issues
- 2.1.1.1 Children as constructive
  - 2.1.1.1.1 In organized contexts
  - 2.1.1.1.2 Schools' involvement in community

(Continued)

(Continued)

2.1.1.1.2.1 Flower beds
2.1.1.1.2.2 Pensioner dinners

2.1.1.2 Children as destructive

2.1.1.2.1 Wild
2.1.1.2.2 Environmental damage
2.1.1.2.3 Litter

2.1.1.3 Children as future/sign of life
2.1.1.4 Young people don't get involved
2.1.1.5 Generations want different things

2.1.2 Inter-racial issues

2.1.2.1 'Us and them'

2.1.2.1.1 Asians unfriendly
2.1.2.1.2 Asians keep to their own comfort zone
2.1.2.1.3 Asians changing nature of community
2.1.2.1.4 Competition for resources

2.1.2.2 Coming together

2.1.2.2.1 Cooking/eating together
2.1.2.2.2 Coming out of comfort zones
2.1.2.2.3 Diversity a good thing
2.1.2.2.4 Asians participating in Broomville activities

2.1.2.3 Difficult/taboo topic

2.1.3 'Broomville don't care'

2.1.3.1 Involvement from outside Broomville
2.1.3.2 People won't get involved

2.1.3.2.1 Asians

2.1.3.3 Excuses (or not) for lack of involvement

2.1.3.3.1 Not lack of information

2.1.4 Contesting the 'Broomville don't care' attitude

2.1.4.1 (Local) Government initiatives cf bottom up community activity
2.1.4.2 Local government has good ideas. But…
2.1.4.3 Doing it from own heart, and pocket
2.1.4.4 Roots of voluntary community action in Christianity

2.2 Physical space and facilities
2.2.1 Physical geography of Broomville

2.2.1.1 Proximity of Village Hall
2.2.1.2 Top and Bottom

(Continued)

(Continued)

2.2.1.2.1 Long way to walk
2.2.1.2.2 Two communities in one

2.2.2 Green environment

2.2.2.1 Improvements to environment
2.2.2.2 Better than other similar (multi-cultural) areas
2.2.2.3 Ownership of environmental improvements (children)

2.2.3 Urban mess

2.2.3.1 Too many takeaways

2.2.3.1.1 Destroying community

2.2.3.2 Lack of cleanliness

2.2.4 Facilities

2.2.4.1 Good bus service
2.2.4.2 Poor main road
2.2.4.3 Other venues for activities

2.2.5 Diversity

2.2.5.1 +ve re diversity of people
2.2.5.2 Diversity of worship
2.2.5.3 Diversity of activities

2.2.5.2.1 Plenty
2.2.5.2.2 Not enough

3. UNDERSTANDING AND PERCEPTION OF BHP
3.1 Understanding of wider BHP activities

3.1.1 Involvement in BHP planning

3.2 Finding out about BHP activities
3.3 Impact of lottery funding

3.3.1 On Broomville in general
3.3.2 On specific services at BHP

3.4 Facilities at Village Hall

3.4.1 Issues re rooms
3.4.2 Access to Village Hall

A. WORLD GONE DOWN THE PLUGHOLE
(INTEGRATIVE THEME)

B. GETTING OLDER
(INTEGRATIVE THEME)

Figure 24.2 Final template from the community group participation study

Deletion

The top-level theme Quality of Group was deleted at version four of the template and the second-level theme Our Purpose as a Group (under Us as a Group) was removed in the final version. This was because, as the analysis progressed, we increasingly observed that, in terms of our research aims, the most important aspect of how people saw their groups was the balance (and at times tension) between a tendency to 'look inwards' at processes and relationships and a willingness to 'look outwards' to how the group related to lives beyond the meetings and to the wider community.

Merging

On the initial template under Perceptions of Broomville we included as a second-level theme World Gone Down the Plughole. This captured the view that the world in general was a less safe, friendly and comfortable place to live in than it had been in the past. We distinguished such views from specific comments about how Broomville had declined, which we captured under the integrative theme Shrinkage. The quotes below illustrate the two themes:

> *World Gone Down the Plughole*
>
> But where is nice to live these days? Where do, do you feel safe, any, any of you, well I can't go out at night. (Maureen, Exercise Group)
>
> *Shrinkage*
>
> I mean the shops up there are frankly not worth bothering, they're very expensive and they haven't got the variety ... You've got to leave Broomville, get out of Broomville to get your stuff, now. (Roger, Coffee Morning Group)

As we developed the template further we became increasingly uncertain as to whether the distinction made above was a meaningful one. Eventually we decided to merge the two themes together, using the World Gone Down the Plughole title as we felt it better encapsulated the tone of participants' comments.

Changing the scope

Having deleted the top-level theme Quality of Group (see above), we made changes in scope to the subsidiary theme Caring for Each Other and its sub-themes.

We concluded that the notion of 'caring' in the groups was best seen as an aspect of their ethos and therefore reversed the hierarchical order here on the final template. This enabled us to get a clearer understanding of the differences in ethos between the groups than was the case when ethos was subsumed under the notion of 'caring'.

Changing the higher order classification

The previous example involved a change in the higher order classification as well as a change in the scope for the themes, since Ethos of Group moved into the second-level theme Looking Inward. This created a potential difficulty in that aspects of ethos that concerned how groups related to the world beyond them could have been neglected. We addressed this by constructing a third-level theme under Looking Outwards entitled Spreading/Sharing the Ethos.

The 'final' template

One of the most difficult decisions to make when constructing an analytical template is where to stop the process of development. It is possible to go on modifying and refining definitions of codes almost ad infinitum, but research projects inevitably face external constraints which will mean that there is not unlimited time to produce an 'ideal' template. The decision about when a template is 'good enough' is always going to be unique to a particular project. However, no template can be considered 'final' if there remain any sections of text that are clearly relevant to the research question but stay uncoded.

Interpreting and Presenting Template Analysis

Interpretation

Developing a template and using it to code a set of transcripts does not represent the end of the process of analysing and interpreting the data. If the themes are simply listed and the main findings summarized under each this will result in a very flat description of the data. Exactly how to go about drawing together an interpretation of the coded data depends on the aims and content of the particular study. I will offer some guidelines and examples that may serve as a useful starting point.

Listing codes

I usually find it useful at an early stage to compile a list of all codes occurring in each transcript, with some indication of their frequency. The distribution of codes within and across transcripts can help to draw attention to aspects of the data that warrant further examination. For example, if a theme occurs prominently in all but one of a set of interview transcripts, it may be revealing to look closely at the one exception. Or if certain themes occur frequently in the transcripts of one sub-set of the sample but hardly ever in another, whether this may exemplify a meaningful difference in views or experiences between the two should be considered. Note, though, that while frequencies of themes and the patterns of their distribution may suggest areas for closer examination, they cannot in and of themselves tell us anything meaningful.

Selectivity

There is always the need to be selective in identifying which themes to examine in depth. It is important not to rush to a decision about which key themes should be the focus, and it should not automatically be assumed that any a priori themes retained in the final template should be included among these. Equally, prioritizing themes to focus on should not be based on mere frequency, as explained above. Rather the task is to consider carefully how each theme (or cluster of themes) sheds light on the topic of interest.

Openness

The need to be selective in analysing and interpreting data must be balanced against the need to retain openness towards it. The researcher must not be so strongly guided by the initial research questions that all themes that are not obviously of direct relevance are disregarded. Themes that are judged to be of marginal relevance can play a useful role in adding to the background detail of the study, without requiring a lengthy explication. More problematic are those themes that are clearly of great importance to participants, but which seem to lie well outside the scope of the study. In such cases, there should be a careful consideration of whether the investigation of the 'excluded' theme casts any significant light on the understanding of central themes in the study. If it does, then it should be included in the interpretation.

Relationships between themes

Whether or not the template has been designed to incorporate integrative themes and/or other lateral links, as the interpretation proceeds consideration should be given to whether there are relationships between themes that need to be highlighted. In the community group participation study, for instance, we recognized that some of the intergenerational and inter-racial issues (themes 2.1.1 and 2.1.2 on the final template, Figure 24.2) were manifest in the intra-group dynamics (theme 1.1.3) and reflected this in our report (King et al., 2009). Sometimes it will be sufficient to draw out such connections in the findings and discussion of the write-up. Alternatively, as Crabtree and Miller (1999) suggest, maps, matrices and other diagrams can be used to explore and display template analysis findings.

Presentation

The final task is to present an account of the interpretation of the data. As with other stages of template analysis, it would be wrong to try to define one single 'correct' way to do this. The nature of the data, the type of document to be produced (including its word length) and, critically, the intended readership need to be considered. All the same, it is possible to identify three approaches to presentation, any one of which might prove useful.

1 *A set of individual case studies, followed by a discussion of the differences and similarities between cases.* This gives the reader a good grasp of the perspectives of individual participants. However, where there are a relatively large number of participants, this format can be confusing for the reader and repetitive, and it does rely on there being sufficient space to provide an adequate description of each case.

2 *An account structured around the main themes identified, drawing illustrative examples from each transcript (or other text) as required.* This tends to be the approach that most readily produces a clear and succinct thematic discussion. The danger is one of over-generalization, and losing sight of individual experiences.

3 *A thematic presentation of the findings, using a different individual case study to illustrate each of the main themes.* This can be a useful synthesis of approaches (1) and (2) above; the key challenge is to select the cases in a way that fairly represents the themes in the data as a whole.

Whatever approach is taken, the use of direct quotes from the participants is essential. These should normally include both short quotes to aid the understanding of specific points of interpretation and more extensive passages, giving readers a flavour of the original texts.

Advantages and Disadvantages of the Technique

Arguably, the greatest advantage of template analysis is that it is a highly flexible approach that can be modified for the needs of any study. It does not come with the heavy baggage of prescriptions and procedures and, as such, is especially welcome to those who want to take a phenomenological and experiential approach to organizational research. At the same time, the principles behind the technique are easily grasped by those relatively unfamiliar with qualitative methods and so it can be a valuable introduction to the whole field. Template analysis works very well in studies that seek to examine the perspectives of different groups within an organizational context – for example, different professions working in a collaborative setting or different grades of staff affected by a particular organizational change. Finally, the discipline of producing the template forces the researcher to take a systematic and well-structured approach to handling the data.

The strong emphasis on the coding structure in template analysis may be seen as a disadvantage by some researchers, for two rather contrasting reasons. On the one hand, this emphasis may seem potentially to stand in the way of a personal engagement with the data for those whose preferred style is a very open, unstructured engagement with texts. On the other hand, some may be too easily seduced into focusing excessively on the details of template construction, neglecting the crucial point made earlier that developing the template is a means to an end (making sense of the data) and not the purpose of the analysis in itself. In response to both these positions I would argue that the flexibility of template analysis should allow researchers to tailor it to suit their own style and stance towards qualitative data analysis, though in the end as with any analytical technique this will not suit everyone.

Conclusion

Template analysis has become a widely used technique for the thematic analysis of qualitative data, in organizational studies and beyond. The main reasons for its popularity, I would suggest, are its combination of a clear, structured and systematic approach with the flexibility to adapt it to specific needs – both in terms of the content of particular studies and the epistemological positions used. I hope this chapter has given a sense of how researchers new to the technique might go about employing it in their own research; and that those already familiar with the technique may have garnered some new ideas for how to creatively develop their analytical practice.

Further Reading

Examples of research using template analysis include: Gollop, Whitby, Buchanan and Ketley (2004), King, Bell, and Thomas (2004), Poppleton, Briner, and Kiefer (2008) and Waring and Wainwright (2008).

General texts on thematic analysis include: Braun and Clarke (2006), King and Horrocks (2010) Chapter 9: 'An introduction to interview data analysis', and Nadin and Cassell (2004).

References

Au, W. (2007) 'High-stakes testing and curricular control: a qualitative metasynthesis', *Educational Researcher*, 36 (5): 258–267.

Braun, V. and Clarke, V. (2006) 'Using thematic analysis in psychology', *Qualitative Research in Psychology*, 3: 77–101.

Charmaz, K. (1995) 'Grounded theory', in J.A. Smith, R. Harré and L. van Langenhove (eds), *Rethinking Methods in Psychology*. London: Sage.

Corbin, J. and Strauss, A. (2008) *Basics of Qualitative Research: Techniques and Procedures for Developing Grounded Theory* (3rd edn). London: Sage.

Crabtree, B.F. and Miller, W.L. (1999) 'Using codes and code manuals: a template organizing style of interpretation', in B.F. Crabtree and W.L. Miller (eds), *Doing Qualitative Research* (2nd edn). Newbury Park, CA: Sage.

Department of Health (1999) *Saving Lives: Our Healthier Nation*. London: HMSO.

Donnelly, R. (2008) 'Careers and temporal flexibility in the new economy: an Anglo-Dutch comparison of the organisation of consultancy work', *Human Resource Management Journal*, 18 (3): 197–215.

Gibbs, G. (2002) *Qualitative Data Analysis: Explorations with NVivo*. Buckingham: Open University Press.

Glaser, B. (1992) *Emergence vs Forcing: Basics of Grounded Analysis*. Mill Valley, CA: The Sociology Press.

Glaser, B. and Strauss, A.L. (1967) *The Discovery of Grounded Theory*. New York: Aldine Publications.

Gollop, R., Whitby, E., Buchanan, D. and Ketley, D. (2004) 'Influencing sceptical staff to become supporters of service improvement: A qualitative study of doctors' and managers' views', *Quality and Safety in Health Care*, 13: 108–114.

Howard, R., Avery, A. and Bissell, P. (2008) 'Causes of preventable drug-related hospital admissions: a qualitative study', *Quality and Safety in Health Care*, 17: 109–116.

Kenny, E.J. and Briner, R.B. (2010) 'Exploring ethnicity in organisations', *Equality, Diversity and Inclusion: An International Journal*, 29 (4): 348–363.

Kent, G. (2000) 'Understanding the experiences of people with disfigurements: an integration of four models of social and psychological functioning', *Psychology, Health and Medicine*, 5 (2): 117–129.

Kidd, J.M. (2008) 'Exploring the components of career well-being and the emotions associated with significant career experiences', *Journal of Career Development*, 35 (2): 166–186.

King, N. (2008) 'What will hatch? A constructivist autobiographical account of writing poetry', *Journal of Constructivist Psychology*, 21 (4): 274–287.

King, N., Bell, D. and Thomas, K. (2004) 'Family carers' experiences of out-of-hours community palliative care: a qualitative study', *International Journal of Palliative Nursing*, 10 (2): 76–83.

King, N., Carroll, C., Newton, P. and Dornan, T. (2002) '"You can't cure it so you have to endure it": the experience of adaptation to diabetic renal disease', *Qualitative Health Research*, 12 (3): 329–346.

King, N. and Horrocks, C. (2010) *Interviews in Qualitative Research*. London: Sage.

King, N., Kirkby-Geddes, E. and Bravington, A. (2009) *Evaluation of the Impact of Paddock Pathways to Health Membership on Beneficiaries' Health, Well-being and Social Functioning*. Centre for Applied Psychological Research, University of Huddersfield.

Langdridge, D. (2004) *Introduction to Research Methods and Data Analysis in Psychology*. Harlow: Pearson Education.

Madill, A., Jordan, A. and Shirley, C. (2000) 'Objectivity and reliability in qualitative analysis: realist, contextualist and radical constructionist epistemologies', *British Journal of Psychology*, 91: 1–20.

Nadin, S. and Cassell, C. (2004) 'Using data matrices', in C. Cassell and G. Symon (eds), *Essential Guide to Qualitative Methods in Organizational Research*. London: Sage.

Nash, C.S. and Sproule, J. (2009) 'Career development of expert coaches', *International Journal of Sports Science & Coaching*, 4 (1), 121–138.

Pope, C., Ziebland, S. and Mays, N. (2000) 'Qualitative research in healthcare: analysing qualitative data', *British Medical Journal*, 320: 114–116.

Poppleton, S., Briner, R.B. and Kiefer, T. (2008) 'The roles of context and everyday experience in understanding work–non-work relationships: A qualitative diary study of white- and blue-collar workers', *Journal of Occupational and Organizational Psychology*, 81 (3): 481–502.

Smith, J.A., Flowers, P. and Larkin, M. (2009) *Interpretative Phenomenological Analysis: Theory, Method, Research*. London: Sage.

Stratton, P., McGovern, M., Wetherell, A. and Farrington, C. (2006) 'Family therapy practitioners researching the reactions of practitioners to an outcome measure', *Australian and New Zealand Journal of Family Therapy*, 27 (4): 199–207.

Strauss, A. and Corbin, J. (1990) *Basics of Qualitative Research: Grounded Theory Procedures and Techniques.* London: Sage.
Symon, G. and Cassell, C. (eds) (1998) *Qualitative Methods and Analysis in Organizational Research.* London: Sage.
Taylor, G.W. and Ussher, J.M. (2001) 'Making sense of S&M: a discourse analytic account', *Sexualities*, 4: 293–314.
Waring, T. and Wainwright, D. (2008) 'Issues and challenges in the use of template analysis: Two comparative case studies from the field', *The Electronic Journal of Business Research Methods*, 6 (1): 85–94, available online at www.ejbrm.com.
Wimalasiri, V., Beesley, N., Cheyne, A. and Daniels, K. (2008) 'Social construction of the aetiology of designer error in the UK oil and gas industry: a stakeholder perspective', *Journal of Engineering Design*, 21 (1): 49–73.

8 Discourse Analysis and Discursive Research

Cliff Oswick

Introduction

It has been suggested that 'discourse is a process of meaning-making through talk and text' (Oswick, forthcoming) and that discourse analysis is 'the study of how meanings are produced, and of which meanings prevail in society' (Iedema, 2008: 389). Cunliffe (2008: 81) goes further and suggests that: 'Discourse analysts study the structures of meaning, expressions, themes, routine ways of talking, and rhetorical devices used in constructing reality'. The overarching inference that can be derived from these assertions is that discourse analysis is concerned with processes of social construction (i.e. meaning-making) through the study of language and language-use.

Discourse analysis cannot easily be reduced down to a single technique. Instead, it should be regarded as constituted through a bundle of methods that can be used to analyse talk and text. On this basis, it is better to think in terms of 'discursive analyses' rather than 'discourse analysis'. Although there might be varieties of discourse analysis, there are two overriding features that distinguish it from other language-based approaches. First, with discursive research the interest in language-use extends beyond a narrow focus on the use of a specific word or words. Hence, approaches such as 'content analysis' (Neuendorf, 2002; Krippendorff, 2004) and 'corpus linguistics' (McEnery and Wilson, 1996; Biber et al., 1998), which typically focus on an aggregated analysis of word frequency, fall outside of the scope of discourse analysis. The common feature of discourse-based approaches is that they consider language at the level of a statement or series of statements rather than simply considering the pattern and prevalence of usage of an individual word (or sample of words) as the unit of analysis. Put differently, discursive approaches privilege the consideration of words in combination (i.e. as a string of words that convey meaning) as opposed to more micro-oriented language-based approaches, which consider words in isolation.

The second, and related, generic feature of discursive approaches that distinguishes them from cognate methods is that they are attuned to aspects of context when examining an extract of written text or an episode of verbal interaction (Keenoy et al., 1997). The process of contextualizing discursive events can take various guises depending on the particular form of discourse analysis undertaken. So, for example, an 'intertextual analysis' (Allen, 2000) would be likely to concentrate on the historical context within which a particular text can be located while a 'critical discourse analysis' (Fairclough, 1992; 1995) might foreground the socio-political context of a particular discursive event. Notwithstanding different points of contextual emphasis, the overarching feature of discursive approaches is that they move beyond the text (whether verbal or written) and consider aspects of the wider context. In effect, this differentiates discursive analyses from forms of 'conversation analysis' (Silverman, 1993; Psathos, 1995; and see Greatbatch and Clark, in this volume) where the focus of inquiry is more narrowly defined and attention is firmly fixed on the text itself and contextualization is often limited to a description of the immediate physical locale in which the focal episode of interaction is taking place (Oswick and Richards, 2004).

There are five main parts to the remainder of this chapter. First, some of the epistemological and ontological issues that prefigure and inform the decision to employ a discursive research design are outlined. Second, several discourse-based methods, applicable to organizational research, are explored. The third section considers some of the practical issues around choosing a sample of discursive material as a basis for analysis. Fourth, a brief example of a study is offered to provide a grounded illustration of how discursive research can be undertaken. Finally, some concluding remarks are offered and some suggested further reading is provided.

Research Design Issues

Prior to selecting a particular discursive method it is important to consider some wider aspects of research design (Boje et al., 2004). These issues include: the primary point of emphasis of the analysis (i.e. the focus of engagement); the limits of the scope of discourse analysis to be undertaken (i.e. the level of engagement); and, the epistemological commitments of the researcher (i.e. the mode of engagement). It may be helpful to consider each of these issues separately.

The focus of discursive engagement

In keeping with other research methods, discourse analysis can be regarded as a means (i.e. a vehicle) to arrive at specified research ends (i.e. a destination). However, the desired research outcomes of discourse analysis can vary. For some, discourse analysis is a means to organizational research ends, but for others it is a means to discursive research ends. Put differently, some researchers are primarily interested in understanding language-use and, as such, organizations are merely the sites at which discourse analysis takes place. By contrast, other researchers are interested in utilizing discourse analysis as a means to better understand organizational phenomena (i.e. leadership processes, organizational culture, power relationships and so on). In effect, we can think in terms of organizational scholars who do discourse and discursive scholars who do organizations.

For our purposes, the content of this chapter is primarily aimed at organizational scholars who wish to use discourse analysis as part of the repertoire of methods available to interrogate organizing processes and organizational practices. That said, discourse analysis is not amenable to studying all organizational phenomena. In particular, discourse analysis does not lend itself to the study of aspects of organizations and organizing that are not easily gathered or represented through language. Hence, discourse analysis is often not the best means for capturing attitudinal data. It is also not well equipped to address spatial and visual data that are not already pre-defined and prescribed in verbal terms. Discourse analysis is, however, suited to research situations where there is a process of social interaction or social engagement (Phillips and Hardy, 2002). In some instances this engagement manifests itself as verbal communication (e.g. conversations, briefings, interviews, meetings, presentations, announcements). In others, it occurs either in a written form *within* organizations (e.g. reports, manuals, newsletters, corporate websites, press releases, e-mail correspondence, advertisements) or in a written form *outside* of organizations (e.g. academic journals and books, media coverage, activist and protest leaflets and websites, public blogs, government-produced material and so on).

Levels of discursive engagement

We can conceive of discourse analysis as operating at different, but non-competing, levels ranging from a micro-focus on the 'fine grain' use of language (e.g. situated talk or a close reading of a single text) through to a macro-emphasis on the 'big picture' of perspectives and ideologies (i.e. grand narratives and meta-discourses such as feminism and neo-liberalism). This categorization is consistent with Potter and Wetherell's (1987) identification of four versions of discourse analysis: (1) the micro-discourse approach; (2) the meso-discourse approach; (3) the grand discourse approach; and (4) the mega-discourse approach. The notion of levels of analysis is also discernible in Alvesson and Karreman's (2000) distinction between discourse analysis with a small 'd' and discourse with a big 'D' where 'discourse' (with a lower case 'd') is characterized as being 'myopic' (i.e. a close-range interest in a local-situated context) and 'Discourse' (with a capital 'D') is described as 'grandiose' (i.e. long-range interest in a macro-systemic context). Discursive work that is more macro-oriented tends to draw upon philosophy, politics, history and social theory. By contrast, the interest in micro-oriented discourse analysis has developed out of the sociolinguistic tradition and, in particular, ethnomethodology (Garfinkel, 1967).

In addition to the extremes of micro and macro levels of discourse, there are intermediate or meso-levels of discursive inquiry. Meso-level discourse analysis falls between the fine grain and the big picture. As such, it typically involves a process of extrapolating from a cluster of situated texts or discerning patterns of emergent themes. The study of workplace stories and narratives would be an example of meso-level discursive analysis insofar as this type of approach occupies a middle position, which is somewhat removed from the immediacy of a single, focal text, yet it does not go so far as to seek to offer a more abstract and distanced macro-systemic perspective (Boje, 2001).

Having indicated that discourse analysis can occur at a number of levels, it is important to highlight that the delineation of levels is not absolute. Indeed, as will be demonstrated later, some approaches simultaneously operate at more than one level. It is also possible to combine different discursive approaches that have an emphasis on different levels in order to undertake forms of cross-level analysis.

Modes of discursive engagement

Discursive approaches can be used towards different epistemological and ontological ends (i.e. positivistic, critical and poststructuralist). When used in a positivist way, discourse analysis seeks to establish a coherent reality or an uncontested truth (i.e. a single meaning). Here discourse analysis is positioned as a means of establishing the definitive or unequivocal reading of a particular text or social situation (Keenoy et al., 1997). It is fair to say that this mode of discursive engagement is not prevalent in organizational research. This is largely because positivistically oriented scholars often find discourse analysis to be inherently ambiguous and therefore it is difficult to pin down meaning to a single account. In short, discourse analysis does not readily lend itself to positivist purposes.

Arguably, discourse analysis is far more suited to research that is critically orientated. Critical forms of discourse analysis draw attention to the contested nature of meaning and the discursive exercise of power (Grant et al., 2004b). Nested within a critical management agenda, this perspective explores the existence of a hegemonic struggle between a privileged discourse and a marginalized discourse (Mumby and Stohl, 1991). In effect, this orientation foregrounds the study of how and why certain views and accounts dominate while others are suppressed or silenced (Grant et al., 2010). As opposed to the single meaning resulting from positivist research, a critical approach to discourse analysis tends to reveal a bi-vocal contestation arising from opposing readings of a discourse or discourses (i.e. contested meanings). Within the critical community, organizational researchers have utilized discourse as a means of questioning dominant interests (e.g. to raise issues of race and gender, governance, corporate social responsibility, business ethics, and workers' rights as well as to challenge corporate capitalism).

Finally, a poststructuralist approach to discourse engages with multiple interpretations of reality and the indeterminacy of meaning. In contrast to a positivist approach, which concentrates on a unified account of a text(s), or a critical approach, which reveals competing discourses (i.e. bi-vocal opposition), a poststructural approach is far more plurivocal in orientation and it highlights multiple discourses (Boje et al., 2004). In effect, poststructuralist forms of discourse analysis are relativistic in orientation and, as such, they tend to reveal a repertoire of interpretations (i.e. multiple co-existing meanings).

Discursive Approaches

Having discussed some of the precursory aspects of discourse analysis (i.e. varying levels of discursive engagement and different epistemological orientations), we now consider the actual methods available to undertake forms of discourse analysis. There is a wide range of techniques that can be used as part of discourse-based research. However, this chapter will not offer a detailed treatment of either conversation analysis, narrative analysis or document analysis – three approaches that are closely related to discourse analysis – as these can be found in other chapters in this volume. That said, it is worth briefly mentioning that conversation analysis and detailed forms of documentary analysis can sometimes be utilized as sub-components of discursive research in instances where the analysis extends beyond an interactional episode or an individual text in order to generalize about issues of social context, processes of meaning-making and the nature of power relations. So, for example, 'critical discourse analysis' (Fairclough, 1992) – which will be discussed more fully below – typically integrates aspects of conversation analysis as part of a wider and more encompassing approach. Equally, narrative analysis (Reissman, 1993; Boje, 2001; and see Maitlis, in this volume) can cross over into the realms of discourse analysis in instances where the data used are gathered via naturally occurring talk or pre-existing written texts rather than through other mechanisms, such as interviews, observation or autoethnography.

Notwithstanding the wide variety of methods that can be captured under the umbrella of discourse analysis, we will primarily focus our attention on four approaches. Treatments of the less prominent discursive approaches, which have been excluded from this chapter (such as rhetorical analysis, dialogic analysis, tropological analysis, analysis of the coordinated management of meaning and interaction analysis), can be found in the *Sage Handbook of Organizational Discourse* (Grant et al., 2004a). The approaches to be discussed in this section can be summarized as deconstruction, Foucauldian-inspired analysis, critical discourse analysis and intertextual analysis.

Deconstruction

Deconstruction is a philosophical approach originally developed by Jacques Derrida. It can be described as micro-level discursive technique insofar as it involves a 'close reading' of a single text (Derrida, 1976; 1978). Currie (1998: 45) has observed that: 'Rather than seeking to stabilize, reduce or close down discourse, a deconstructive reading opens up complexity and uses it to problematize previous attempts at oversimplification'. In this regard, deconstruction is antithetical to positivist forms of discourse analysis and is instead predisposed to critical and/or poststructural modes of engagement.

It is difficult to be absolutely prescriptive about processes of deconstruction. As Kilduff and Keleman (2004: 261) have pointed out: 'The deconstructive process is adaptable to the exigencies of the text in question and deconstruction, therefore, cannot be boiled down to a formula or a method'. There are, however, some points of common or typical focus for the deconstructive process. These foci include: identifying binary oppositions (e.g. points of contradiction or opposition); a consideration of the examples used (e.g. in terms of partiality or representativeness); issues of absence and presence within the text (e.g. what is included and what is excluded); aspects of hierarchical ordering; and discrepancies within the text. For a comprehensive discussion of how to apply deconstruction to organizational research, readers should consult *Deconstructing Organizations* (Kilduff, 1993).

Foucauldian-inspired analysis

Michel Foucault's contribution to discourse analysis has been seen as highly influential (see, for example, Alvesson and Karreman, 2000; Fairclough, 2003; Dick, 2004; Cunliffe, 2008; Iedema, 2008). Like deconstruction, Foucauldian-inspired forms of discourse analysis have their roots in philosophy (Foucault, 1972; 1980; 1984). However, in terms of the level, this form of analysis operates at the other end of the spectrum to the close reading approach of deconstruction.

Cunliffe (2008: 81) has highlighted that Foucauldian-informed analysis explores 'how discursive practices constitute both objectivities (social institutions, knowledge) and subjectivities (identities and actions)'. Although concentrating on discursive practices, this form of engagement nevertheless remains relatively broad and abstract insofar as it is not aimed at a detailed analysis of texts. Rather, as Fairclough (2003: 123) points out: 'the concern is more a matter of discerning the rules which "govern" bodies of texts and utterances'.

In effect, Foucauldian-style discourse analysis centres on the study of 'discursive formations'. The analysis of these formations involves the identification, contemplation and articulation of the abstract semantic features of a discourse (or discourses) and/or sets of abstract linguistic themes (Iedema, 2008).

Critical discourse analysis

Critical discourse analysis (CDA) has been developed by Norman Fairclough (see Fairclough, 1992; 1995; 2003). It explicitly embraces a 'critical' epistemology and it challenges the delineation of macro-, meso- and micro-levels of discursive engagement. As Fairclough (1995: 97) explains:

> It [CDA] facilitates the integration of 'micro' analysis and 'macro' analysis. It is moreover a critical approach to discourse analysis in the sense that it sets out to make visible through analysis, and to criticise, connections between properties of texts and social processes and relations (ideologies, power relations) which are generally not obvious to people who produce and interpret those texts.

CDA is positioned as an approach in which a discursive event is seen as being three dimensional insofar as it is 'simultaneously a piece text, an instance of discursive practice, and an instance of social practice' (Fairclough, 1992: 4). As a result, the analysis of discourse requires: (1) an examination of the language in use (*the text dimension*); (2) an identification of the processes of textual production and consumption (*the discursive practice dimension*); and (3) a consideration of the institutional factors surrounding the event and how they shape the discourse (*the social practice dimension*).

CDA seeks to establish connections between different levels of discursive aggregation and different levels of analysis. Hence, we can envisage that:

> a piece of discourse is embedded within sociocultural practice at a number of levels; in the immediate situation, in the wider institution or organization, and at a societal level. For example, one can read an interaction between marital partners in terms of their particular relationship, relationships between partners within the family as an institution, or gender relationships in the larger society. (Fairclough, 1995: 97).

Typically the analysis of the 'text dimension' in CDA encompasses the use of 'fine grain' situated approaches such as conversation analysis or ethnomethodology (e.g. an episode of interaction between marital partners). The 'discursive practice dimension' involves moving beyond the immediate situation to consider the 'who', 'when' and 'where' of text production and consumption (including aspects of genre, issues of authorship, the positioning of stakeholders within the text and the intended audience). Finally, the 'social practice dimension' considers the wider institutional and political landscape in which a discursive event is located in terms of issues of power and hegemony (e.g. the way in which the gendered nature of society might constrain and configure both the situation-specific interaction between marital partners and processes of marital interaction more generally). Ultimately, CDA is concerned with issues of power and ideology and it is particularly suited to forms of discursive inquiry that seek to address how local texts are influenced by wider contextual factors and vice versa.

Intertextual analysis

Intertextuality can been described as being concerned with the extent to which a given text has embedded within it elements of other texts. Allen (2000: 5) points out: 'Intertextuality seems such a useful term because it foregrounds notions of relationality, interconnectedness and interdependence in modern cultural life'. Intertextual analysis focuses upon identifying, analysing and synthesizing from parts of a focal text in terms of the earlier sources and other voices, which are either implicitly or explicitly incorporated and presented within that text (Keenoy and Oswick, 2004). Given that intertextual analysis initially focuses on the actual content of a text, it could be described as a micro-level approach to discourse analysis. However, because it is concerned with the interpenetration and/or interrelationship of a text with other texts, it is perhaps more appropriate to think of intertextual analysis as a meso-level approach.

Although originally developed as a technique among literary scholars (Kristeva, 1980; Bakhtin, 1981), it has also proved to be an effective approach to studying non-fictional texts. Indeed, in extolling the virtues of applying intertextual analysis to organizational research, Keenoy and Oswick (2004: 136) suggest: 'It provides a means of, at least tentatively, apprehending the embedded, interwoven, and multivocal nature of discursive events and enables us to develop more complex and context-sensitive understandings of the episodes of discourse we choose to analyze'.

Intertextual analysis has historical overtones insofar as it has a temporal and retrospective emphasis by exploring the nature of a contemporary text in relation to a previous text (or texts). This approach can be utilized to establish the patterns of continuity or discontinuity of discursive themes and perspectives over time. Equally, it can be used to establish connections between previously unconnected texts. There are a number of ways of doing intertextual analysis. Drawing upon and extending the work of Gerard Genette (1992; 1997), it is possible to identify two different forms of intertextual analysis. First, there is what might be described as 'overt intertextuality' via the examination of 'the actual presence of one text within another' (Genette, 1997: 1–2). This involves the explicit incorporation of another text(s) within the focal text through direct quotation and/or reference. On this basis, it is often possible to draw interesting inferences regarding the influences, positioning and genealogy of a text by locating it in relation to a body of work.

Second, there are forms of 'covert intertextuality' that can be meaningfully investigated. Here the analysis focuses on more implicit connections or resonances with other texts. The practice of textual borrowing and importation can take the form of either content similarities (e.g. adopting comparable positions, using similar phrases or terminology) or genre replication, including: style of exposition, the actual layout of text (fonts size, use of headings, etc.) and the media employed (e.g. a report, general announcement or podcast). Analysing processes of 'covert intertextuality' can be usefully employed in a variety of ways. For example, it is possible to interrogate a company's espoused aims and goals by comparing them to those contained within other corporate mission statements in terms of content and style of presentation.

Choosing a Text (or Texts)

There is a danger in being too prescriptive about how to go about selecting suitable discursive material. There are, however, some important issues to consider when choosing a sample, or samples, of spoken or written text. To begin with, there is the question of what constitutes a text. For our purposes, a text is a pre-existing extract of written discourse or episode of spoken discourse. The keyword here is 'pre-existing' because discourse analysis involves the scrutiny of a language-based artifact (e.g. a company document, a promotional video, a tape-recording of a presentation or transcribed data). Moreover, the established convention in discourse analysis is that the researcher is not an active participant in the production of the discourse that he or she then seeks to analyse. So with regard to written material it should be a document that has not been authored or co-authored by the researcher and spoken material should be 'naturally occurring talk' in which the analyst is not directly involved (Potter and Wetherell, 1987). Hence, for example, transcribed material that is gathered by a researcher through semi-interviews can obviously be explored in terms of language use. However, purists would argue that it should not be regarded as 'discourse analysis' (Johnstone, 2002; Fairclough, 2003). Whether or not we subscribe to this demarcation of discourse, involvement in the discourse one seeks to then analyse is potentially problematic. Not least because, if discourse is about meaning-making it is difficult to step back and analyse meaning (and indeed infer meaning) from a conversation where the analyst has co-constructed the meaning as an interlocutor (e.g. would a topic have arisen had the researcher not raised it? Did the researcher's involvement intentionally or unintentionally steer the direction of the conversation? Is the process tautological?) The overriding implication is that data that are to be analysed through discourse analysis should be gathered in a non-participatory way (i.e. as texts that exist independently of the researcher).

A further consideration, in terms of text selection, is the need to ensure that there is an alignment between the sample of discursive material, the discursive method employed and the epistemological position taken. So, for example, if one adopted a critical epistemological stance and used deconstruction as a method, this combination would have two significant implications for the selection of discursive material. First, the need for a 'close reading', which is central to deconstruction, would mean that the analysis is likely to focus on a single text. Second, in order to accommodate critical interrogation, it is likely that the selected text is inherently partial in nature and/or represents dominant interests and a deconstruction is therefore likely to focus on the existence of privileged voices and the marginalization or subordination of alternative accounts. An overview of the connection between issues of sample and the other various aspects of discursive engagement is provided in Table 26.1.

Doing Discourse Analysis: An Example

In this section we provide an illustration of how discourse analysis can be undertaken. The example used is a study of the discursive construction of

Table 26.1 A summary of discursive approaches, orientations and emphases

Discursive approach	Level of analysis	Mode of discursive engagement	Typical form of sample and textual emphasis
Deconstruction	*Micro-level*: a detailed and text-focused close reading	Critical	A single written text – focusing on points of contradiction (and inclusions *vs* exclusions)
		Post-structural	A single written text – focusing on discrepancies, ambiguities and multiple readings
Foucauldian analysis	*Macro-level*: a broad and abstract engagement with discursive formations	Critical and post-structural	A range of texts – a focus on discerning the rules that govern bodies of texts and a consideration of the abstract semantic features of a discourse(s)
Critical discourse analysis	*Multi-level*: links the detailed use of language with wider social and political practices	Critical	A single discursive event (either spoken or written) – problematical connections between the properties of a text and the social processes and institutional practices in terms of issues of ideology and power
Intertextual analysis	*Meso-level*: considers a focal text in relation to other preceding texts	Positivist	A longitudinal chain of texts – revealing continuity, progress and/or coherence over time
		Critical	Juxtaposing a text with another text – revealing contradictions and oppositions
		Post-structural	A web or weave of texts – revealing multiple accounts and interpretations

equality, diversity and inclusion (Oswick, 2010). The primary aim of research was to identify and analyse the respective emphasis upon, and popularity of, equality, diversity and inclusion as subtly different approaches to tackling discrimination in employment. The study adopted a critical orientation and it incorporated two main strands of inquiry. It involved both the broad analysis of published work on equality, diversity and inclusion (i.e. an academic discourse) and the detailed scrutiny of a small sample of corporate videos appearing on the YouTube website (i.e. a corporate discourse). The rationale for this approach was explained as follows:

> The two sources used have been chosen because they facilitate different discursive levels of analysis (i.e. macro-level patterns and micro-level interaction). This is important insofar as it enables connections to be made, and

> inferences to be drawn, between the everyday, situated use of language (written or spoken) and the more generalized, abstract meta-discursive perspectives which are informed and reinforced through these localized interactions and texts. (Oswick, 2010)

In effect, the research combined some elements of Foucauldian analysis (i.e. a macro-level analysis involving an abstract engagement with a range of texts) with CDA (i.e. using video clips as specific discursive events and seeking to understand the wider social and institutional practices within which these were embedded).

The identification of meta-discursive trends

The analysis of academic work involved a broad interrogation of the Social Science Citation Index (SSCI) over four decades in order to identify the general pattern of usage of the concepts of equality, diversity and inclusion. This broad interrogation involved keyword, topic and thematic searches of the SSCI database.

The results showed that a discernible pattern of publication was evident. First, equality was the most popular area of enquiry in the period from 1970 through to 1990. Second, the general level of interest in equality had remained more or less constant since 1990, but at that point an interest in diversity overtook equality and started to climb steeply as well as increase throughout the period between 1990 and 2010 (albeit that such interest began to flatten out during the past decade). Finally, inclusion was the least popular of the three areas of academic interest, but interest in this had increased in a significant and enduring way since the late 1990s. So, in summary, we can say that equality was initially the most popular anti-discrimination discourse, but one that has been increasingly overshadowed by a burgeoning interest in diversity, with some signs that inclusion is starting to emerge as a popular discursive formation.

Uncovering micro-discursive patterns

The focus of the analysis of detailed discursive events was video clips uploaded on YouTube in 2008 and 2009. The sample comprised of 18 videos in which company representatives talked about their organization's approach to equality, diversity and/or inclusion. The content of the videos was transcribed and the data were analysed in terms of their general narrative theme (e.g. a discernible emphasis on either equality, diversity or inclusion), discursive patterns (e.g. language-use aimed at differentiating, privileging and/or downplaying particular anti-discriminatory approaches) and aggregated content (e.g. how frequently the terms equality, diversity and inclusion were used).

The discursive analysis of the spoken discourse revealed several interesting findings. Of particular note was the absence of talk about 'equality' and 'equal opportunities'. Only three out of the 18 videos contained any discussion of equality with the remaining 15 videos all focusing on issues of diversity and inclusion. Beyond this, the discourse of the corporate representatives revealed a significant pattern to their respective positioning of diversity and inclusion. More specifically, inclusion was generally presented as more relevant, critical and/or important to organizations than diversity (i.e. ten videos presented it as more relevant/important, four videos presented it as equally relevant/important and only one presented diversity as more relevant/important). Within the specific articulations of corporate representatives it was apparent that diversity was presented in a taken-for-granted way while inclusion was portrayed as a strategic imperative. This can be seen in the assertion made by Mr H (the CEO of a community organization):

> Inclusion is important because it is really about how we as local [company name] reflect the diversity of our community. It's about our ability to be able to bring people to our mutual table.

The purchase of inclusion is similarly reinforced, and further extended, in the comments of Ms L (the Director of Global Inclusion and Diversity at a large software company). She observed:

> Diversity is what you see when you get a group of people together. Whenever there is a different person in the room from you, you got [*sic*] a diverse group going on. But what do we do with it? So, it's how we leverage the fact we bring different perspectives, that we bring different cultures and backgrounds together and what we do when we get those folks together, how that promotes innovation and helps us work as a better multicultural global organization ... I think that's the inclusion part of the equation.

Ms L's observations are typical of those presented by a number of the videos. The pro-inclusion discourse positions diversity as inevitable and unavoidable (i.e. as a given). This is implied in Ms L's suggestion that: 'Whenever there is a different person in the room from you, you got [*sic*] a diverse group going on'. However, inclusion is not an ever-present phenomenon and it involves making a choice. In effect, it is the means by which the latent potential of diversity can be operationalized and utilized (or as Ms L frames it in corporate-speak: 'Leveraged'). Hence, in terms of anti-discrimination initiatives, the discourse of diversity becomes subtly marginalized and the discourse of inclusion becomes privileged as the primary means of facilitating the achievement of corporate goals and socially desirable outcomes.

Discursive conclusions

The overriding conclusion that can be derived from the macro-discursive study of academic texts and the micro-discursive study of the public accounts of practitioners is relatively consistent. There is a discernible shift in discursive prominence from equality to diversity and an emerging movement towards inclusion. Moreover, the temporal formation of anti-discrimination discourses exhibits a pattern which is similar to that found in the literature on management fads and fashions. As Abrahamson and Eisenman (2008: 719) have observed: 'Lexical shifts over time serve to differentiate a fashion from its predecessor, creating a sense of novelty and progress from the earlier to the later fashions'. Arguably, it is perhaps the sense of progress, newness and leverage offered by successive discursive transitions from equality to diversity to inclusion that makes them so attractive to both management academics and practitioners.

Implications for discursive research

There are two main inferences that can be drawn from the study presented. First, it provides a two-pronged illustration of the importance of aligning discursive methods with a specific level of engagement and a desired mode of engagement. We can see that the study used a more micro-oriented approach (i.e. CDA) to capture the detail of the interaction and a more macro-oriented approach (i.e. Foucauldian-inspired analysis) to explore wider trends and broader discursive formations.

Second, the study demonstrates the scope for combining discursive methods (i.e. CDA and Foucauldian-inspired analysis). The concurrent deployment of different discursive techniques can, as in the case of the above example, be utilized to capture data pertaining to different levels of analysis. Equally, discursive methods used in combination can offer either contrasting or complimentary insights when applied to discursive material gathered at the same level of analysis (e.g. deconstruction in combination with conversation analysis).

Conclusion

Discourse analysis is more than just a simplistic focus on organizational communication (i.e. the study of communication media or how organizational stakeholders interact). It is also more than a prescriptive means of scrutinizing secondary data sources (i.e. organizational documents and artifacts) as an obligatory, but necessarily supplementary, element of a wider research project(s). Discourse analysis comprises a range of language-oriented approaches that can be meaningfully deployed to study organizations and organizational phenomena. In particular, discursive approaches are especially valuable mechanisms for studying the more subjective and intangible parts of organizational and social life (e.g. aspects of power, affiliation, identity, conflict, culture and ideology).

Finally, having previously identified the potential for combining discursive approaches, it is also important to highlight that there is considerable scope for using discourse analytic methods in combination with other qualitative approaches (e.g. interviews, observational techniques, sociograms and so on). So, for example, the study of the enduring pattern of relationships between individuals revealed by social network analysis (Scott, 1992) can be enhanced by considering the actual dynamics of interaction that can be apprehended through discourse analysis. This, in turn, leads to richer and more sophisticated insights into a given social situation. Beyond the benefits of understanding relationships through discourse and vice versa, we can also derive fresh insights into agency and positionality by simultaneously deploying discursive techniques and stakeholder analysis (Burgoyne, 1994). In summary, there are many creative ways in which a rich array of discursive approaches can be triangulated with other qualitative research methods.

Further Reading

For a comprehensive treatment of discourse and discourse analysis readers should consult Jaworski and Coupland (1999) or Schriffin et al. (2001). Texts that specifically focus on discourse analysis from an organizational perspective are provided by Grant et al. (2004a) and Phillips and Hardy (2002). More information on the question of contrasting levels of discursive engagement can be found in Alvesson and Karreman's (2000) article in *Human Relations*. Finally, the following sources offer an elaboration on the main discursive approaches discussed in this chapter: deconstruction (Kilduff, 1993); intertextual analysis (Allen, 2000); Foucauldian discourse analysis (Arribas-Ayllon and Walkerdine, 2008); and critical discourse analysis (Fairclough, 1995).

References

Abrahamson, E. and Eisenman, M. (2008) 'Employee management techniques: transient fads or trending fashions?', *Administrative Science Quarterly*, 53 (4): 719–744.

Allen, G. (2000) *Intertextuality*. London: Routledge.

Alvesson, M. and Karreman, D. (2000) 'Varieties of discourse: on the study of organizations through discourse analysis', *Human Relations*, 53 (9): 1125–1149.

Arribas-Ayllon, M. and Walkerdine, V. (2008) 'Foucauldian discourse analysis', in C. Willig and W. Stainton-Rogers (eds), *The Sage Handbook of Qualitative Research in Psychology*. London: Sage.

Bakhtin, M. (1981) *The Dialogic Imagination: Four Essays*, trans. C. Emerson and M. Holquist. Austin, TX: University of Texas Press.

Biber, D., Conrad, S. and Reppen, R. (1998) *Corpus Linguistics: Investigating Language Structure and Use*. Cambridge: Cambridge University Press.

Boje, D. M. (2001) *Narrative Methods for Organizational and Communications Research*. London: Sage.

Boje, D.M., Oswick, C. and Ford, J.D. (2004) 'Language and organization: the doing of discourse', *Academy of Management Review*, 29 (4): 571–577.

Burgoyne, J.G. (1994) 'Stakeholder analysis', in C. Cassell and G. Symon (eds), *Qualitative Methods in Organizational Research: A Practical Guide*. New Delhi: Sage.

Cunliffe, A.L. (2008) 'Discourse analysis', in R. Thorpe and R. Holt (eds), *The Sage Dictionary of Qualitative Management Research, Handbook of Organizational Discourse*. London: Sage.

Currie, M. (1998) *Postmodern Narrative Theory*. New York: St Martin's Press.

Derrida, J. (1976) *Of Grammatology*. Baltimore, MD: Johns Hopkins University Press.

Derrida, J. (1978) *Writing and Difference*. Chicago, IL: University of Chicago Press.

Dick, P. (2004) 'Discourse analysis', in C. Cassell and G. Symon (eds), *Essential Guide to Qualitative Methods in Organizational Research.* London: Sage.

Fairclough, N. (1992) *Discourse and Social Change.* Cambridge: Polity Press.

Fairclough, N. (1995) *Critical Discourse Analysis: The Critical Study of Language.* London: Longman.

Fairclough, N. (2003) *Analysing Discourse: Textual Analysis for Social Research.* London: Routledge.

Foucault, M. (1972) *The Archaeology of Knowledge.* New York: Pantheon.

Foucault, M. (1980) *Power/Knowledge: Selected Interviews and Other Writings 1972–1977.* New York: Pantheon.

Foucault, M. (1984) 'The order of discourse', in M. Shapiro (ed.), *The Language of Politics.* Oxford: Blackwell.

Garfinkel, H. (1967) *Studies in Ethnomethodology.* Englewood-Cliffs, NJ: Prentice-Hall.

Genette, G. (1992) *The Architext: An Introduction,* trans. J. Lewin. Berkeley, CA: University of California Press.

Genette, G. (1997) *Palimpsests: Literature in the Second Degree,* trans. C. Newman and C. Doubinsky. Lincoln: University of Nebraska Press.

Grant, D., Hardy, C., Oswick, C. and Putnam, L. (eds) (2004a) *Sage Handbook of Organizational Discourse.* London: Sage.

Grant, D., Hardy, C., Oswick, C. and Putnam, L. (2004b) 'Organizational discourse: exploring the field', in D. Grant, C. Hardy, C. Oswick and L. Putnam (eds), *Sage Handbook of Organizational Discourse.* London: Sage.

Grant, D. Iedema, R. and Oswick, C. (2010) 'Discourse and critical management studies', in M. Alvesson, T. Bridgman and H. Willmott (eds), *The Oxford Handbook of Critical Management Studies.* Oxford: Oxford University Press.

Iedema, R. (2008) 'Discourse analysis', in S.R. Clegg and J.R. Bailey (eds), *International Encyclopedia of Organization Stuidies.* Thousand Oaks, CA: Sage.

Jaworski, A. and Coupland, N. (eds) (1999) *The Discourse Reader.* London: Routledge.

Johnstone, B. (2002) *Discourse Analysis.* Malden, MA: Blackwell Publishing.

Keenoy, T. and Oswick, C. (2004) 'Organizing textscapes', *Organization Studies,* 25 (1): 135–142.

Keenoy, T., Oswick, C. and Grant, D. (1997) 'Organizational discourses: text and context', *Organization,* 4 (2): 147–157.

Kilduff, M. (1993) 'Deconstructing organizations', *Academy of Management Review,* 18: 13–31.

Kilduff, M. and Kelemen, M. (2004) 'Deconstructing discourse', in D. Grant, C. Hardy, C. Oswick and L. Putnam (eds), *Handbook of Organizational Discourse.* London: Sage.

Krippendorff, K. (2004) *Content Analysis: An Introduction to its Methodology* (2nd edn). London: Sage.

Kristeva, J. (1980) *Desire in Language: A Semiotic Approach to Literature and Art,* trans. T. Gora, A. Jardine and L. Roudiez. New York: Columbia University Press.

McEnery, T. and Wilson, A. (1996) *Corpus Linguistics: An Introduction.* Edinburgh: Edinburgh University Press.

Mumby, D. and Stohl, C. (1991) 'Power and discourse in organization studies: absence and the dialectics of control', *Discourse and Society*, 2 (3): 313–332.

Neuendorf, K.A. (2002) *The Content Analysis Guidebook*. Beverley Hills, CA: Sage.

Oswick, C. (2010) 'The social construction of diversity, equality and inclusion: an exploration of academic and public discourses', in G. Healy, G. Kirton and M. Noon (eds), *Equality, Inequalities and Diversity: From Global to Local*. London: Palgrave, pp. 18–36.

Oswick, C. (forthcoming) 'Discourse', in M. Tadajewski, P. Maclaran, E. Parsons and M. Parker (eds), *Key Concepts in Critical Management Studies*. London: Sage.

Oswick, C. and Richards, D. (2004) 'Talk in organizations: local conversations, wider perspectives', *Culture and Organization*, 10 (2): 107–123.

Phillips, N. and Hardy, C. (2002) *Discourse Analysis: Investigating Processes of Social Construction*. Newbury Park, CA: Sage.

Potter, J. and Wetherell, M. (1987) *Discourse and Social Psychology*. London: Sage.

Psathos, G. (1995) *Conversation Analysis: The Study of Talk-in-Interaction*. Beverley Hills, CA: Sage.

Reissman, C.K. (1993) *Narrative Analysis*. Newbury Park, CA: Sage.

Schriffin, D., Tannen, D. and Hamilton, H.E. (eds) (2001) *The Handbook of Discourse Analysis*. Oxford: Blackwell Publishing.

Scott, J. (1992) *Social Network Analysis*. Newbury Park, CA: Sage.

Silverman, D. (1993) *Interpreting Qualitative Data: Methods for Analysing Talk, Text and Interaction*. London: Sage.

9 Case Studies in Organizational Research

David A. Buchanan

Personal Research Experience 1: The Case of the Polish Call-girls

> You are the new professional services manager for a computer company. Margins on hardware have fallen. Revenue growth will come from selling business solutions and consulting services. Growth in your section will take staff away from the sales area. On your third day in the job, the company's most successful sales manager approaches you, unprovoked, insults you, and threatens to have you removed from the company whenever he wants. He is on the same management grade and you both report to the same company director. He generates 40 per cent of the company's turnover, and high levels of commission, from one customer whose buyer is a close personal friend of his. He is in his mid-30s, recently married, and about to start a family. He consistently tries to block your contacts with this major customer. You discover through a trick that he is capturing your email traffic, and probably that of other managers. He is undermining your credibility with your own staff with rumours and innuendo. You also know that he incurs high expenses on overseas trips that generate no new sales. On a joint business development trip to Poland, he arranges for two call-girls to come to your hotel room, apparently planning to take photographs with which to discredit you. (Buchanan and Badham, 2008: 111)

Casual conversations can have unanticipated consequences. I mentioned my interest in researching organization politics, a topic where controversy and sensitivity can inhibit frank and honest discussion. 'You should speak to my husband Brian', said Carla. 'He's dealing with an issue at work at the moment. I'm sure he'd be willing to tell you about it'. Meeting with Brian for about an hour, he explained his relationship with a senior colleague in his new organization, the devious political tactics used by this manager to interfere with Brian's new role and how Brian was responding. I recorded and transcribed the conversation and returned it to Brian out of courtesy and for an accuracy check. He called back to say thanks for the transcript, which had helped him to think through the issues; he had been placed by his colleague in an awkward interpersonal and professional position. However, he explained that 'things have moved on', so we met again, and the process was repeated. I now had over two hours of narrative concerning the use of extreme political tactics directed at Brian, the tactics that he had used in response and the outcomes of this exchange.

I had no research project plan at this point, no funding. My aim was to gather interesting information, collect anecdotes for the classroom, generate ideas for further research and perhaps develop a teaching case. While considering these options, the call for papers for the British Academy of Management's annual conference appeared. Why not develop Brian's experience into a case study? I submitted the paper to the conference expecting it to be rejected; a single case, a thin sliver of one person's experience, no information from others, poor contextualization (this had to remain anonymous), lacking methodological rigour. To my surprise, the paper was favourably reviewed and the conference presentation went well. I revised it for the *British Journal of Management*, again anticipating rejection.

The paper was accepted (Buchanan, 1999): 'The logic of political action: an experiment with the epistemology of the particular'. The last part of the subtitle concerned the single case underpinning the argument; there was no representative sample. There were two 'experiments' in the subtitle. One concerned the exploration of what could be learned from such limited evidence. The second concerned whether an academic journal would publish this. These experiments appear to have been successful.

This experience suggests that case study research based on a single individual is publishable. Not all journal editors and referees are sympathetic, however, and it is usually necessary to justify this approach, to a degree that is not expected of positivist researchers using quantitative methods, even when they are putting sophisticated parametric statistical analysis to use on ordinal-scale data.

This also illustrates how, in practice, the textbook logic of literature review, questions, research design and data collection can be subverted. I was already familiar with much, but not all, of the literature on organization politics. In this area, a positivist tradition dominates, based on surveys (e.g. Ferris et al., 2002; 2007). One focus of this work has concerned the Perceptions of Organization Politics (POPS) scale (Ferris et al., 2005), but to judge from the output of those researchers, they appear never to have spoken to managers or other employees about their perceptions of politics. I think that this is unsatisfactory. I also knew that politics was typically defined as self-serving, deviant, damaging behaviour. Brian's response to the 'dirty tricks' had been to use political tactics to benefit the organization, his department, his personal reputation and his value to the company. Challenging current definitions, here was an example of constructive political behaviour (Buchanan, 1999: 85).

In his standard text on case studies in social research, Robert Yin (2009) devotes a chapter to 'designing case studies'. He argues that, 'you need a plan or *research design*' (Yin, 2009: 25), with five components: questions, propositions, unit(s) of analysis, logic linking data to propositions and criteria for interpreting findings. This may be one way to conduct case study research, but is not the only way. With Brian's narrative, the interesting questions (beyond, 'What's happening here?') were formed after the case was documented. Case researchers may often have to consider retrospectively, 'What questions does this case study allow us to answer?', as well as the questions they originally posed.

What Makes a Case?

What constitutes a case study has been a matter for some debate. Yin's (2009: 18) definition is:

> A case study is an empirical inquiry that investigates a contemporary phenomenon in depth and within its real-life context, especially when the boundaries between phenomenon and context are not clearly evident.

While case studies can be pre-defined in focus and scope, they can also be emergent and self-defining. As well as being able to design studies as Yin prescribes, researchers must also be able to spot the interesting, the different, the unusual, the novel, the surprising – the black swan which challenges the theory that 'all swans are white' (a representative sample of black swans is unnecessary). A case study can become an example of something different from what was originally intended, as a second illustration, described later, demonstrates. The 'phenomenon' in Yin's definition thus covers a range of possibilities. There is no single correct answer to the question of, 'What makes a case?' Examples with units of analysis other than the individual include:

- *Organizations*: the longitudinal study of the chemicals manufacturing company ICI by Andrew Pettigrew (1985) is a benchmark in both methodology and the study of organizational change. Based on interviews, informal conversations, documents and observation, this study established processual-contextual perspectives on change, since developed by others, notably Patrick Dawson (2003). Pettigrew traced the experiences of five divisions of ICI, making this a 'nested' case study, of those divisions, and their interactions, in the organization.

- *Change processes*: Donde Plowman and colleagues (2007) studied an American church over a protracted period of change. This began in a minor way and was 'amplified' through several mechanisms to generate a radical shift in mission and activity, from a sedate 'silk stockings' church, to one that served a wider population, including minorities and the homeless. This study challenges the view that radical change has to be a managed, top-down process dependent on leadership. Data for this study were obtained through interviews, newspaper articles, church documents and grant applications, websites and informal observation.

- *Decision processes*: the decisions of the American president John F. Kennedy and his advisers in 1962 during the Cuban Missile Crisis, which brought the world close to nuclear holocaust, were analysed by Graham Allison (1969 and 1971). His account relies on published academic sources in international politics and policy analysis, a biography of Kennedy, government papers and the *New York Times*. He contrasts three models of decision-making: rational policy, organizational process and bureaucratic politics models. He notes that critical strategic decisions are not above politics and that 'bargaining games' influence key decisions.

- *Respondent validation mechanisms*: organizational researchers often feed back their findings to participants, to check accuracy and interpretations. Although this process can raise problems, 'respondent validation' or 'member review' mechanisms are under-researched. From personal experience, Karen Locke and Ramakrishna Velamuri (2009) present a case of respondent validation, concerning research exploring resistance to corrupt practices in an Indian organization. Their case narrative describes what happened when their findings were fed back; company managers did not like what was said and demanded changes. This analysis allows the researchers to explore the problems that respondent validation can generate, along with options for addressing these issues.

- *Events*: why in 1994, over Northern Iraq, did two US Air Force F-15 fighter jets shoot down two US Army Black Hawk Helicopters, killing all 26 passengers and crew, in perfect flying conditions, with no hostile action nearby, watched by a coordinating AWACS aircraft overhead? Scott Snook (2000) develops a multi-level case analysis, exploring individual, group, organizational and contextual explanations. He develops a theory of 'practical drift', explaining how operations depart from written procedures, thus contributing to such incidents. The work of Charles Perrow (1999) is based on case studies of different types of disasters, leading to the theory of 'interactive complexity'. The study by Diane Vaughan (1996), of the Challenger shuttle launch decision, is a study both of this tragic event and its multiple (technical and organizational) causes, and also of the fatal launch decision.

These examples of different units of analysis illustrate the potential of case studies, which is limited only by the researcher's ingenuity. We have single cases, nested cases, multiple cases – the topics and combinations are endless; this list has no closure.

The case study is a research design and not a method. The case study may rely on a single method for collecting data; interviews are popular. But case studies are more often a multi-methods design, combining quantitative and qualitative data. In his chapter on 'collecting case study evidence', Yin (2009: 102) focuses on six methods: documentation (see Lee, in this volume), archival records, interviews (see Alvesson and Ashcraft, in this volume), direct observations, participant observation (see Brannan, in this volume) and physical artefacts. He adds that films, photographs, videotapes (see Vince and Warren, in this volume), 'street' ethnography, psychological testing and life histories can also be relevant.

Yin's list is far from complete. Snook (2000: 15–16) lists the sources for his 'friendly fire' case as follows:

> [O]fficial government documents, archival records, interviews, physical artefacts, gun target footage, videotapes, audio tapes, training records, maintenance records, technical reports, trial transcripts, AWACS data tapes, internal Department of Defence (DOD) memoranda, press releases, newspaper clippings, congressional hearings, criminal investigations, conference briefings, flight records, mishap reports, personnel records, military flight plans, oil analyses, medical evaluations, psychological evaluations, human factors reports, optics reports, crash site analyses, equipment teardowns, weather observations, accident site photographs, witness statements, regulations, directives, maps, communications logs, intelligence briefings, task force airspace control

> orders, pre-mission briefs, flight logs, lists of corrective actions taken, and DOD fact sheets.

As a commissioned officer in the US Army, Snook had experience of combat and had been wounded by 'friendly fire' on Grenada in 1983. For this study, he also analysed two commercial videos, one from an Iraqi news team, on the scene, and another made by the ABC news magazine *Prime Time Live* including interviews with key players. Snook (2000: 17) also reports that:

> I obtained a copy of the F-15 gun-sight-video footage of the shootdown that includes not only video, but also an audio record of the tragedy from the cockpit of the trail F-15. I also analysed a copy of video footage taken by a commercial camcorder inside the AWACS. This camera was focused on an extra controller console in the AWACS during the shoot-down and graphically captured the same radar screen available to AWACS controllers during the incident.

Snook's data concerned an event lasting only eight minutes. Case researchers often complain of 'data overload' (Dawson, 1997). While some sources are common, it is the phenomenon itself, the context in which it is set and the research aims that decide which methods and data are relevant. This includes non-traditional data such as newspapers, radio programmes and television documentaries, if these are useful, albeit partial, sources of relevant information. Sources that are partisan or biased can also be valuable, as these reflect stakeholder positions and interpretations, which influence the views and decisions of other actors in the drama and often help to shape the outcomes.

We could add data sources from personal reflection, autoethnography (see Humphreys and Learmonth, in this volume), survey questionnaires, diary studies, focus groups (see Kandola, in this volume), informal conversations and respondent validation briefings. The appropriate sources depend on the case and on the investigative skills of the researcher, seeking evidence and clues, wherever they can be found.

The Current Status of Case Research

In his foreword to the fourth edition of Yin's text (2009: viii), Donald Campbell stresses the importance of experimental control in research, observing that scientific certainty is jeopardized 'in out-of-doors social science', and carping about 'the ambiguities of non-laboratory settings'. Surely it is the desire to understand the ambiguity of the great outdoors that makes social and organizational research intriguing and worthwhile?

Donald Campbell and Julian Stanley (1966) were responsible for sowing the first seeds of suspicion regarding the status of case studies, in their seminal work on research design. They defined the 'one-shot case study' as a design in which a group is studied after having been subjected to some form of intervention that was presumed to have caused change. Suppose the outcome was successful. How do we know that it really was the intervention that caused that outcome, and not some other set of factors, such as events and conditions in the environment, a general trend occurring anyway (maturation), or chance? Unless we have a comparison group operating under the same conditions over the same period, but not subjected to the intervention, then we cannot be sure. They concluded that, 'such studies have such a total absence of control as to be of almost *no scientific value*' (Campbell and Stanley, 1966: 6), adding that, 'it seems *well-nigh unethical* at the present time to allow case studies of this nature' (1966: 7).

Thomas Cook and Donald Campbell (1979) later weakened these arguments, replacing 'case study' with the clumsier 'one-group posttest-only design'. While noting the lack of control, comparison, and observation prior to treatment, they conceded that the characteristics of case study designs in social science partially addressed those problems. These are not studies in which a single variable is measured at one point in time, and 'the case study as normally practiced should not be demeaned by identification with the one-group posttest-only design' (Cook and Campbell, 1979: 96). On the contrary, the 'posttest' phase of most case studies usually explores multiple factors, the researcher has rich contextual knowledge and 'intelligent presumptions can be made about what this group would have been like' in the absence of the intervention (1979: 96).

Today, methods texts have mandatory chapters on case studies. Robert Stake (1994 and 2000) has chapters in both editions of the *Handbook of Qualitative Research* (Denzin and Lincoln, 1994 and 2000). Jean Hartley (2004) wrote the chapter in the *Essential Guide to Qualitative Methods in Organizational Research* (Cassell and Symon, 2004). Andrea Ellinger et al. (2005) offer a dry account in *Research in Organizations: Foundations and Methods of Inquiry* (Swanson and Holton, 2005). Louise Fitzgerald and Sue Dopson (2009) explore comparative case study designs in *The Sage Handbook of Organizational Research Methods*

(Buchanan and Bryman, 2009). Here are two typical assessments: Hartley (2004: 323 and 332) states 'there is growing confidence in the case study as a rigorous research strategy', and 'case study research can be engaging, rewarding, stimulating and intellectually challenging', while Fitzgerald and Dopson (2009: 481) argue 'case study research is a valuable and developing research design with significant potential to contribute to They argue organizational studies', and 'case study designs have been undervalued'.

These assessments are some distance from 'unscientific and unethical'. Contemporary commentary, however, is uneven and there are many journal editors and academic reviewers who are not impressed by case studies (or qualitative research in general). Terri Scandura and Ethlyn Williams (2000) reviewed the methods reported in studies published in the *Academy of Management Journal*, *Administrative Science Quarterly* and *Journal of Management*, from 1985 to 1997. They noted a drop in the use of surveys, laboratory experiments and simulations, and an increase in field studies (cases). They criticized this trend because field studies lacked the precision and control that ensure internal validity and generalizability. They argued that organizational researchers 'need to question whether studies with ambiguous conclusions can say much about the settings in which they occur. It may be that, without rigour, relevance in management research cannot be claimed' (Scandura and Williams, 2000: 1263). Kathleen Eisenhardt and Melissa Graebner (2007: 26) also describe case designs as a 'complement to mainstream deductive research', indicating that they are not 'mainstream'.

These debates are not about designs or methods. They arise from the conflict between positivist and constructivist epistemologies. The former are wedded to a nomothetic, variance-based, hypothetico-deductive logic, and the latter to an inductive, idiographic, interpretative agenda often linked to processual theoretical perspectives. Positivists do not like small idiosyncratic samples; constructivists have a different approach to developing understanding of social and organizational phenomena. We will revisit these issues in the discussion of generalizing from case study evidence.

The researcher considering a case study approach, however inventive in technique and relevant to the project, is by no means guaranteed a safe passage through the stages of funding body appraisal, ethical approval and journal peer review. This does not mean that we should abandon case designs. We need to develop compelling justifications for their use, detailed descriptions of the design in practice and novel, interesting and important findings.

Personal Research Experience 2: The Case of the Missing Project Leads

> Distributed change agency typically involves small teams and senior groups. In this qualitative study of service improvements in the treatment of prostate cancer at an acute hospital, Grange, change roles were distributed more widely, with responsibilities 'migrating' among a large informal cast supporting four central characters. This distribution appears to have been triggered by the change goals and substance, and by the network organization through which services were delivered. Cross-case comparisons with other hospitals, Henley and Norwood, suggest that a combination of factors contributed to the development of a distributed approach. Analytical generalization invites speculation concerning the transferability of this model, with 'nobody in charge', to other settings. (Buchanan et al., 2007: 1065).

From 2002 to 2005, I worked with a team funded by part of the UK National Health Service. Using a case study approach, this project explored the roles of managers and doctors implementing strategic changes in six hospitals and five primary care organizations. Three of the hospital case studies concerned cancer services and the other three involved maternity; the primary care cases focused on diabetes services. Data sources included website downloads, organization documents, observation at key meetings and interviews. Within-case analysis was complemented with cross-case comparisons; this account focuses on within-case analysis at one site.

The fieldwork was divided across the team, and I worked mainly at Grange, a hospital with an annual budget of £80 million, and 1,600 staff. Grange also belonged to the regional Glenelg cancer network. Each case focused on an area that had experienced change. At Grange this concerned prostate cancer services, provided by the department for general surgery and urology, which had an annual budget of £4 million, diagnosing 200 cases of prostate cancer a year, and employing five consultant surgeons and two consultant urologists.

The 21 interviews at Grange covered four themes; respondent background, role interpretation, relationships and service improvements – including the nature and objectives of changes, project management structures and outcomes. We knew that Grange had made significant improvements to their prostate cancer services. They had reduced the waiting time from referral to treatment from around six months to two weeks (the speed of treatment influences survival). Although facing the same pressures, the other two cancer service sites had not made such improvements, so Grange was a 'maverick' or an 'outlier'. Although the waiting time target of two weeks appeared simple, the changes required to meet it were complex, involving new equipment and facilities, new roles and the redesign of processes. So how had these changes been managed so successfully?

The research problems at this site began with the interview questions concerning project management structures. Who was the project manager or lead? Who were the members of the project team? We also knew from other healthcare research that complex multi-layered management structures typically accompany change initiatives like this. However, our interviewees at Grange could not answer these questions, because there were no project managers and no project team. Content analysis of the interview transcripts stalled, because the answers to those questions were missing.

I then focused the analysis on answers to the question, 'Who were involved in implementation roles?' This revealed that four individuals had been particularly influential, but at different stages in the process, and that a further 23 individuals had played major roles, along with 26 other managerial, administrative and clinical groups, including patients, patient representatives and other organizations across the cancer network. What emerged was a picture of a change process in which roles were dispersed not only across the target organization, Grange, but also across other organizations as well. Different individuals and groups had taken responsibility for different aspects of the change at different times, handing over that responsibility to others as necessary. Comparing the change management process at Grange with a conventional implementation guide (Gustafson et al., 2003) showed that they had ignored the textbook, but had been successful anyway.

I was familiar with some of the literature on 'distributed leadership' (Gronn, 2002; Bennett et al., 2003). That work was mostly conceptual and rooted in experience in education. Grange offered an empirical case study of 'distributed change agency' in healthcare. I wrote the paper with colleagues as a single case study and we submitted this to the *Human Relations* journal. Two of the three referees questioned the value of the single case. We were invited to 'revise and resubmit'. It was not possible within the journal's word limit to present the other cases in detail, so we developed a table to contrast the experience of Grange with that of the Henley and Norwood hospitals on contextual, structural, managerial, clinical, processual and substantive dimensions, and the outcomes. Those comparative dimensions were derived partly from processual-contextual perspectives on change and partly from the data. With this and other minor revisions, the paper was accepted (Buchanan et al., 2007).

The title of the paper, 'Nobody in charge', reflected the main finding. The argument was similar to that in Plowman et al. (2007), although those researchers adopted a different theoretical lens. Grange was an example of a 'nested' case study, of a clinical service within a surgical directorate within an acute hospital. This was also one of multiple case studies (Stake, 2006; Fitzgerald and Dopson, 2009) where findings could be combined and contrasted with results from other sites. The case that emerged from this study was not what was originally planned. It was not to be a study of distributed change leadership. It should instead have concerned the relationships between managers and doctors.

What's the 'So What?'

In their guidelines for authors, the editors of *Harvard Business Review* advise contributors that they are looking for the 'So what?', the 'aha' – the compelling insight. This is good advice, whatever the journal, and has implications for case selection and data analysis.

Case selection

Having established the subject of interest and the (initial) research questions, and having decided that a case study design is appropriate, how does the researcher select the appropriate case or cases? The conventional answer is that cases should be representative of the phenomenon under investigation. And that may involve a 'safe' decision rule. However, we have to consider what can be learned from further study of the typical, the commonplace. Kathleen Eisenhardt (1989) and Andrew Pettigrew (1990) both argue that researchers should consider choosing extreme situations, critical incidents, social dramas, 'polar' types, outliers and mavericks, where the experience of the phenomena under investigation is intense and visible. Case selection thus often relies on theoretical sampling: on what should we focus our attention in order to develop our understanding of this phenomenon?

As the examples in this chapter suggest, however, case studies can also be 'self-selecting', emerging from opportunities and evidence. I did not anticipate that Brian's story would produce a case study of constructive political behaviour. I did not predict that the Grange Hospital experience would produce a case study of distributed change leadership. The 'So what?' in both cases emerged during the analysis.

Data analysis

Yin (2009: 126) admits that the analysis of case study data is difficult, 'because the techniques still have not been well defined'. Eisenhardt (1989) made that observation 20 years ago. Given the variety of forms that case studies can take and the range of sources from which data can be drawn, the development of standardized analytical strategies would be challenging. There are of course established methods for analysing many of the kinds of quantitative and qualitative data that typically inform case studies. But this suggests a fragmented approach to the analysis of, say, interviews and documents, and does not deal with how data can be analysed to capture and interpret the holistic integrity of a case. While statistical methods and content or template analysis (see King, in this volume) are useful, we need to find other ways in which to analyse what is often a significant volume of case study data.

A useful first step is to develop a *case description*, without the clutter of referencing and without systematic analysis. What should be included in this case description? Everything – including details that are not (perceived to be) relevant (at this stage) and aspects of the context in which the phenomenon is embedded. What is the purpose of this description? This is a form of data reduction, crafting the information overload into a coherent account, which then becomes the platform for analysis and the basis for reports and publications. This is a 'base document' from which analyses, selective descriptions, explanations and new theories can be 'mined'. The description, which often takes the form of a narrative, will probably never be published in this form, although it may be fed back to research participants for comment. It is during this step that the 'aha' often appears, based on an anomaly, on something unusual or surprising, on the unexpected – a 'black swan'.

Yin (2009) suggests five other analytical techniques:

1 *Pattern matching*: comparing the pattern in the case or cases with one predicted in other commentary. The comparison of the approach to change implementation at Grange with the model of Gustafson et al. (2003) is an example of pattern matching (Buchanan et al., 2007: 1082).

2 *Explanation building*: generating propositions or hypotheses about causal patterns and links for further investigation. The closing section of 'Nobody in charge', identifying the conditions under which distributed change agency is appropriate, is an example of explanation building (Buchanan et al., 2007: 1083–1085).

3 *Time-series analysis*: tracking event sequences over time, comparing actual and theoretically predicted patterns, often in the form of narrative. Ann Langley (1999 and 2009) and Brian Pentland (1999) describe techniques for analysing temporally-based process data.

4 *Logic models*: this also involves matching actual with predicted outcomes, over a series of iterations, with immediate, intermediate and ultimate outcomes. This approach is often used to evaluate interventions, such as the introduction of novel classroom activities to improve academic performance.

5 *Cross-case synthesis*: comparing data from different cases across a uniform framework. 'Nobody in charge' provides an example comparing three hospitals on several factors (Buchanan et al., 2007: 1072–1073). This explains why Grange was successful and the other two hospitals were not.

These techniques are neither rigid nor exclusive. They can be used and developed in different ways, depending on the setting, and can be applied in parallel to the same data.

Theory testing

Case studies are traditionally categorized as descriptive, exploratory or explanatory (Yin, 2009). These headings capture only part of the case study potential. Cases can develop and test theory and in many instances the 'So what?' has fundamentally altered perceptions of the field. The designation of case studies as 'not mainstream' is painfully inappropriate.

The 'So what?' of the case may lie in the development of theory for further exploration. Cases have thus been described as 'pre-research' reconnaissance, generating ideas for 'real research' by conventional (rigorous, positivist, deductive) means. The use of case studies to test theory is not widely appreciated. Alex Bitektine (2008) describes prospective case study designs in which theory-based hypotheses concerning a social or organizational process are first developed, to be compared at a pre-determined time in the future with the observed process outcomes. Brian Pentland (1999) and John Hassard and David Buchanan (2009) respectively explore the use of fictional narratives and feature films, treated as case studies, to test organization theory.

The reputation of case studies as plausible research designs has probably been damaged by their association with case teaching in organization and management. Clayton Christensen and Paul Carlile (2009) argue that case studies can be used in the classroom inductively to develop, test and improve theory. The first step involves observation, description and the formulation of constructs. The second step concerns building frameworks and typologies based on the attributes of the phenomenon. The third step is to develop models expressing the relationships between attributes and observed outcomes.

Case Study Myths

Let us dispose of two myths surrounding case study research.

The myth of triangulation

Case studies involve multi-methods research, one of the advantages of which is the ability to use many sources of evidence as corroboration, to triangulate facts, to develop converging lines of inquiry, to produce more accurate accounts (Yin, 2009: 115–116). But as David Buchanan and Patrick Dawson (2007) argue, with regard to organizational change, the accounts of those involved vary and compete with each other. These divergences arise from differences in experience and because accounts can be politically inspired, and designed for specific audiences, to encourage particular decisions and behaviours. They argue that it is useful to expose the polyphonic, polysemic nature of organizations; many voices, many meanings. Many voices are silenced by prevailing power structures and relationships, and one role of the researcher is to give those voices expression. See, for example, the accounts by Hazen (1993), O'Connor (1995) and O'Leary (2003).

The myth of non-generalizability

The claim that, 'you can't generalize from a single case', displays a lack of understanding of both case study research and concepts of generalization. With a single case, or a small number of cases, one cannot rely on statistical methods to calculate whether one can extrapolate sample findings to a wider population. For most of the cases cited here, it is not even clear what that wider population comprises. Generalizability, or external validity, concerns the application of findings to settings other than the one studied. While establishing the internal validity of a study – did that cause generate this effect? – is a matter of logical deduction (Campbell and Stanley, 1966), assessing external validity is a matter of judgement. Is it reasonable to claim that these findings, this argument, those relationships, apply in other settings? Going beyond a statistical generalization, there are at least four other modes in which case study findings are generalizable.

1 *Moderatum generalizations*. This term was coined by Malcolm Williams (2000: 138) to refer to speculative associations: 'If characteristics point to particular structures in one situation, then one can hypothesize that the existence of such structures in a further situation will lead to at least some similar characteristics [. . .] Though there may be evidence of a shared reality as experienced, or shared underlying structures, the complexity of these structures and the possibility of agency to transform them, means that generalizations can be only moderate ones'. Eisenhardt (1989) and Langley (1999) also claim that it is possible to identify low-level patterns and develop generalizations with eight to ten cases.

2 *Naturalistic generalization*. Robert Stake (1994: 240) notes that, 'The reader comes to know some things told, as if he or she had experienced them. Enduring meanings come from encounter, and are modified and reinforced by repeated encounter'. The process through which we learn from case (and other) accounts and apply them to our own context, Stake defines as naturalistic generalization, which is similar to the concept of transferability (Lincoln and Guba, 1985). With a study of organization development interventions, say, or research into managerial politics, the reader naturally considers, would those methods work in my company, can I adopt those behaviours?

3 *Analytical refinement*. The findings from case research do not generalize from sample to population, but from experience and observation to theory. Suppose we have a concept of political behaviour as self-serving and damaging. Now we have a case in which politics benefit the company. Our concept may still apply to some instances, but it is inaccurate and must be revised. Suppose we have a model which says that, to be successful, change must be implemented in a certain manner. Now we have a case of an organization which departed from that model, but was nevertheless successful. We need to revise the model. Haridimos Tsoukas (2009) refers to this process as analytical refinement (also called analytical generalization). This relies on the case study being an example of the phenomenon under investigation. It is important to note that this does not involve proving or disproving theories, but does involve broadening our understanding with the accumulation of fresh observations.

4 *Isomorphic learning*. Accidents and disasters are unique, which may be why the 'lessons learned' from such incidents are often not implemented in comparable settings. Analysis of the findings of inquiries, however, shows that the same lessons and recommendations keep recurring. Technical issues (the shuttle's 'O-ring') are typically outweighed by organizational and managerial factors (training, management style, communications). Brian Toft and Simon Reynolds (2005: 66 and 72–75) thus argue that the lessons from an event can be applied in other settings. They refer to this as isomorphic learning, which includes event isomorphism (separate incidents, identical hazards), cross-organizational isomorphism (different organizations, same sector), common mode isomorphism (different sectors, similar processes) and self-isomorphism (sub-units operating in similar ways).

These forms of generalization are neither discrete nor mutually exclusive. Isomorphic learning is a form of naturalistic generalization, applied to particular incidents with regard to organization and management practice. Analytical refinement and naturalistic generalization may both apply to most organizational case studies.

Challenges and Prospects

Case study designs are well established in organizational research, but they are not universally accepted. The challenge is to ensure that the approach is seen as valid and valuable across the research community. One test will be the acceptance of case study papers by journal editors without the need for a 'boilerplate' paragraph repeating the justification for these designs. One threat to this agenda is the evidence-based management movement, which encourages a traditional positivist, variance-based approach. Another threat concerns the procedures of research ethics committees, which expect adherence to pre-specified protocols rather than the flexible departures, following lines of enquiry as they arise, which are a strength of case designs. The two key texts on case study designs are authored outside the field of organization studies. Robert Stake's interests lie with the evaluation of educational programmes. Robert Yin's background combines history and experimental psychology. While the issues that their texts address are generic, organizational research presents a different profile of opportunities, constraints and expectations (Buchanan and Bryman, 2007). Case study research designs in organization studies would benefit from having their own champions.

Further Reading

For practical and theoretical advice on the use, selection, conduct, analysis and writing of case studies in organizational research, the best starting point is still Robert Yin's (2009) text, which doctoral examiners and journal referees will probably expect to see in your list of references (but use selectively and critically).

For further methodological guidance, with regard to the use of cases to test and develop theory, and to the use of multiple and comparative case designs, refer to Bitektine (2008), Eisenhardt and Graebner (2007) and Fitzgerald and Dopson (2009).

There are many exemplary research (as opposed to teaching) case studies available. The (2007) paper by Donde Plowman and colleagues is particularly interesting as it is based on a single qualitative case, but was published in a journal that is traditionally biased towards quantitative positivist research design. The book by Scott Snook (2000) is also based on a single case, an incident lasting only eight minutes, offering an extraordinarily rich multi-level processual explanation for what went wrong. Snook's approach to his case data presentation, analysis and the development of explanation can be applied to a wide range of other less extreme organizational research settings.

References

Allison, G.T. (1969) 'Conceptual models and the Cuban missile crisis', *The American Political Science Review*, 63 (3): 689–718.

Allison, G.T. (1971) *The Essence of Decision: Explaining the Cuban Missile Crisis*. Boston, MA: Little, Brown.

Bennett, N., Wise, C. and Woods, P. (2003) *Distributed Leadership*. Nottingham: National College for School Leadership.

Bitektine, A. (2008) 'Prospective case study design: qualitative method for deductive theory testing', *Organizational Research Methods*, 11 (1): 160–180.

Buchanan, D.A. (1999) 'The logic of political action: an experiment with the epistemology of the particular', *British Journal of Management*, 10 (special conference issue): 73–88.

Buchanan, D.A., Addicott, R., Fitzgerald, L., Ferlie, E. and Baeza, J. (2007) 'Nobody in charge: distributed change agency in healthcare', *Human Relations*, 60 (7): 1065–1090.

Buchanan, D.A. and Badham, R. (2008) *Power, Politics, and Organizational Change: Winning the Turf Game* (2nd edn). London: Sage.

Buchanan, D.A. and Bryman, A. (2007) 'Contextualizing methods choice in organizational research', *Organizational Research Methods*, 10 (3): 483–501.

Buchanan, D.A. and Bryman, A. (eds) (2009) *The Sage Handbook of Organizational Research Methods*. London: Sage.
Buchanan, D.A. and Dawson, P. (2007) 'Discourse and audience: organizational change as multi-story process', *Journal of Management Studies*, 44 (5): 669–686.
Campbell, D.T. and Stanley, J.C. (1966) *Experimental and Quasi-Experimental Designs for Research*. Chicago, IL: Rand McNally and Company.
Cassell, C. and Symon, G. (eds) (2004) *Essential Guide to Qualitative Methods in Organizational Research*. London: Sage.
Christensen, C.M. and Carlile, P.R. (2009) 'Course research: using the case method to build and teach management theory', *Academy of Management Learning and Education*, 8 (2): 240–251.
Cook, T.D. and Campbell, D.T. (1979) *Quasi-Experimentation: Design and Analysis Issues for Field Settings*. Chicago, IL: Rand McNally College Publishing Company.
Dawson, P. (1997) 'In at the deep end: conducting processual research on organizational change', *Scandinavian Journal of Management*, 13 (4): 389–405.
Dawson, P. (2003) *Reshaping Change: A Processual Approach*. London: Routledge.
Denzin, N.K. and Lincoln, Y.S. (eds) (1994) *Handbook of Qualitative Research*. Thousand Oaks, CA: Sage.
Denzin, N.K. and Lincoln, Y.S. (eds) (2000) *Handbook of Qualitative Research* (2nd edn). Thousand Oaks, CA: Sage.
Eisenhardt, K.M. (1989) 'Building theories from case study research', *Academy of Management Review*, 14 (4): 532–550.
Eisenhardt, K.M. and Graebner, M.E. (2007) 'Theory building from cases: opportunities and challenges', *Academy of Management Journal*, 50 (1): 25–32.
Ellinger, A.D., Watkins, K.E. and Marsick, V.J. (2005) 'Case study research methods', in R.A. Swanson and E.F. Holton (eds), *Research in Organizations: Foundations and Methods of Inquiry*. San Francisco, CA: Berret-Koehler Publishers Inc, pp. 327–350.
Ferris, G.R., Adams, G., Kolodinsky, R.W., Hochwarter, W.A. and Ammeter, A.P. (2002) 'Perceptions of organizational politics: theory and research directions', *Research in Multi-Level Issues Volume 1: The Many Faces of Multi-Level Issues*: 179–254.
Ferris, G.R., Treadway, D.C., Kolodinsky, R.W., Hochwarter, W.A., Kacmar, C.J., Douglas, C. and Frink, D.D. (2005) 'Development and validation of the political skill inventory', *Journal of Management*, 31 (1): 126–152.
Ferris, G.R., Treadway, D.C., Perrewé, P.L., Brouer, R.L., Douglas, C. and Lux, S. (2007) 'Political skill in organizations', *Journal of Management*, 33 (3): 290–320.
Fitzgerald, L. and Dopson, S. (2009) 'Comparative case study designs: their utility and development in organizational research', in D.A. Buchanan and A. Bryman (eds), *The Sage Handbook of Organizational Research Methods*. London: Sage, pp. 465–483.
Gronn, P. (2002) 'Distributed leadership as a unit of analysis', *Leadership Quarterly*, 13 (4): 423–451.
Gustafson, D.H., Sainfort, F., Eichler, M., Adams, L., Bisognano, M. and Steudel, H. (2003) 'Developing and testing a model to predict outcomes of organizational change', *Health Services Research*, 38 (2): 751–776.

Hartley, J. (2004) 'Case study research', in C. Cassell and G. Symon (eds), *Essential Guide to Qualitative Methods in Organizational Research*. London: Sage, pp. 323–333.
Hassard, J.S. and Buchanan, D.A. (2009) 'From *Modern Times* to *Syriana*: feature films as research data', in D.A. Buchanan and A. Bryman (eds), *The Sage Handbook of Organizational Research Methods*. London: Sage, pp. 620–635.
Hazen, M.A. (1993) 'Towards polyphonic organization', *Journal of Organizational Change Management*, 6 (5): 15–26.
Langley, A. (1999) 'Strategies for theorizing from process data', *Academy of Management Review*, 24 (4): 691–710.
Langley, A. (2009) 'Studying processes in and around organizations', in D. A. Buchanan and A. Bryman (eds), *The Sage Handbook of Organizational Research Methods*. London: Sage, pp. 409–429.
Lincoln, Y.S. and Guba, E.G. (1985) *Naturalistic Inquiry*. Beverly Hills, CA: Sage.
Locke, K. and Velamuri, S.R. (2009) 'The design of member review: showing what to organization members and why', *Organizational Research Methods*, 12 (3): 488–509.
O'Connor, E.S. (1995) 'Paradoxes of participation: textual analysis and organizational change', *Organization Studies*, 16 (5): 769–803.
O'Leary, M. (2003) 'From paternalism to cynicism: narratives of a newspaper company', *Human Relations*, 56 (6): 685–704.
Pentland, B.T. (1999) 'Building process theory with narrative: from description to explanation', *Academy of Management Review*, 24 (4): 711–724.
Perrow, C. (1999) *Normal Accidents: Living With High-Risk Technologies*. New Jersey: Princeton University Press.
Pettigrew, A.M. (1985) *The Awakening Giant: Continuity and Change in ICI*. Oxford: Basil Blackwell.
Pettigrew, A.M. (1990) 'Longitudinal field research on change: theory and practice', *Organization Science*, 1 (3): 267–292.
Plowman, D.A., Baker, L.T., Beck, T.E., Kulkarni, M., Solansky, S.T. and Travis, D.V.T. (2007) 'Radical change accidentally: the emergence and amplification of small change', *Academy of Management Journal*, 50 (3): 515–543.
Scandura, T.A. and Williams, E.A. (2000) 'Research methodology in management: current practices, trends, and implications for future research', *Academy of Management Journal*, 43 (6): 1248–1264.
Snook, S.A. (2000) *Friendly Fire: The Accidental Shootdown of US Black Hawks Over Northern Iraq*. Princeton and Oxford: Princeton University Press.
Stake, R.E. (1994) 'Case studies', in N.K. Denzin and Y.S. Lincoln (eds), *Handbook of Qualitative Research*. Thousand Oaks, CA: Sage, pp. 236–247.
Stake, R.E. (2000) 'Case studies', in N.K. Denzin and Y.S. Lincoln (eds), *Handbook of Qualitative Research* (2nd edn). Thousand Oaks, CA: Sage, pp. 435–454.
Stake, R.E. (2006) *Multiple Case Study Analysis*. New York: The Guilford Press.
Swanson, R.A. and Holton, E.F. (eds) (2005) *Research in Organizations: Foundations and Methods of Inquiry*. San Francisco, CA: Berret-Koehler Publishers Inc.
Toft, B. and Reynolds, S. (2005) *Learning from Disasters: A Management Approach* (3rd edn). Houndmills, Basingstoke: Palgrave Macmillan.

Tsoukas, H. (2009) 'Craving for generality and small-N studies: a Wittgensteinian approach towards the epistemology of the particular in organization and management studies', in D.A. Buchanan and A. Bryman (eds), *The Sage Handbook of Organizational Research Methods*. London: Sage, pp. 285–301.
Vaughan, D. (1996) *The Challenger Launch Decision: Risky Technology, Culture, and Deviance at NASA*. Chicago: University of Chicago Press.
Williams, M. (2000) 'Interpretivism and generalization', *Sociology*, 34 (2): 209–224.
Yin, R.K. (2009) *Case Study Research: Design and Methods* (4th edn). Thousand Oaks, CA: Sage.

10 Using Documents in Organizational Research

Bill Lee

Introduction

Qualitative research involving fieldwork is often costly. Documentary analysis by contrast may involve few costs apart from the researcher's time (c.f. Rapley, 2007: 12). Moreover, documents are manifold, playing an important role in organizational life, providing details of policies, procedures, prospective plans such as investment appraisals and records of events such as minutes of meetings. There are many additional documentary sources about organizations, including newspaper reports, government abstracts, tribunal records of misdemeanours and pressure groups' objections to developments. It is, thus, possible to use documents to address a broad range of research questions. As many documents are readily available and endure over time, the research questions and answers may cover a much longer period than may be possible when other research methods are used.

Yet documents have often been under-utilized in research into organizations, vis-à-vis their availability. This may be related in part to a belief that documents are too readily available to be of any real use; either the really interesting questions have already been asked of the documents or the number of documents available is now so great that it has become almost impossible to organize an enquiry to make a sufficiently succinct and meaningful statement on the basis of an analysis of documents about an organization. The ready availability of documents – especially given the materials that are now digitized for collection through the internet – obviously causes problems. But documents also offer numerous opportunities for research and obstacles to their use may reside in not knowing how to source, verify and analyse them to answer research questions.

This chapter aims to consider how questions may be formulated and answered by the systematic collection and analysis of documents. The remainder of the chapter proceeds in the following way. First, the question of what is a document will be considered. Thought will then be given to how to scope research by defining relevant research questions and how to gather the documents to help provide answers to those questions. Attention will then be turned to how to conduct different types of analysis of documents depending on one's epistemology and illustrations of studies involving documents will be drawn from the author's work.

Defining a Document

Hodder (2003: 703) has described a document as 'mute evidence ... [which] unlike the spoken word, endures physically and thus can be separated across space and time from its author, producer and user'. Hodder's definition captures the way in which documents allow information to be transposed across time and geographical distance. However, it is questionable whether all documentary records should be considered as 'mute'. There has been an increasing variety of forms of records that have been kept over the past 150 years that do not store only the written word, but are able to project both sound and vision, including film, digital versatile discs, compact discs, pages in cyberspace, etc. Many are not mute in the sense of giving off no sound, although they may be unheard and unseen unless the researcher includes their manifest qualities in the research design.

It is important to consider whether any message either represented in – or symbolized by – a document may be universally understood, or subject to different interpretations. Prior (2003: 2) argues documents involve 'creators (agents, writers, publishers, publicists and so on), users (readers, or receivers) and settings. All three realms are implicated in the emergence of documentation'. Prior's definition introduces the potential for an author's intended meaning, when creating a document, to vary from the understanding that users derive from the document, which could be influenced by the regulatory and institutional setting including language, belief systems and legal requirements. Prior (2008) subsequently highlights how documents may take on the role of actants – i.e. hybrids of objects and actors. When seen in this way, documents have relational properties with other actors, helping to structure relationships both between the documents and the actors and between different actors where the documents are employed. Thus, Prior (2008: 824) says, 'documents serve not merely as containers of content, but as active agents in episodes of interaction and schemes of social organization'.

It may, thus, be argued that a document is a durable repository for textual, visual and audio representations that may be retained and used in different times and spaces, creating the possibility that the meanings of the representations may be interpreted differently – and employed accordingly – by the user, partly because of variations between the regulatory and institutional setting of the producer and user of the document. The user may either be the researcher or another actor in a setting where the documents are employed and the employment of those documents may – or may not – advantage some parties or disadvantage others.

Scoping Research with Documents

The choice of research question will depend in part on the researcher's epistemological position – see below – and whether that position puts greater emphasis on documents' properties as repositories, or also recognizes their potential constitutive capabilities. Different authors (Bricknell, 2008; Prior, 2008) have identified different types of research question that may be considered using documents. Examples include:

- For what purpose were the chosen documents designed?
- How effectively have the chosen documents been designed to realize the purpose for which they were intended?
- Do all documents of a particular genre cover the same issues in the same way?
- Are people interpreting the documents in ways intended by the authors and what are the consequences if they are not doing so?
- How do the contents of documents – such as regulations and policies – help to structure relationships between those parties affected?

- How are people constructing and using documents to project a particular view of themselves or others?
- What insights might documents provide about broader processes on the phenomena in which we are interested?

The different types of research questions require that the researcher conducts either a survey of a population of a particular type of document, a case study of a particular phenomenon using documents, or considers individual cases of different types of documents. As the collection of documents can be inexpensive, a study involving documents is most likely to be useful if documents can provide a pertinent way of addressing the research question when (a) other sources are not sufficient in number or adequate *per se* and (b) documents are available in an ample enough number to provide a sensible answer. Subsidiary considerations depending on the research question include the following:

- If a survey of particular types of documents is being considered, is the total population involved in a particular phenomenon – such as the companies adopting a particular human resource policy of interest – known?
- Are the documents in that population easily accessible?
- If case studies are being considered, either of particular documents or of a particular event or phenomenon using documentary evidence, would the documents that are studied be recognized as sufficiently credible to provide a commentary?
- If one is studying the potential constitutive qualities of documents, is there evidence available to show the impact of the documents?

If documents are an appropriate and ample source to provide a credible answer to the research question, the investigation may go ahead. Of course, the answer to the questions may be 'only partly'. If, however, there are other sources of evidence available to address the parts of research questions that documents are unable to address satisfactorily, a research strategy may be devised in which documents are used in conjunction with other methods.

Collecting Documents

The collection of documents will depend in part on whether the chosen research question addresses the whole population that has to be surveyed, or considers a particular event, organization or phenomenon that requires the study of one or more cases. In both situations, the development of the internet has helped to transform the document collection process. If a survey of organizations is to be conducted and the full composition of that population is known, it may be possible to visit those organizations' websites to download the documents. For example, lists of the top 100 and 250 FTSE companies are widely available. Such organizations' websites are located easily by simply entering their names into a search engine. Many documents such as annual accounts and financial reports, corporate social responsibility reports, product range and historical details are generally available through corporate websites. Internal documentation such as employment policies, collective agreements with trade unions, market intelligence and accounting practices may not be so easily accessible. Nevertheless, documents that are not considered to be commercially sensitive may be made available by a corporation on request if the researcher writes to them, specifying in concise detail what he or she is looking for.

A lot of material may also be available via the internet when the research question requires the conduct of one or more case studies of a particular event, organization or phenomenon. General search engines such as Google facilitate drawing on global resources and an inestimable number of documents. There are two major problems with this approach. First, there will not be a catalogue for all of the information that is available and an initial search using a single term relating to the phenomenon of interest may yield hundreds of thousands of references. Thus, it may be necessary to focus the search more and more narrowly by combining the original search term with others that are related to the research questions until the number of references becomes more manageable. Secondly, although it may be possible to attribute some data to original sources, the validity and origins of some other web pages may be indeterminate, requiring that the information that is reported be authenticated by reference to another source. Useful sources *per se* – that could also help authenticate information in sources that cannot be attributed – are newspapers.

An extensive set of newspapers may be accessed through the Newspaper Subset of the British Library's catalogue (see http://catalogue.bl.uk). Many academic libraries subscribe to *NewsBank*, which provides access to electronic copies of the majority of the UK's daily and Sunday newspapers. *NewsBank* has a search facility that allows the retrieval of all articles on a chosen topic that appeared in any of the newspapers during a period specified by the researcher. Individual newspapers may also have their own indexes – including overseas ones such as the *New York Times* – that may be searched on-line for articles on particular events or organizations. Other important sources of documentation that could help with research are available through government-sponsored websites in the UK. Documents on current government policies may be found at www.direct.gov.uk. Details of documents about historic events, companies and phenomena may be found at www.nationalarchives.gov.uk. Information on parliamentary debates and the emergence of legislation is available through Hansard (see www.publications.parliament.uk/pa/pahansard.htm). There are also important academic sources of documents that are either available, or there is a catalogue of information, through the internet. This includes research conducted by others that is stored at the UK data archive at Essex (see: www.data-archive.ac.uk). Additionally, there is Archives Hub, which provides descriptions of around 200 archives held in UK universities and colleges and a number of research institutes and museums (see: www.archiveshub.ac.uk/). An important emergent facility is the British Library's Management and Business Portal, which provides access to a broad range of sources including the British Library's digital collection. This can be accessed via www.mbsportal.bl.uk/index. A guide to digital datasets relevant to management and business studies may be found on the site at www.mbsportal.bl.uk/taster/subjareas/resmethods/bl/116166datasets_MBS_SA.pdf.

Not all catalogues have been digitized, so a visit to an archive will sometimes be necessary. When visiting archives, it is important to go prepared. Having identified the relevant archive, check:

- The times that the archive is open to the public.
- What proofs of identity will be required for membership of the archive or for access to its records.
- Whether the documents that are required are kept at the archive where there is public access or at a remote location that will necessitate the items being ordered several days in advance of the planned visit.
- How many documents may be accessed at any one time.

Some documents are extremely precious, so many personal belongings such as portable computers, books, ink pens, food and drink may not be permitted in the reading rooms. There are also likely to be restrictions on what items may be photocopied and so it is essential to take writing materials. If information is noted from a source, an extremely clear record of where the information was obtained should be kept in order to provide references when using those data in subsequent work. (For a more extensive discussion of preparations for – and the problems of – conducting research in archives, see Walker, 2004.)

Analysing Documents and Some Illustrations

Once the documents have been collected, a preliminary form of analysis may be necessary to establish whether they should be considered reliable and authentic in the sense of remaining in the form produced by the original author. With contemporary documents, it may be possible to check with the original author whether these have been altered in any way. If the document is sourced from an archive, the archive may have records of provenance that will indicate the article's authenticity. If, however, the document has been obtained from another source and it is not possible to check with the original author that the document is authentic, it may be necessary to consider a number of questions to assess its usefulness. These should include:

- Can the source from which the document was obtained be seen as reliable?
- What was the history of the document before it was obtained?
- Was the document complete as originally constructed or had some of it been partially destroyed, edited or tampered with?
- Is it plausible that the person who produced the document may have wanted to produce a document for the designated purpose?
- Are there other documents that might help to verify the authenticity – and enhance an understanding – of the original document?
- Are those other documents accessible and – if so – through which channels?

Once the authenticity of the documents has been considered, further analysis is likely to be necessary in order to formulate answers to the research questions. There are many different ways of analysing documents (see, for example, Lincoln, 1980; Prior, 2008). The taxonomy of documentary analyses used below will be based around four epistemological positions in qualitative research, adapted broadly from Johnson et al. (2006). These will each be linked to particular methods of documentary analysis, with

Table 22.1 Epistemological position and form of documentary analysis

Epistemology	Form of analysis
Positivism	Objective content analysis that may be quantitative or qualitative. Survey or case study
Interpretive approaches including phenomenology	Ethnographic content analysis of cases
Critical theory	Chronological case study that recognizes a dialectical relationship between text and outcome
Constructivism	Discourse analysis of text

illustrations from the author's work. However, neither the epistemological positions, nor the forms of analysis associated with them here, should be viewed as mutually exclusive of each other. It is possible for the different epistemological positions to inform the same project at different stages, just as it is possible for someone working from one epistemological position to use a method associated with another position in a different way. Table 22.1 provides a summary of the different types of epistemological position and associated forms of documentary analysis. Each will be considered in turn.

Positivist approach

Positivists view a reality that exists independent of observers. An objective, observational language parallels that reality and allows an understanding of the meaning of that reality by analysing what is said. Content analysis provides a tool for understanding meanings that are reported in documents. Those meanings are not considered to be contestable if systematically derived. Thus, Berelson (1952: 18) says: 'Content analysis is a research technique for the objective, systematic ... description of the manifest content of communication'. A logical corollary is that the meaning may be measured in some form. This may be by quantifiable measures such as the *frequency* with which something appears that may indicate the *importance* of a topic afforded by the document and the *balance of favourable and unfavourable references* which may provide a measurement of the *bias* or *direction* of the document (Krippendorff, 2004: 59). However, it might also involve a more qualitative analysis in terms of gradations such as *qualifications* or *provisos*, which will give an indication of the *intensity* or *strength* of the concerns (see Krippendorff, 2004).

The process of applying content analysis is likely to be a sequential one involving a unilinear progression from document collection, analysis and interpretation (Altheide, 1987: 67). A positivist approach may involve a case study of a document or a survey of a population of documents. Where a survey is conducted, sampling techniques may be used to 'answer the research question with sufficient confidence' (Krippendorff, 2004: 121). Content analysis requires the development of a framework to code and help transform the evidence from documents into answers to specified research questions. Holsti (1969) suggests five principles to create a reliable taxonomy for coding. First, the categories used to classify text should be derived from variables in the research questions or hypotheses of the researcher. Second, the categories that are created must be exhaustive, at least along the important criteria, so that each unit of text – such as a sentence, paragraph or article – may be put into one category or another. Third, categories should be mutually exclusive, so that each unit of text will be placed in only one cell in the process of categorization. Fourth, categories will be independent of one another, so the assignment of one unit of text will not lead to the immediate assignment of another. Fifth, the categories should be derived from a single classification principle, so that levels of analysis that are conceptually different should be kept so.

An example here is Lee and Cassell's (2004) content analysis of information for union learning representatives (ULRs) on trade union websites. This was conducted because Catherine Cassell and I were planning an interview study (see Alvesson and Ashcraft, in this volume) to explore the introduction of ULRs and their facilitation of workplace learning opportunities. That study emerged within a programme of research that led to numerous publications (e.g. Cassell and Lee, 2007; 2009; Lee and Cassell 2008), so this case shows how documentary research can fit into a broader research strategy. In preparing for interviews, we wanted to find out how trade unions supported ULRs. As the most readily available form of support was trade union websites, we surveyed these in preparation for our later research. We decided to conduct a systematic content analysis of UK trade union websites to address the following two research questions: 1) how easy would it be for ULRs to access information to carry out their role from their union's website? And 2) what information would ULRs be able to obtain from this source?

We obtained a list of TUC-affiliated trade unions and conducted a Google search to identify whether each had a website. This allowed us to make our research questions more concise by considering only TUC-affiliated trade unions with websites and we conducted a full census of those trade unions. Consistent with a positivist approach, we assumed a single definition of ease of access to information that was related simply to the design of the website. Thus, we ignored other factors that might have affected whether individual ULRs could obtain that information, such as whether: lay officials had personal computers; they were sufficiently confident in their use of those computers; those computers were linked to the internet; the internet connection was made through an exchange that provided a strong uninterrupted connection; and the personal computer had a sufficiently large hard drive to download information quickly. Consistent with Holsti's guidance, we derived the categories for classifying the content of trade union websites from our research questions above, formulated criteria relating to ease of access and defined a full range of information that could help ULRs conduct their role.

To confirm some notion of objectivity for the framework and the validity of its use, we each analysed the same small set of websites initially. The level of consistency between our analyses suggested a confirmation of these issues. This exercise also allowed us to iterate our framework to ensure it was exhaustive for our purposes, i.e. that all issues relevant to the research questions were listed under appropriate categories, with the default options for the respective research questions being that access to a site required a membership number or no useful information could be found anywhere on the site. These categories were ultimately mutually exclusive, so that websites either had pages dedicated to ULRs or they did not. Similarly, they either had other pages that contained information that were useful to ULRs or they did not. The categories were kept independent of one another, so – for example – the absence of a page dedicated to ULRs did not presuppose that there would be no information of use to ULRs elsewhere on the site. Our categories were organized along a single classification principle, so that levels of analysis that were conceptually different – such as the ease with which information could be obtained and the types of information available – were kept separate. Although the information could be measured quantitatively, such as by the number of topics on which ULRs could gather information, we were also able to provide a more qualitative understanding by describing the process that ULRs would have to undertake in order to access the information and the type of information that they might be able to obtain, be it learning materials, guidance on workplace organization for learning, legal rights, etc.

Interpretive approaches

Interpretive approaches – such as phenomenology – are concerned with the ways in which people experience their world in the specific contexts that they occupy. By implication, social meanings are at the centre of any analysis. Thus, documents contain signs and symbols that have to be interpreted. Moreover, the ways in which the signs and symbols are formatted will be subjected to the conventions that prevail in a particular culture. Any interpretation of what those signs are intended to symbolize, or how they are received, must be linked to the culture in which the author prepares the document and the reader digests its contents. Such an understanding is derived from an 'ethnographic content analysis' (Altheide, 1987) and involves reading the text and focusing on 'situations, settings, styles, images, meanings and nuances presumed to be recognizable by the human actors/speakers involved' (Krippendorff, 2004: 16; see also Altheide, 1987: 68). An ethnographic content analysis will involve taking cases of documents and making constant comparisons between them to 'check, supplement, and supplant prior theoretical claims by simultaneously obtaining categorical and unique data for every case studied in order to develop analytical constructs' (Altheide, 1987: 68). Thus, unlike the unilinear process in positivist forms of content analysis, ethnographic content analysis is both reflexive and circular with data being used to develop concepts throughout the process of analysis.

A method akin to ethnographic content analysis was adopted for a study of the alleged damaging effects of accounting on new technology (Lee, 1996; Jones and Lee, 1998). Throughout the late twentieth century, there were suggestions that accounting practices embodied high productivity assumptions, so investment appraisals only allowed new systems that could be justified by increases in volume of output and reductions in labour input, while ongoing cost control measures assumed high levels of output vis-à-vis low levels of labour input with any variance from the low input-high output measure being viewed disparagingly. It was assumed that the high productivity assumptions in accounting techniques either discouraged an introduction of the innovative flexible manufacturing system (FMS) that could manufacture a wide variety rather than large volumes of products, or would lead to inappropriate high-volume manufacturing by any FMS that was introduced.

To assess the validity of these claims, cases concerning companies that had introduced FMS were identified from the trade press and visited. At this time, investment justification documents of FMS and flexible budgets from the departments in which the FMS were deployed were collected to investigate whether accounting methods either discouraged the introduction of FMS or led to their misuse once they were introduced. A form of ethnographic content analysis of documents was an important part of the case studies of the companies. This example thus illustrates how documents can be used as part of case study research (see Buchanan, in this volume). Other methods revealed that, when engineers proposed FMS, they would prepare a document that: described the configuration of FMS; outlined its strengths; detailed the range of products that it was going to manufacture in specified batch sizes at desired levels of system utilization; and conducted a financial appraisal based on the monetary benefits that the specified use of the system would bring against its relative costs. An accountant would check the financial aspects of the proposal and then forward it to a decision-maker. If the FMS was introduced, the assumptions in the initial proposal would be embodied in the flexible budget against which the performance of the system was judged.

The ethnographic content analysis involved, first, drawing a matrix to compare how the initial proposals of FMS had envisaged the performance of each system in quantitative terms of range, batch sizes and machine utilization, to see whether all systems were assumed to have comparable strengths. This revealed three broad motives for FMS. The majority of configurations were introduced to machine a limited range of parts in large batch sizes to realize high levels of system utilization. Another group of systems was introduced to machine a wide range of parts in small batch sizes and assumed lower levels of system utilization. The third group of configurations was introduced to machine a limited range of parts in small batch sizes and also did not emphasize high levels of system utilization. The description of the systems in each document was then compared with all others to establish whether each had been designed to realize particular forms of output. This confirmed that only one of the three different uses above had been embodied in the design of each FMS. The narratives in the documents that described the deployment and strengths of each system were read and variations between them were used to develop the concept of a production strategy embodied in the design and management of the FMS to explain the variations in expected levels of performance between them. These were summarized as 'volume production', 'flexible manufacturing' and the 'just-in-time production' of high value parts. In this way, documents were used iteratively to develop concepts that allowed the understanding that configurations of FMS were not uniform but instead had been constructed to realize different objectives and that accounting techniques had been varied to reflect each configuration's different strengths.

Critical theory

There are many genres of 'critical' theory: Marx's ideas will be drawn on here. Like many subsequent critical theorists, Marx saw the access to power in organizations as unequal. For Marx, a key source of power was control over economic resources. Moreover, access to power is likely to result in an ability to disseminate one's ideas and to persuade others of the value of those ideas, reconstituting the relationship between those with more or less power. Thus, there is a dialectical relationship between power and the ideas expressed in documents. This position is consistent with a view of documents as being both a repository of information and constitutive of relationships involving people affected by those documents' contents. A range of techniques could be used to analyse documents' constitutive role.[1] A case study method is used here (see Buchanan, in this volume). If a case study is organized chronologically, it is possible to envisage a sequence of events involving the composition and use of the documents and an assessment of their impact in the reconstitution of relationships. It is useful to have a set of rules to guide the composition of the case. Various authors (e.g. Lincoln, 1980: 34–35) have provided suggestions for what these rules might cover. These include:

- Clear criteria for the selection of case studies to ensure that the cases chosen are the appropriate ones for addressing the research questions, rather than being ones that will simply produce the answers that the researcher wants. Of course, the universe of possible cases may be one if the phenomenon investigated is unique.
- A checklist or a clear set of themes intended to ascertain information about certain outcomes of interest. These themes will emerge from the research problem.
- A set of decision rules to help ensure consistency in what is classified as part of each theme.

As the method is being applied to appraise the constitutive quality of documents, one might also ask 'What if?' questions of whether outcomes following the publication or use of documents would have occurred without the intervention of the document.

Lee's (2010) document-based case study investigated how the UK government's experiment with Individual Learning Accounts (ILAs) was evaluated by regulators and the impact that those regulators had on the demise and

[1]For example, Prior (2008) uses social network analysis as part of actor-network theory.

abandonment of ILAs. Gramsci's interpretation of Marx was used to explain how the Conservative administrations of 1979–1997 had introduced policies of purchasing state-financed services from independent bodies through markets. These markets were overseen by state-appointed regulators that had the authority to produce reports about the provision of those services. ILAs were introduced by the Labour government that replaced the Conservative administrations. The Labour government continued to use markets to deliver services, but also sought to facilitate lifelong learning by creating ILAs that offered everyone state monies to purchase learning. Registration for ILAs occurred faster than anticipated, so the scheme soon ran out of funds. There were suggestions that the scheme had been defrauded by unscrupulous learning providers and members of parliament asked regulators to investigate. Although the government promised to reintroduce ILAs, it took several years before a more limited, targeted scheme of financial assistance for learning was introduced. This suggested the question: what role did the regulators who reported on the demise of ILAs play in this scenario?

Four sets of regulators produced formal reports about ILAs. These were the Education and Skills Select Committee (E&SSC), the National Audit Office, the Public Accounts Committee and the Parliamentary Ombudsman. The reports were read initially to get a sense of their contents and to identify relevant themes to help extrapolate information that could answer subsidiary questions of the above general research question. These subsidiary questions were: 1) how had the different regulators perceived the ILA experiment? And 2) what had been the impact of their pronouncements? The first question was addressed by asking: did the reports provided a bias of strengths over weaknesses in references to ILAs? In what areas did references to strengths and weaknesses appear – such as education and learning or financial management? What were the perceived outcomes of those strengths and weaknesses? And what were the suggested solutions to any weaknesses? Through a further reading of the reports, an entire checklist of terms relating to education and learning, financial management, problems with the scheme and solutions to problems were listed. For example, terms relating to problems included abuse, fraud, financial loss, poor quality learning and unscrupulous providers, while terms relating to solutions included audit, registration of providers, accreditation of providers, etc.

A set of decision rules was formulated to guide the subsequent analysis of the reports. This included the following:

- Count each reference to any of the specified terms.
- Read each sentence and paragraph in which the term appears and document the reference as either: an education and learning strength or weakness; a positive or negative financial management facet; a positive or negative outcome; a financial management, educational quality or some other type of solution to a negative outcome.
- Note any quantification of the financial value of any alleged fraud and abuse and of the number of people that are claimed to be involved.
- Make note of whether the reference appears in witness statements or whether the information has appeared in the formal report and so can be seen to have the regulators' approval.
- Read through reports in their entirety to ensure that the bias of references reflects the full content of the report and no important issues have been omitted.

This analysis was performed for each report so that a chronology could be mapped which showed that while the first report by the E&SSC questioned the evidence of fraud and called for a re-introduction of ILAs, the latter reports blamed the government department that oversaw the scheme for insufficient financial controls, which allowed several hundred fraudsters to pose as learning providers and defraud the scheme by £97 million. These reports also accepted a later government decision to replace universal ILAs by a smaller targeted scheme. The question was asked 'what if' the regulators had not made their interventions. A newspaper search of prosecutions revealed that the risk of financial abuse had been vastly overstated. A newspaper search also revealed that the relevant government department was wary of ambitious universal schemes because of the regulators' criticisms. In this way, it was possible to highlight the potential constitutive nature of the regulators' reports.

Constructivist approaches

Constructivists[2] see social reality as constructed and sustained in the course of social interactions. Language plays an important role in these social interactions and should be perceived as constitutive of relationships and of the identities of people involved in those relationships. Constructivists may use

[2]See Cunliffe (2008) for an easy-to-understand distinction between the way in which postmodernists and constructivists may use discourse analysis differently.

discourse analysis (see Oswick, in this volume) to understand how language represented by text in documents has mediated in – and helped to constitute – social actions. It is not easy to outline a clear set of rules for conducting discourse analysis. Phillips and Di Domenico (2009: 560) argue: 'The breadth of textual analysis that could be used ... and the diversity of the phenomenon under investigation means that ... researchers need to develop an approach that makes sense in the light of their particular study *and* establish a set of arguments to justify the particular approach they adopt'. Although different authors will adopt different ways of conducting discourse analysis and use different terms to describe what they are doing, analyses are often conducted at one or more of the following levels. First, there is the context in which the interaction involving the discourse takes place and how that interaction gives rise to a specific social order. Second, there is the general direction of the account in the discourse and its implicit morality and assumptions. Third, there are the particular techniques that are used in the discourse to convey impressions of scale, importance, insignificance or to bring the discourse to an end. Here, I will apply discourse analysis to an interpretation of the regulators' reports that were discussed above.

Regulators' reports are composed by a committee after they have collected evidence from a range of sources, including 'expert' witnesses. Texts of reports will contain the narrative of regulators and statements from witnesses. The text involving the collection of evidence could be divided up into exchanges to identify who said what to whom and the role of each of those participants as either witnesses or members of the committee. By analysing how members of the committee asked questions, pressed for answers and reprimanded witnesses for taking too long to answer a question, an understanding could be achieved of how those members helped to construct the nature of a committee and its investigations. Similarly, analysis of responses from witnesses into such categories as 'refinement' (through a response that states conditions under which assumptions in a question hold), 'over-compliance' (through unqualified answers directed only to the terms of the question), 'evasion' (by providing a response that does not address a question), or 'denial' (of any knowledge, etc.), could be used to understand how witnesses helped construct the order of the committee.

Alternatively, the accounts of individual witnesses could be read. The view of each witness could be constructed around a conceptual pro forma derived from a reading of the types of questions and evidence provided in the report. This could include what the ILA monies were for, how actual use varied from the prescription for the use of monies, who was responsible for the variations, how did those people achieve such a variation and what were the consequences of that variation? By analysing the text of individual witnesses or the narrative of a report in this way, it would be possible to see how one or more accounts were constructed to suggest some individuals were responsible for a subversion of the aims of the ILA scheme. An analysis could be conducted on each component sentence of the text to identify the devices used by different witnesses to help construct their respective accounts. Thus, some witnesses offered anecdotes, others made comparisons with past initiatives and still others drew analogies between their situation and others in different contexts. For example, one witness to the E&SSC suggested that he stood alongside '*bona fide* trainers [that] had to fight arrivistes whose only interest in training was its ability to earn them quick money for no effort'. Although there was no physical combat involved, the image portrayed is one of 'good' providers having to struggle against 'bad' ones. The relative success of different witnesses in getting their viewpoint accepted could be assessed by investigating the extent to which the regulators endorsed opinions akin to those of different witnesses.

Conclusion

This chapter has explained what constitutes a document and shown how to scope research involving documents, gather relevant documents and analyse those documents once they have been collected. Attention has been given to how particular types of analysis complement different epistemological approaches. However, the framework provided is a heuristic device and it is important to realize that authors will use different types of epistemological approach according to the research question that they are asking and the reason why they are asking that question. Indeed, illustrations of documentary analysis where different epistemological assumptions are apparent have been drawn from the author's work. Nor should it be assumed that studies will contain only one form of documentary analysis. While a different body of the author's research has been used to illustrate one corresponding form of analysis, several forms of analysis – and epistemological position – could feature in the same body of work. For example, the study of the influence of accounting on the introduction and deployment of FMS was presented as an interpretive study that required an ethnographic content analysis. However, the investment appraisal documents had a constitutive dimension as their assumptions were embodied in the cost control mechanisms that guided the operation of the FMS. The studies do illustrate that documentary analysis is a rule-guided process, so it is important to compose, apply and report procedures and selection criteria for the inclusion and exclusion of information when seeking answers to research questions. Formulation and a systematic application of rules can help to justify the approach adopted.

Further Reading

When read in conjunction with each other, Krippendorff (2004) and Prior (2003) provide useful overviews of different approaches to the analysis of documents from different epistemological positions. A useful source for understanding the underlying methodologies and related epistemologies informing the organization of the wide range of documents that are available is the long-standing *Journal of Documentation*. Many excellent studies of organizations that draw on the use of documents may also be found in *Discourse and Communication*. Documents do take on a variety of forms and there are numerous useful readings that are dedicated to different types or uses of documents. Walker (2004) provides an informative and entertaining discussion of the trials, tribulations and joys of conducting archival research. Alazewski (2006) also provides a useful introduction to diaries as a research method. Documents may contain visual representations as well. Vince and Warren's chapter in this collection provides some insights into methods for analysing visual representations.

References

Alazewski, A. (2006) *Using Diaries for Social Research*. London: Sage.

Altheide, D.L. (1987) 'Ethnographic content analysis', *Qualitative Sociology*, 10 (1): 65–77.

Berelson, B. (1952) *Content Analysis in Communicative Research*. New York: Free Press.

Bricknell, D. (2008) 'Historical analysis', in R. Thorpe and R. Holt (eds), *The Sage Dictionary of Qualitative Management Research*. London: Sage, 108–109.

Cassell, C. and Lee, B. (2007) 'Re-vitalising learning and development? Exploring the role of the trade union learning representative', *Personnel Review*, 36 (5/6): 781–799.

Cassell, C. and Lee, B. (2009) 'Trade union learning representatives: progressing partnership?', *Work, Employment & Society*, 23 (2): 213–230.
Cunliffe, A.L. (2008) 'Discourse analysis', in R. Thorpe and R. Holt (eds), *The Sage Dictionary of Qualitative Management Research*. London: Sage, pp. 81–82.
Hodder, I. (2003) 'The interpretation of documents and material culture', in N.K. Denzin and Y.S. Lincoln (eds), *Handbook of Qualitative Research*. London: Sage. pp. 703–716.
Holsti, O.M. (1969) *Content Analysis for the Social Sciences and Humanities*. Reading, MA: Addison-Wesley.
Johnson, P., Buerhring, A., Cassell, C. and Symon, G (2006) 'Evaluating qualitative management research: towards a contingent criteriology', *International Journal of Management Reviews*, 8 (3): 131–156.
Jones, T.C. and Lee, B. (1998) 'Accounting, strategy and AMT investment', *Omega*, 26 (6): 769–783.
Krippendorff, K. (2004) *Content Analysis: An Introduction to Its Methodology* (2nd edn). Thousand Oaks, CA: Sage.
Lee, B. (1996) 'The justification and monitoring of AMT: an empirical study of 21 installations of FMS', *Management Accounting Research*, 7 (1): 95–118.
Lee, B. (2010) 'The Individual Learning Account experiment in the UK: a conjunctural crisis?' *Critical Perspectives on Accounting*, 21 (1): 18–30.
Lee, B. and Cassell, C. (2004) 'Electronic routes to change? A survey of website support for trade union learning representatives', *International Journal of Knowledge, Culture and Change Management*, 4: 701–711.
Lee, B. and Cassell, C. (2008) 'Employee and social reporting as a war of position and the union learning representative initiative in the UK', *Accounting Forum*, 32 (4): 276–287.
Lincoln, Y.S. (1980) 'Documentary analysis and record utilization: new uses for old methods', paper presented at the Annual Meeting of the American Educational Research Association, Boston, April.
Phillips, N. and Di Domenico, M. (2009) 'Discourse analysis in organizational research: methods and debates', in D.A. Buchanan and A. Bryman (eds), *The Sage Handbook of Organizational Research Methods*. London: Sage.
Prior, L. (2003) *Using Documents in Social Research*. London: Sage.
Prior, L. (2008) 'Repositioning documents in social research', *Sociology*, 42 (5): 821–836.
Rapley, T. (2007) *Doing Conversation, Discourse and Document Analysis*. London: Sage.
Walker, S. (2004) 'The search for clues in accounting history', in C. Humphrey and B. Lee (eds), *The Real Life Guide to Accounting Research*. Oxford: Elsevier, pp. 5–21.

11 Mixed Methods in Organizational Research

Alan Bryman

INTRODUCTION: THE RISE OF MIXED METHODS RESEARCH

Mixed methods research is an approach to the research process that is in an ambiguous position. The ambiguity arises from several factors but two are worth mentioning at the outset. First, it is in an ambiguous position, because it is not always obvious what it denotes. There is a growing tendency for it to refer to research that combines quantitative and qualitative research methods. However, methods can be combined within both quantitative research and qualitative research, as well as between them. In spite of the fact that this is generally recognized, mixed methods research has come to denote a distinctive approach that entails various modes of bringing together quantitative and qualitative research (e.g. Brannen, 2008: 54). Indeed, it is increasingly depicted as a research strategy in its own right that sits alongside quantitative and qualitative research (Denscombe, 2008; Greene, 2008; Johnson and Onwuegbuzie, 2008). In this chapter, the convention of reserving the term 'mixed methods research' for research integrating quantitative and qualitative research will be followed. Second, it is in an ambiguous position, because it is simultaneously an old and a new approach to organizational and social research. Old because it has been around in different forms for many years; new because interest in it has burgeoned in recent years. This burgeoning of interest can be discerned in such indicators as: the arrival of new journals dedicated to mixed methods research – the *Journal of Mixed Methods Research* and *International Journal of Multiple Research Approaches* (http://mra.e-contentmanagement.com/ – accessed on 14 April 2008); a handbook of mixed methods research (Tashakkori and Teddlie, 2003); a regular conference series organized by the Homerton School of Health Studies, UK, which attracts an international audience; special issues of established journals (e.g. *International Journal of Social Research Methodology*, 8(3), 2005; *Qualitative Research*, 6(1), 2006; *Research in the Schools*, 13(1), 2006); and a stream of books and edited collections dedicated to mixed methods research (Bergman, 2008; Bryman, 2006b; Creswell and Plano Clark, 2007;

Greene, 2007; Plano Clark and Creswell, 2008; Tashakkori and Teddlie, 1998).

Further evidence of the growing interest in mixed methods research is the fact that a content analysis of articles in the social sciences that had used a mixed methods approach (see Exhibit 30.1) revealed over three times as many articles in 2003 than in 1994 (Bryman, 2008a). This content analysis derived from a search of articles in the Social Sciences Citation Index. While the rise in the number of mixed methods articles almost certainly reflects the growth in the publishing of social science more generally, it is also possible if not likely that it is also to do with a real upsurge of work based on the approach. Of further interest to the organizational researcher is that, over the period in question, articles in the field of organization and management as the primary discipline made up the third largest group of articles by primary discipline (Bryman, 2006a). The percentages of all articles in each disciplinary area were: sociology (36%); social psychology (27%); management and organizational research (23%); geography (8%); and media and cultural studies (7%). Indeed, several other authors in this volume have drawn attention to the significance of mixed methods in the field (e.g. see Fitzgerald and Dopson, Chapter 27, this volume). However, some authors express disappointment at the lack of penetration of mixed methods in the field. Writing about management and organizational research, Currall and Towler (2003) have suggested that 'procedures for linking qualitative and quantitative techniques within a single study have received little attention' (p. 514) and argue that a 'perusal of the management literature over the past ten years suggests that a combination of methods is still rare' (p. 520).

Mixed methods research and the paradigm wars

One of the chief reasons for the relatively recent upsurge of interest in mixed methods research is the fact that it has only relatively recently come to be regarded as a legitimate approach. One of the main impediments to undertaking mixed methods research for many social scientists has been that combining quantitative and qualitative research has been seen as illegitimate on epistemological (and often ontological) grounds. Because of a tendency to see the methods associated with quantitative research as inherently or predominantly drenched with positivism and for the

EXHIBIT 30.1: Conducting mixed methods research on mixed methods research.

At several points in this chapter, reference will be made to Bryman's (2006a, 2007a) research on mixed methods research. This was in fact a study that employed mixed methods research to examine mixed methods research. Two of the main objectives for doing this research were:

1 To gain an understanding of mixed methods research practice in terms of such issues as: kinds of research methods used, disciplinary area, whether the quantitative preceded the qualitative component or vice versa, etc.
2 To gain an understanding of the contingencies of mixed methods research practice in terms of such issues as: why mixed methods research was chosen, problems encountered, lessons learned, etc.

In order to realise the first objective, a content analysis of 232 mixed methods research articles was conducted to map the general characteristics of mixed methods research in terms of a variety of features. From semistructured interviews, I wanted to glean the perspectives of mixed methods researchers in their own terms. The content analysis was designed to give a sense of the public face of mixed methods research, while the interviews were an attempt to get inside the heads of its practitioners in order to tease out how and why they used mixed methods research and their reflections on their own and others' practices. As such, this study of mixed methods research employed both a quantitative method – traditional quantitative content analysis – and a qualitative method – semistructured interviews – to examine different aspects of mixed methods research.

methods associated with qualitative research as inherently or predominantly drenched with interpretivism (e.g. phenomenology), combining quantitative and qualitative research was viewed as impossible because of their incompatibility. To underline this, quantitative and qualitative research were often depicted as paradigms, following Kuhn, and as such were deemed to be *ipso facto* incommensurable. At best, if quantitative and qualitative research *were* combined in research, it was viewed as turning qualitative research into an adjunct of quantitative research and hence positivism. Even quite recently, mixed methods research has been described as 'positivism in drag' (Giddings, 2006). Thus, although there has been a rise in the use of mixed methods research, this should not be taken to signal that the paradigm wars have given way to paradigm peace. For one thing, concerns about the epistemological problems associated with combining quantitative and qualitative research have not gone away completely and sometimes resurface (as signalled by the recency of the 'positivism in drag' comment). Indeed, in the present volume, Yanow and Ybema (Chapter 3, this volume) make the point that the mere existence of mixed methods research does not signal that the epistemological issues have been resolved or surmounted. They argue that combining quantitative and qualitative research does not signal that the underlying epistemologies are being somehow combined, though this position presumes a necessary association between research methods and epistemological positions. This view can be disputed on the grounds that methods are not necessarily associated with particular epistemologies; it is the *use* that is made of them that is crucial. A questionnaire may lend itself to the kinds of research question that are often asked within a positivist frame of reference but that does not mean that it should solely be viewed in this way. The other reason for doubting that the paradigm wars have abated is that they can be viewed as resurfacing in a different guise. Developments such as the rise of systematic review (see Denyer and Tranfield, Chapter 39, this volume) and of 'Bush science', as it is sometimes called in some quarters of the social sciences, are testament to lingering or new forms of the paradigm wars (Bryman, 2008a).

In place of the paradigm wars and their underlying philosophical principles, pragmatism has emerged as the foundational philosophy of much mixed methods research (e.g. Denscombe, 2008; Maxcy, 2003). As a philosophy, pragmatism is viewed as freeing the researcher to select whichever methods and data sources that might reasonably be used to explore a research problem in pursuit of rigorous and comprehensive findings. It is no coincidence that this stance has found particular favour among practitioners in applied fields like evaluation and educational research, where the over-riding emphasis tends to be on dealing with practical research problems. While organizational research *could* be construed as an applied field, it is striking that discussions in the pages of the *Academy of Management Journal* of the relevance of management studies generally imply that it is an area that is predominantly concerned with the solution of theoretical problems than with applied ones. Nonetheless, as previously noted, mixed methods research has a considerable following in organization studies.

The development of mixed methods research

It has been suggested that mixed methods research has proceeded through distinct phases. Creswell and Plano Clark (2007) have proposed that there have been four stages of development:

(1) A *formative period* associated with early explorations of ways of combining quantitative and qualitative research as well as discussions of the use of more than one quantitative research technique, usually within an explicit or implicit triangulation framework.
(2) A *paradigm debate period*, which explored the foundations of quantitative and qualitative research and whether it is feasible to combine them. These discussions have mainly

occurred in the 1970s and 1980s. My own work (Bryman, 1988) is situated in this period by the authors.

(3) A *procedural development period* that is mainly associated with exploring how mixed methods studies have been and can be designed. Debates about paradigms did not disappear but the emphasis changed to exploring the doing of mixed methods research. This work is mainly associated with the late 1980s through the start of the new millennium.

(4) An *advocacy as separate design period* associated with the new millennium whereby mixed methods researchers began to advocate it as a new and distinctive design in its own right.

In many ways, the third and fourth periods are likely to overlap considerably as not all practising researchers with an interest in mixed methods research will be inclined to treat it as a separate approach in its own right. Thus, we can expect that procedural development is likely to continue alongside the articulation of mixed methods research and its advocacy as a distinct design.

Classifying mixed methods research

There has undoubtedly been a greater preparedness to regard mixed methods research as a legitimate endeavour in the social sciences in recent years. However, the precise roles that quantitative and qualitative research are supposed to play in relation to each other are many. For one thing, mixed methods research subsumes a variety of research designs. Thus, it has become quite commonplace to distinguish mixed methods projects in terms of: *sequence* – whether the quantitative component precedes the qualitative or vice versa or whether they occur more or less concurrently; and *priority* – whether the quantitative component is more important than the qualitative component or *vice versa* or whether they have more or less equal weighting. A consideration of these two elements yields a typology whose component cells vary considerably in the frequency with which they are found in published research.

Indeed, following the early initiative of Morse (1991), writers on mixed methods have developed a distinctive notation to express the various possibilities offered by these considerations. Writers use 'quan' and 'qual' to refer to the different components of a mixed methods study and use upper or lower case to reflect the relative weighting of those components. They use arrows to signify which element precedes the other or a plus sign to express simultaneity. Thus, for example, QUAN + QUAL signifies a design in which the quantitative and qualitative are of equal weight and conducted concurrently, as in a triangulation design (see the following section). QUAN → qual signifies a design in which the quantitative component is the lead one and precedes the qualitative component. This might occur with a design emphasizing complementarity (see the following section) where the emphasis is on quantitative findings and the qualitative data are used to shed light on and explain them.

Considering where a particular mixed methods study falls in terms of these two dimensions is not without problems. First, there are issues of judgement involved – for example, deciding whether the quantitative and qualitative components differ in importance may not be easy to establish in many cases. Second, what is to count as mixed methods research can be difficult to resolve. For example, if a researcher conducts a survey that entails mainly a quantitative research orientation and if the questionnaire or interview schedule includes some open questions to which predominantly textual responses are given and these are analysed using a method of qualitative data analysis, does this count as mixed methods research (Bryman 1992)? Definitional issues bedevil methodological discussions and mixed methods research is obviously not immune to this tendency (Holmes, 2006).

Establishing typologies of mixed methods research along these lines has been particularly popular among North American writers. A somewhat different way of classifying mixed methods research has been to explore the various reasons or rationales for conducting it. This has been a feature of both North American writers (e.g. Greene et al., 1989; Creswell and Plano Clark, 2007) and European writers (e.g. Bryman, 1988, 2006a; Hammersley, 1996; Niglas, 2004; O'Cathain et al., 2007). The emphasis on rationales is highly compatible with the focus on priority and sequence and many writers express design types that reflect rationale in these terms.

The investigation of researchers' reasons for conducting mixed methods research is usually arrived at inductively from an examination of published research. In some cases, this investigation has been conducted through a relatively informal analysis of published research (e.g. Bryman, 1988; Hammersley, 1996). However, other students of mixed methods research have conducted more formal analyses. Such authors have content analysed mixed methods articles in order to establish the relative frequency with which different bases for conducting mixed methods research can be found.

The Greene et al. (1989) scheme has probably been one of the most frequently employed classifications for this purpose. This scheme identifies five justifications for combining quantitative and qualitative research:

(1) Triangulation. This is to do with establishing the convergence, corroboration, and/or correspondence of results from different methods. In the context of mixed methods research, triangulation is to do with seeking corroboration between quantitative and qualitative data.
(2) Complementarity. This occurs when the researcher 'seeks elaboration, enhancement, illustration, clarification of the results from one method with the results from another' (Greene et al., 1989: 259).
(3) Development. Entails seeking 'to use the results from one method to help develop or inform the other method, where development is broadly construed to include sampling and implementation, as well as measurement decisions' (Greene et al., 1989: 259).
(4) Initiation. Entails seeking 'the discovery of paradox and contradiction, new perspectives of [sic] frameworks, the recasting of questions or results from one method with questions or results from the other method' (Greene et al., 1989: 259).
(5) Expansion. Entails seeking 'to extend the breadth and range of enquiry by using different methods for different inquiry components' (Greene et al., 1989: 259).

One of the chief advantages of this classification is that it is parsimonious and uses generic categories. Thus, the fact that the typology was developed in relation to the authors' field of interest – evaluation research – does not preclude its being employed in relation to other fields. Indeed, it was employed by both Bryman (2006a) and Niglas (2004) in connection with their content analyses of five social science fields and educational research respectively. When Greene et al. (1989) applied the scheme to content analyse evaluation studies, each article was coded in terms of a primary and a secondary rationale. Other classificatory schemes have been developed (see Creswell and Plano Clark, 2007, Table 4.1 for a useful overview). In his content analysis of mixed methods articles, Bryman (2006a) preferred an approach that draws finer distinctions between possible bases for doing mixed methods research.

A further distinction that has been suggested is between the stated intentions of doing mixed methods research and how it is used in practice. This distinction has been a focus of the work of both Greene et al. (1989) and Bryman (2006a), with the latter distinguishing between rationale and practice: the rationale refers to the reasons given for combining quantitative and qualitative research; practice is to do with 'the ways in which quantitative and qualitative research[es] were actually combined' (Bryman, 2006a: 104). When this distinction is drawn and mixed methods articles are content analysed in terms of both rationale and practice, it is found that the two are often out of phase with each other. In other words, it is not always possible to establish how mixed methods research is actually used from a knowledge of the rationale that authors provide; similarly, knowing how mixed methods research has been used may not relate well to the way

Table 30.1 Rationales for mixed methods research using the Greene et al. (1989) scheme

Category	Rationale	%	Practice
Triangulation	7.8		12.5
Complementarity	28.9		44.8
Development	10.3		8.6
Initiation	0.4		1.3
Expansion	25.4		31.5
Not stated/other	27.2		1.3

All percentages are based on 232 cases – see Exhibit 30.1

it is rationalized by researchers. Two factors seem to lie behind this finding. First, in around a quarter of mixed methods articles, no rationale was provided, but it is nearly always possible to divine how quantitative and qualitative research were combined (see Table 30.1). Second, researchers appear to find more uses of mixed methods research than an examination of the rationales that they provide would lead the reader to expect. It would seem that when confronted with the two sets of data, more and often different possibilities open up than had been envisaged. In many ways, this points to much of the excitement as well as the unpredictability of a great deal of mixed methods research.

Table 30.1 provides previously unpublished findings relating to the content analysis of social science articles referred to in Exhibit 30.1 for both rationale and practice. It shows the distribution of articles in terms of just the primary rationale using the Greene et al. scheme (see column for 'Rationale'). In just over a quarter respectively of all articles, no rationale was provided. Complementarity and expansion were the most frequently cited primary rationales with 29% and 25% respectively of all articles mentioning each of them as a primary rationale. Triangulation and development were less commonly mentioned, while initiation was extremely uncommon. The latter was also the case in Greene et al. (1989) but was even more so in the data reported here. Turning to the actual uses of the integration of quantitative and qualitative research, Table 30.1 (column for 'Practice') provides the primary use in terms of the Greene et al. scheme. All of the frequencies are greater, because the category of 'not stated' virtually disappears. Most striking is that nearly half of all articles can be subsumed into the complementarity category. In terms of the Greene et al. scheme, this is by far the most prominent primary approach to the integration of quantitative and qualitative research.

When the data for the 'practice' column in Table 30.1 using the Greene et al. scheme are contrasted with comparable data from Greene et al. (1989) and Niglas (2004), we find that the pattern is closer to Niglas's examination of educational research articles than to the analysis of evaluation research articles by Greene et al. Similarly to Niglas, complementarity is the most common use of mixed methods research, followed by expansion. In the examination of evaluation research articles by Greene et al., it was the other way around, in that expansion was more common that complementarity. In the case of all three studies, then, these two uses of mixed methods research were the most common forms.

Table 30.2 takes the analysis of these data somewhat further with another previously unpublished analysis. This table presents

Table 30.2 Rationales for mixed methods management and organizational research using the Greene et al. (1989) scheme

Category	MOR	%	Other
Rationale			
Triangulation	18.9		4.5
Complementarity	24.5		30.2
Development	17.0		8.4
Initiation	1.9		0.0
Expansion	20.8		26.8
Not stated/other	17.0		30.2
N=	53		179
Practice			
Triangulation	22.6		9.5
Complementarity	37.7		46.9
Development	13.2		7.3
Initiation	3.8		0.6
Expansion	20.8		34.6
Not stated/other	1.9		1.1
N=	53		179

All percentages are based on 232 cases – see Exhibit 30.1
MOR = management and organizational research

the proportion of articles falling within Greene et al.'s five categories for articles in the management and organizational research (MOR) field versus the rest. The table presents the analysis for both rationale and practice. This table does indeed highlight some differences between MOR and the rest of the social sciences. At the level of rationale, MOR practitioners are noticeably more likely than other social scientists to use mixed methods research for the purpose of triangulation and development and are also noticeably less prone to not stating the purpose of doing mixed methods research. At the level of practice, the findings for triangulation and development are repeated. The findings for rationale and practice suggest that MOR practitioners are somewhat less likely to use mixed methods research for purposes of complementarity and expansion. On the one hand, these findings point to the existence of disciplinary differences in the uses to which mixed methods research is put, but, on the other hand, they point to areas where MOR practitioners might seek to extend their thinking about the possibilities with respect to integrating quantitative and qualitative research.

A classification of rationales for mixed methods research

We will now return to the issue of rationales in mixed methods research and use some examples from organization studies to illustrate the five-fold classification used by Greene et al. (1989). The aim will be to explore how mixed methods research is being used in organizational research through the examination of illustrations of a mixed methods approach.

Triangulation

As previously noted, triangulation is one of the most frequently encountered terms employed in a mixed methods research context to the extent that it is sometimes employed in a manner that suggests that it is seen as more or less synonymous with the combining of quantitative and qualitative research. However, Greene et al. employ the term appropriately to refer to exploring whether the results from two or more research methods converge (Webb et al., 1966). We can see the operation of triangulation in both Exhibits 30.2 and 30.3.

In Exhibit 30.2, Fey and Dennison (2003: 698–699) propose that the findings from the case studies 'supported' and 'mirror' the quantitative findings. In Exhibit 30.3, triangulation was also a feature but the picture is somewhat complex. At one of the case study firms (referred to as PC), Yauch and Steudel (2003) were able to use their quantitative data to reinforce their qualitative findings. However, at the other firm – BEC – the quantitative data were not able to identify cultural factors that impeded the introduction of cellular manufacturing. In part, this appears to have been due to a limitation of the quantitative measurement scale employed, which, the authors suggest, means that for some companies this scale may not be appropriate. Thus, in one of the firms, the quantitative data could be used to corroborate the qualitative findings but in the other firm, they could not. Nonetheless, the authors propose that using a mixed methods approach can help to give a study like theirs 'greater validity ... through data triangulation' (2003: 479).

Complementarity

Evidence of complementarity can be discerned in both Exhibits 30.2 and 30.3. With regard to the former, Fey and Denison say at one point that the 'qualitative elaboration' stage helped them to 'see many interesting and unanticipated insights that were hiding behind [their] quantitative analyses' (2003: 702). This was especially the case with respect to uncovering some of the cultural factors that helped them to understand the data relating to quantitative patterns, suggesting departures from the American model with respect to their Russian organizations. As noted in Exhibit 30.3, Yauch and Steudel (2003) explicitly employed the Greene et al. classification and rationalized the use of a mixed methods approach largely in terms of triangulation (see previous

EXHIBIT 30.2: Mixed methods research in a cross-national context.

Fey and Denison (2003) report the findings of a mixed methods study that explored the relationship between organizational culture and effectiveness in the context of whether theory and findings stemming from the US can be applied to Russia. This was one of the studies included in Bryman's (2006a) content analysis. Fey and Denison's investigation was guided by three research questions: whether the US model is applicable to Russia; what differences in findings can be discerned concerning the culture-effectiveness relationship between the two countries; and the meaning and applicability in Russia of the concepts developed for examining culture and effectiveness in the US. The first two research questions were explored with a quantitative study of 179 Russian firms; the third through four qualitative case studies. Denison had previously developed measures to study four cultural traits exhibited by effective organizations: involvement (empowerment); consistency (strong cultures); adaptability (responsive to customers); and mission (sense of direction). These scales and measures of effectiveness were employed in questionnaires by senior managers. While the model was broadly validated, some differences were found between the Russian and previous US findings, e.g. in Russia adaptability and involvement were the main correlates of effectiveness, whereas in the US it tended to be mission. Fey and Denison argue that there is a risk that the researcher could wrongly assume that the cultural traits mean the same things in Russia as they do in the US. To consider this possibility, they conducted semistructured interviews with managers in a subsample of four of the firms, which were purposively selected. The authors note that the qualitative case study findings confirmed the quantitative ones. They also suggest that the case studies 'served to ground the theoretical concepts in the realities of the Russian context' and helped to identify aspects of the findings that were consistent with the US model and also ones that 'were not fully anticipated by the model' (p. 701). In addition, they propose that the qualitative findings helped to 'illustrate' some of the model's constituent concepts. They conclude that the insights from both the quantitative and the qualitative findings 'enabled [them] to both validate the model and to provide a more complete understanding of the dynamics of organizational cultures in the Russian context' (p. 702).

EXHIBIT 30.3: Mixed methods research and the introduction of cellular manufacturing.

Yauch and Steudel (2003) report the findings of a mixed methods study that, like Exhibit 30.1, explores organizational culture and was also one of the articles in Bryman's (2006a) content analysis. The authors draw on the work of Greene et al. (1989), which is referred to in the main text, to make sense of their findings. The goal of the study 'was to identify key cultural factors that aided or hindered a company's ability to successfully implement manufacturing cells' (p. 467). The authors conducted two exploratory case studies to explore the cultural factors that contributed to or impeded the process of converting from traditional to cellular manufacturing processes. The two case-study firms (referred to as PC and BEC) were both new to cellular manufacturing. The case studies entailed participant observation, examination of documents, and group interviews with organizational members at a variety of levels. For the quantitative component of the investigation, an established scale – the Organizational Culture Inventory (OCI) – was employed in each company. The OCI was administered to a random sample of both managers and nonmanagerial employees. The authors drew up an assessment of the strengths and weaknesses of both sets of findings but of particular significance for this summary of the research is the authors' assessment of their mixed methods findings. Yauch and Steudel found that at PC, a factor that has an adverse effect on implementation was 'avoidance', which refers to a tendency not to take responsibility for one's actions so that one is not blamed. This cultural factor was uncovered through the qualitative research and then confirmed through the quantitative evidence. The qualitative findings revealed the beliefs and assumptions that lay behind avoidance while the quantitative findings are deemed to have provided greater precision in explaining it and also helped with naming it. At BEC, a cultural factor referred to as 'rigid group boundaries' was identified through the qualitative data as an impediment to implementation. This cultural trait was to do with a tendency for organizational members to form barriers between groups that made it difficult for them to interact. However, rigid group boundaries was not revealed through the administration of the OCI, because this inventory is not designed to measure it! Yauch and Steudel propose that they were able to triangulate their findings at PC but at BEC the OCI did not reveal a particular cultural style. However, in addition, the combination of quantitative and qualitative research allowed the researchers to explore different aspects, and to some extent levels, of organizational culture. As they put it: 'Although the quantitative analysis identified behavioral norms for the organization as a whole, the qualitative analysis was necessary to get at the underlying reasons for this behavior' (p. 477).

section) and complementarity. They write, for example:

> Using a combination of qualitative and quantitative techniques revealed different aspects of organizational culture. Although the quantitative analysis revealed behavioral norms for the organization as a whole, the qualitative analysis was necessary to get at the underlying reasons for this behavior. Thus, the use of mixed methods created a deeper understanding of the organization ... Defining key cultural factors at the artefact level fit within the quantitative research paradigm, whereas the qualitative paradigm was needed to investigate the lived experience of managers and employees within the organization at the level of values and underlying assumptions. (Yauch and Steudel, 2003: 477)

Development

An interesting slant on development is provided by Yauch and Steudel (2003) in connection with what they feel they *should* have done. As noted in Exhibit 30.3, at the firm referred to as BEC, a cultural factor described as 'rigid group boundaries' (a tendency for organizational members to form barriers between groups that made it difficult for them to interact) was identified through the qualitative data as impeding implementation. However, this cultural factor was not revealed through the administration of the quantitative instrument used to measure organizational culture, because this inventory is not designed to measure that particular factor. Yauch and Steudel make an interesting point when they write: 'If the primary goal is to increase validity, an instrument should be selected *or developed* that specifically asks about the cultural aspects of the organization that have been identified through the preliminary qualitative work' (2003: 476, emphasis added). Essentially, what these authors seem to be proposing is that from the point of view of seeking to triangulate quantitative and qualitative findings, the exercise might have worked better had the quantitative measure of organizational culture been one that had been developed out of prior qualitative findings. This kind of use of mixed methods research can be found in an article by Myers and Oetzel (2003) which is both frequently referred to and reprinted in Creswell and Plano Clark (2007). In this study, the researchers conducted semistructured interviews with a variety of organizational participants to develop the concept of organizational assimilation. The interviews revealed six dimensions of assimilation: familiarity with others; acculturation; recognition; involvement with the organization; job competency; and adaptation and role negotiation. Myers and Oetzel then developed a questionnaire scale to reflect these six dimensions. The scale comprised 61 items. The six dimensions were validated when the questionnaire was administered to a sample and construct validity was established when several hypotheses concerning organizational assimilation were supported.

An element of development could also be discerned in Fey and Denison's (2003) research in that the choice of the four case-study firms was undertaken with reference to what was already known about them through the quantitative data that had been collected.

Initiation

As the findings described in Tables 30.1 and 30.2 suggest, initiation is not a common basis for doing mixed methods research at the level of either rationale or practice and, as is noted in the foregoing section, it is uncommon in a variety of areas. However, Exhibit 30.4 provides an interesting illustration of initiation in practice. While the example used in Exhibit 30.4 was clearly not planned in a manner consistent with what Greene et al. mean by initiation, that is how it turned out. The authors were forced to salvage their overall research project by rethinking the nature of their research questions by collecting qualitative data. Fortunately, they resisted the temptation to write up their research as a purely quantitative research study in which a negative relationship was hypothesized and then confirmed through their quantitative findings (Sutton and Rafaeli, 1992). Instead, they collected qualitative data to understand their quantitative data better.

EXHIBIT 30.4: Using mixed methods research to rescue a quantitative research project.

This exhibit is a favourite exemplar of mixed methods research in the organizations field and one I have used before (Bryman and Bell, 2007). It is Sutton and Rafaeli's (1988) study of the relationship between the display of positive emotions and organizational effectiveness. While a fascinating example of a mixed methods study, it is also a saga of academic endurance. Sutton and Rafaeli were afforded the opportunity to examine the organizational impact of the display of positive emotions when they were given access to data collected by a convenience store chain from a sample of 576 of its stores. The data had been collected by observation as part of an evaluation of the courtesy of its clerks. Sutton and Rafaeli hypothesized that stores where there was a high incidence of the display of positive emotions (smiling, thanking, eye contact, etc.) would have higher levels of sales. The researchers found that there was indeed a relationship between emotional display and sales but it was *negative*. In other words, the display of positive emotions was associated with lower levels of store sales. Sutton and Rafaeli then conducted a qualitative investigation 'to help explain the unexpected negative relationship' (p. 471). Four stores were purposively sampled as case studies based on their levels of sales and on the display of positive emotions. Data were collected by observation, semistructured interview, brief periods of participant observation and other qualitative methods. The qualitative data confirmed that the relationship was a negative one, but that sales was an independent rather than a dependent variable. In other words, because they tended to be busier, check-out clerks in stores with high sales typically had less time for the display of positive emotions. The quantitative data were reanalysed and this inference was supported. The experience of doing this research led the authors to appreciate the virtues of using both quantitative and qualitative methods (Sutton and Rafaeli, 1992).

Expansion

Although not a study in the field of organizational research, Exhibit 30.1 provides an example of a study 'using different methods for different inquiry components' (Greene et al., 1989: 259). The traditional quantitative content analysis was employed in order to reveal the nature of published mixed methods studies. As such, it was concerned to uncover the formal characteristics of mixed methods research in terms of such features as: the research methods and research designs employed, the main disciplines, whether the quantitative or the qualitative component was primary, and the rationales for using mixed methods research. The goal of the qualitative interviews was to get at the nature of mixed methods practice from the perspective of practitioners, looking at such issues as the contingencies of doing mixed methods research and problems encountered in the course of its implementation.

Mixed methods research and the problem of integration

One issue that has preoccupied methodologists in recent times has been the degree to which the findings deriving from mixed methods findings are genuinely integrated. The term '*mixed* methods research' implies that the quantitative and qualitative components involved in a mixed methods investigation are brought together. For example, in an editorial for the *Journal of Mixed Methods Research*, the journal's editors proposed that one criterion of a good mixed methods article is that the quantitative and qualitative components should be linked:

> Mixed methods research is simply more than reporting two distinct 'strands' of quantitative and qualitative research; these studies must also integrate, link, or connect these 'strands' in some way ... The expectation is that by the end of the manuscript, conclusions gleaned from the two strands are integrated to provide a fuller understanding of the phenomenon under study. (Creswell and Tashakkori, 2007: 108)

A study that asked social policy researchers about the quality criteria that should be applied to mixed methods research found that one of the most frequently mentioned criteria was whether the quantitative and qualitative findings are integrated (Bryman, Becker and Sempik, 2008), while O'Cathain et al. (2007)

propose that it is important for a mixed methods publication to be more than the sum of its constituent parts (see also Tashakkori and Teddlie, 2008: 106, on this point).

Although there is a view that the integration of the quantitative and qualitative findings of a mixed methods project is highly desirable, there is evidence that this does not always happen. Several reasons have been identified for the lack of integration of findings. Most of these were covered in the course of interviews with twenty British mixed methods social researchers (Bryman, 2007a see Exhibit 30.1). Many of the interviewees recognized that quantitative and qualitative findings were often not integrated and typically felt that they themselves were guilty of this. The following were the main factors identified as impeding integration:

- Writing for *different audiences.* Mixed methods researchers sometimes find that they end up writing up the quantitative and qualitative findings for different audiences. This may be associated with the researcher's judgement about the acceptability of certain styles of research or types of data for particular audiences.
- Researchers' *methodological preferences.* Researchers sometimes reveal a tendency to have greater confidence in some types of data than in others. This tendency often reflects being more comfortable with some kinds of data resulting from training.
- The different components of a mixed methods project may follow different *timelines.* As a result, the findings of one component may emerge at a considerably earlier stage than those associated with the other component.
- The *structure of research projects* may mean that it is difficult for integration to be achieved. This can arise when one component of the overall project occupies a much more central role than the other component. A typical example is when the quantitative component is both highly structured and occupies a much more pivotal position than the qualitative component, the style of qualitative data collection may be too constrained by the quantitative research.
- When a mixed methods project is conducted by a team whose members have different *methods skills,* a division of labour within the team may arise that makes it difficult for the skills specialists to work together.
- Sometimes, one set of data may emerge as more *intrinsically interesting* than the other set, with the result that the researcher tends to emphasize the more striking findings.
- Although mentioned by only one interviewee, the presence of an *ontological divide* between the quantitative and qualitative elements can prove a difficulty. This can arise when the qualitative component reflects a strong constructionist position that problematizes the nature and even the existence of the phenomenon being investigated. It can then be difficult to explore this problematized phenomenon with an objectivist research strategy that presumes its existence.
- *Publication issues* can also pose a problem for integrating findings. This can arise because of the preferences of some journals and editors for research approaches that are associated with either quantitative or qualitative research. In this context, it is striking that Currall and Towler (2003) called for a re-evaluation of journal editorial policies as a means of garnering greater acceptance of mixed methods studies.

It may also be that when mixed methods research is being conducted within a framework consistent with expansion in terms of the five-fold classification by Greene et al. (1989), integration may be difficult to achieve. This was certainly the case with the research referred to in Exhibit 30.1, where the quantitative and qualitative components were designed to explore distinct research questions to generate an overall view of the phenomenon of interest.

One further reason for the limited integration of quantitative and qualitative findings in many mixed methods articles may be that there are relatively few guidelines for the writing up of findings deriving from such research and relatively few well known exemplars to draw upon. To the extent that guidelines and exemplars exist in the social sciences, they tend to be identifiable in relation to *either* quantitative or qualitative research. In fact, it could be argued that the emphasis in writing about mixed methods research should shift slightly away from data collection and design and towards the interpretation and representation of findings.

Writing mixed methods research

As previously suggested, one of the issues that needs greater consideration is how mixed methods research should be written up. There are well-established formats for the writing up of quantitative and qualitative research but few guidelines regarding mixed methods research. Creswell and Plano Clark (2007) have offered some helpful suggestions in this connection. They propose the following guidelines:

(1) The writing should be structured so that it is tailored to the kind of mixed methods design employed. Thus, if the study's primary orientation is towards qualitative research, this should be reflected in the approach taken to writing up the findings.
(2) The writing up should 'help to educate the reader about this form of research' (Creswell and Plano Clark, 2007: 152). This implies that key mixed methods terms should be clearly defined and there should be clear references to the mixed methods literature. This suggestion could be linked to the notion that mixed methods research is currently in the throes of an advocacy period (see foregoing section).
(3) Researchers should use visual and other aids to display and help the reader to follow the components of a mixed methods study and their interconnections.
(4) The researcher should aim to generate a unified narrative for the findings. This recommendation reflects the preference among mixed methods researchers for publications that integrate the quantitative and qualitative findings.

In addition, the following additional considerations could be registered:

(1) Creswell and Tashakkori (2007: 108) have proposed that mixed methods articles 'need to be well-developed in both quantitative and qualitative components'. This means that not only should the research have been conducted according to the respective standards or quality criteria of quantitative and qualitative research, but it should also be written up in such a way that it establishes the probity of these components.
(2) Researchers might also consider framing their research at the outset with research questions that reflect a specific orientation to research questions. For example, Tashakkori and Creswell (2007) and Creswell and Plano Clark (2007) refer to 'mixed methods research questions' which explicitly deal with how the quantitative and qualitative components will be mixed. This feature is likely to need to be tailored to the nature of the mixed methods design (see first point in this list). Edmondson and McManus (2007: 1165) advocate employing a mixed methods approach in situations when 'the combination of qualitative data to help elaborate a phenomenon and quantitative data to provide preliminary tests of relationships can promote insight and rigor'. However, this approach to stipulating mixed methods research questions seems to restrict mixed methods research to a rather narrow range of issues.
(3) It should be clear why a mixed methods approach was employed. Researchers should guard against simply presuming that it is obvious why both quantitative and qualitative research were employed on the grounds that more is better. The case for using a mixed methods approach needs to be clearly articulated, not least because in the eyes of many mixed methods researchers, the approach should only be used when relevant to the research questions asked (Bryman, 2006b; Bryman et al., 2008).

One of the impediments to mixed methods writing is that there are few generally accepted exemplary studies. It may be that once these are established, the writing process will become less problematic for researchers than is currently the case. An example of the use of an exemplary mixed methods study to illustrate good practice in this connection, but from outside the field of organizational research, can be found in Bryman (2008b).

CONCLUSION

Mixed methods research generally and in the field of organizational research in particular is at something of a crossroads. On the one hand, there is no doubt that it is attracting a great deal of attention and its popularity continues to grow. Its legitimacy is questioned less frequently than was the case even ten years ago. Indeed, it has the characteristics of a distinct 'community of practice' (Denscombe, 2008). However, there are also countervailing factors that should not be forgotten. In this Conclusion, four are emphasized:

First, the ontological and epistemological issues that previously inhibited mixed methods work have not gone away; they have simply been sidelined in the pursuit of pragmatism. On a personal note, I am not averse to this. As I have said before, I have never believed that a research method necessarily implies a certain epistemological orientation; rather it is the use that is made of the research method that links it to wider issues of epistemology and ontology. The affordances of a research method may predispose its use in connection with particular epistemological or ontological positions, but ultimately it is the use made of the research method that is the principal issue.

Second, as a field, organizational research is still largely dominated by quantitative research, as Bazeley's (2008) informal inspection of recent issues of the *Administrative Science Quarterly* and *Academy of Management Journal* reveals. Bazeley's analysis implies that, in these journals, to the extent that mixed methods research is published, the role of the qualitative component is largely that of handmaiden to the quantitative component. This means that in essence, such journals are only likely to publish a restricted range of forms of mixed methods work and that its wider acceptance may not be as great as some of the more optimistic accounts of the rise of mixed methods research imply. It may also reinforce the previous point about lingering epistemological issues and concerns redolent of the paradigm wars (Bryman, 2008a).

Third, the connection between mixed methods research and research questions remains opaque. There are two aspects to this issue. First, whether there are types of research questions that require or at least imply a mixed methods approach is not entirely resolved. The notion expressed earlier that a mixed methods research question is which stipulates how the quantitative and the qualitative components will be brought together is significant but that relates to the issue of integration. What is still not clear is whether there is a specific kind of research question (that is, over and above how components are to be combined) that implies a mixed methods approach. Second, some writers on and practitioners of mixed methods research seem to suggest that the approach will almost always be superior to monomethod research, whereas others suggest that it should only be used when the research question(s) imply that it should be used (Bryman, 2007b; Bryman et al., 2008). This implies some uncertainty about the status of mixed methods research that needs to be resolved.

Fourth, there are skills issues that have not been fully resolved. What are the necessary skills for being a mixed methods researcher? Most obviously, a mixed methods researcher needs to have skills in both quantitative and qualitative research or when specific skills are not present needs to build a team that can incorporate missing skills. The first of these is often inhibited by the tendency for many researchers either to be trained in either quantitative or qualitative research skills or to have acquired a preference at an early stage for one or the other. The team-building solution can cause problems of integrating the components as suggested before (see also Bryman, 2007a). However, in addition to these issues, the many discussions about the nature of mixed methods research and the various types of design that the term can subsume and about the contingencies of the approach (such as the issue of integration) suggest that a mixed methods skills set is beginning to emerge that is in addition to the abilities that are required for doing both quantitative and qualitative research. In turn, these reflections have implications for the teaching of and training in mixed methods research for future generations, an issue to which writers on research methods are beginning to turn their attention (Creswell et al., 2003).

To some extent, these considerations relate to how writers on and practitioners of mixed methods research want to position themselves and their craft. If the goal is to position mixed methods research as a paradigm that stands alongside quantitative and qualitative research, which certainly seems to be an objective according to several commentators (Denscombe, 2008), deliberation on these and several of the other issues raised in this chapter are pressing. However, in so doing they must be wary of turning mixed methods into a methodological cult. As the second issue raised in this Conclusion suggests, the credibility of mixed methods research is still not as widely accepted as is sometimes supposed, and it is here that there are battles still to be fought.

It could be argued that although just under a quarter of all the articles content analysed in the research described in Exhibit 30.1 are based on mixed methods research, given the large number of journals in the MOR field, it is somewhat surprising that there are not more. It may be that this is what prompted Currall and Towler (2003: 520) to remark that 'a combination of methods is still rare'. MOR would appear to be an ideal field for the proliferation of mixed methods research. Its practitioners are very sensitive to the advantages of applying different paradigmatic approaches and readings of organizational phenomena (as Buchanan and Bryman, Chapter 1; Deetz, Chapter 2; Yanow and Ybema, Chapter 3; Alvesson and Ashcraft, Chapter 4; and Prasad and Prasad Chapter 8, among others in this volume, make clear). Further, qualitative researchers often perceive the mainstream journals as preferring articles based on quantitative research, so it might be that a mixed methods approach would be attractive as a strategic means of getting published (see Buchanan and Bryman, Chapter 1, this volume, on this point). In addition, it may be that mixed methods research is especially suited to the kinds of research questions that are asked in MOR. The fact that organizations can be examined at a variety of levels (sectors, populations, inter-organizational relations, single organization, departments, work groups, etc.) may make a mixed methods approach especially suitable. Research questions may be asked that require an appreciation of macro and micro issues and mixed methods research would be well placed to address them. In addition, the fact that organizational phenomena include combinations of both highly measurable constructs (profitability, size, market share, etc.) and ones which are less directly measurable and hence amenable to both quantitative and qualitative approaches (organizational culture, organizational aesthetics, emotional labour, etc.) would seem to point to several advantages of adopting a mixed methods approach. Also, some areas of MOR are dominated by either a quantitative or a qualitative research approach. Thus, for example, as Bryman and Buchanan note (Chapter 41, this volume), areas like job satisfaction (see Rafferty and Griffin, Chapter 12, this volume) are largely dominated by quantitative research. Other fields like organizational aesthetics (Strati, Chapter 14, this volume) are largely dominated by qualitative research. Again, a mixed methods approach has the potential to increase the range of enquiry for such subfields and enhance the understanding of their respective phenomena. Mixed methods research would seem, then, to offer great potential to organizational researchers, suggesting that while it has been responsible for some important and significant contributions in the field, there is the potential for a great deal more.

REFERENCES

Bazeley, P. (2008) 'Mixed methods in management research', in R. Thorpe and R. Holt (eds), *The SAGE Dictionary of Qualitative Management Research*, London: Sage, pp.133–6.

Bergman, M.M. (ed.) (2008) *Advances in Mixed Methods Research*, London: Sage.

Brannen, J. (2008) 'The practice of a mixed methods research strategy: personal, professional and project considerations', in M.M. Bergman (ed.), *Advances in Mixed Methods Research*, London: Sage, pp.53–65.

Bryman, A. (1988) *Quantity and Quality in Social Research*, London: Unwin Hyman.

Bryman, A. (1992) 'Quantitative and qualitative research: further reflections on their integration', in J. Brannen (ed.), *Mixing Methods: Qualitative and Quantitative Research*, Aldershot: Ashgate, pp. 57–78.

Bryman, A. (2006a) 'Integrating quantitative and qualitative research: how is it done?', *Qualitative Research*, 6(1): 97–113.

Bryman, A. (2006b) *Mixed Methods*, Four-volume set, London: Sage.

Bryman, A. (2007a) 'Barriers to integrating quantitative and qualitative research', *Journal of Mixed Methods Research*, 1(1): 8–22.

Bryman, A. (2007b) 'The research question in social research: what is its role?', *International Journal of Social Research Methodology*, 10(1): 5–20.

Bryman, A. (2008a) 'The end of the paradigm wars?', in P. Alasuutari, L. Bickman, and J. Brannen (eds), *The SAGE Handbook of Social Research Methods*, London: Sage, pp.13–25.

Bryman, A. (2008b) *Social Research Methods* (third edn.), Oxford: Oxford University Press.

Bryman, A. and Bell, E. (2007) *Business Research Methods* (Revised edn.), Oxford: Oxford University Press.

Bryman, A., Becker, S. and Sempik, J. (2008) 'Quality criteria for quantitative, qualitative and mixed methods research: the view from social policy', *International Journal of Social Research Methodology*, 11(4), 261–76.

Creswell, J.W., and Plano Clark, V.L. (2007) *Designing and Conducting Mixed Methods Research*, Thousand Oaks, CA: Sage.

Creswell, J.W. and Tashakkori, A. (2007) 'Developing publishable mixed methods manuscripts', *Journal of Mixed Methods Research*, 1(2): 107–11.

Creswell, J.W., Tashakkori, A., Jensen, K.D. and Shapley, K.L. (2003) 'Teaching mixed methods research: practices, dilemmas, and challenges', in A. Tashakkori and C. Teddlie (eds), *Handbook of Mixed Methods in Social & Behavioral Research*, Thousand Oaks, CA: Sage, pp. 619–38.

Currall, S.C. and Towler, A.J. (2003) 'Research methods in management and organizational research: toward integration of qualitative and quantitative techniques', in A. Tashakkori and C. Teddlie (eds), *Handbook of Mixed Methods in Social & Behavioral Research*, Thousand Oaks, CA: Sage, pp.513–26.

Denscombe, M. (2008) 'Communities of practice: a research paradigm for the mixed methods approach', *Journal of Mixed Methods Research*, 2(3): 270–83.

Edmondson, A.C. and McManus, S.E. (2007) 'Methodological fit in management field research', *Academy of Management Review*, 32(4): 1155–79.

Fey, C.F. and Denison, D.R. (2003) 'Organizational culture and effectiveness: can American theory be applied in Russia?', *Organization Science*, 14(6): 686–706.

Giddings, L.S. (2006) 'Mixed-methods research: positivism dressed in drag?', *Journal of Research in Nursing*,11(3): 195–203.

Greene, J.C. (2007) *Mixed Methods in Social Inquiry*, San Francisco, CA: Jossey-Bass.

Greene, J.C. (2008) 'Is mixed methods social inquiry a distinctive methodology?', *Journal of Mixed Methods Research*, 2(1): 7–22.

Greene. J.C., Caracelli, V.J. and Graham, W.F. (1989) 'Toward a conceptual framework for mixed-method evaluation designs', *Educational Evaluation and Policy Analysis*, 11: 255–74.

Hammersley, M. (1996) 'The relationship between qualitative and quantitative research: paradigm loyalty versus methodological eclecticism', in J.T.E. Richardson (ed.), *Handbook of Research Methods for Psychology and the Social Sciences*, Leicester: BPS Books.

Holmes, C.A. (2006) 'Mixed(up) methods, methodology and interpretive frameworks', Paper presented at the Homerton Mixed Methods Conference, Cambridge.

Johnson, R.B. and Onwuegbuzie, A.J. (2004) 'Mixed methods research: a research paradigm whose time has come', *Educational Researcher*, 33(7): 14–26.

Maxcy, S.J. (2003) Pragmatic threads in mixed methods research in the social sciences: the search for multiple modes of inquiry and the end of the philosophy of formalism. in A. Tashakkori and C. Teddlie (Eds.), *Handbook of Mixed Methods in Social and Behavioral Research* Thousand Oaks, CA: Sage, pp. 51–89.

Morgan, D.L. (1998) 'Practical strategies for combining qualitative and quantitative methods: applications for health research', *Qualitative Health Research*, 8(3): 362–76.

Morse, J.M. (1991) 'Approaches to qualitative-quantitative methodological triangulation', *Nursing Research*, 40(2): 120–3.

Myers, K.K. and Oetzel, J.G. (2003) 'Exploring the dimensions of organizational assimilation: creating and validating a measure', *Communication Quarterly*, 51(4): 438–57.

Niglas, K. (2004) *The Combined Use of Qualitative and Quantitative Methods in Educational Research*, Tallinn, Estonia: Tallinn Pedagogical University Dissertation on Social Sciences.

O'Cathain, A., Murphy, E. and Nicholl, J. (2007) 'Integration and publications as indicators of "yield" from mixed methods studies', *Journal of Mixed Methods Research*, 1(2): 147–63.

Plano Clark, V.L. and Creswell, J.W. (2008) *The Mixed Methods Reader*, Thousand Oaks, CA: Sage.

Sutton, R.I. and Rafaeli, A. (1988) 'Untangling the relationship between displayed emotions and organizational sales: the case of convenience stores', *Academy of Management Journal*, 31 (3): 461–87.

Sutton, R.I. and Rafaeli, A. (1992) 'How we untangled the relationship between displayed emotions and organizational sales: a tale of bickering and optimism', in P.J. Frost and R. Stablein (1992), *Doing Exemplary Research*, Newbury Park, CA: Sage, pp.115–28

Tashakkori, A. and Creswell, J.W. (2007) 'Exploring the nature of research questions in mixed methods research', *Journal of Mixed Methods Research*, 1(3): 207–11.

Tashakkori, A. and Teddlie, C. (1998) *Mixed Methodology: Combining Qualitative and Quantitative Approaches*, Thousand Oaks, CA: Sage.

Tashakkori, A. and Teddlie, C. (eds) (2003) *Handbook of Mixed Methods in Social and Behavioral Research*, Thousand Oaks, CA: Sage.

Tashakkori, A. and Teddlie, C. (2008) 'Quality of inferences in mixed methods research: calling for an integrative framework', in M.M. Bergman (ed.), *Advances in Mixed Methods Research*, London: Sage, pp.101–19.

Webb, E.J., Campbell, D.T., Schwartz, R.D. and Sechrest, L. (1966) *Unobtrusive Measures: Non-Reactive Research in the Social Sciences*, Chicago: Rand McNally.

Yauch, C.A. and Steudel, H.J. (2003) 'Complementary use of qualitative and quantitative cultural assessment methods', *Organizational Research Methods*, 6(4): 465–81.

12 Toward a Definition of Mixed Methods Research

R. Burke Johnson, Anthony J. Onwuegbuzie, Lisa A. Turner

The purpose of this article is to examine how the field of *mixed methods* currently is being defined. The authors asked many of the current leaders in mixed methods research how they define mixed methods research. The authors provide the leaders' definitions and discuss the content found as they searched for the criteria of demarcation. The authors provide a current answer to the question, What is mixed methods research? They also briefly summarize the recent history of mixed methods and list several issues that need additional work as the field continues to advance. They argue that mixed methods research is one of the three major "research paradigms" (quantitative research, qualitative research, and mixed methods research). The authors hope this article will contribute to the ongoing dialogue about how mixed methods research is defined and conceptualized by its practitioners.

Keywords: *mixed methods; mixed methodology; mixed research; multimethod; paradigm; pragmatism*

Mixed methods research (also called *mixed research* in this article) is becoming increasingly articulated, attached to research practice, and recognized as the third major research approach or *research paradigm*,[1] along with qualitative research and quantitative research. In this article, we will show that there might not be a single criterion of demarcation for mixed methods research, but there are several important criteria for thinking about mixed methods research in a narrow or pure sense as well as in a broader or highly inclusive sense. We believe that whereas there might not be a perfect or essentialist definition forthcoming, dialogue and social construction of a workable definition is a worthwhile goal for the field, understanding, of course, that definitions can and will usually change over time as the approach or "research paradigm" continues to grow. The classical pragmatic philosophers (i.e., Peirce, James, Dewey) had it right when they pointed out that the present is always a new starting point.

This article has four related purposes. First, we will review the recent history of mixed methods research to place the forthcoming definitions in recent historical context. Second, we list 19 definitions and summarize them through content analysis and discussion. The summary definition we provide is the result of an online discussion with several leaders in the field. Third, we also provide definitions of qualitative dominant and quantitative dominant mixed methods research. Fourth, we list several issues that might need additional attention as the field advances. We hope that the definitions provided here will be useful as the field continues positioning itself as one of the three methodological or research paradigms (i.e., qualitative research, quantitative research, and mixed methods research).

A Recent History of Mixed Methods Research

Debates about singular or universal truths or approaches to viewing the world (Socrates, Plato), versus multiple or relative truths (the Sophists such as Protagoras and Gorgias), versus balances or mixtures of the extremes (Aristotle's "golden mean" or principle of balance, moderate skepticism, Cicero, Sextus Empiricus), go back, at least, to ancient Western philosophy, and the spirit of these debates lives today in the different views of the three major approaches to social research. According to Plato, Protagoras said that "man is the measure of all things," and in many ways the history of Western philosophy still is debating Protagoras and the other Sophists.[2] This debate continues to affect how we view knowledge, what we look for, what we expect to find, and how we believe we are to go about finding and justifying "knowledge."

We would position mixed research between the extremes Plato (quantitative research) and the Sophists (qualitative research), with mixed research attempting to respect fully the wisdom of both of these viewpoints while also seeking a workable middle solution for many (research) problems of interest. Today, the primary philosophy of mixed research is that of pragmatism. Mixed methods research is, generally speaking, an approach to knowledge (theory and practice) that attempts to consider multiple viewpoints, perspectives, positions, and standpoints (always including the standpoints of qualitative and quantitative research).

Mixed research, in its recent history in the social and behavioral or human sciences, started with researchers and methodologists who believed qualitative *and* quantitative viewpoints and methods were useful as they addressed their research questions. For the first 60 years or so of the 20th century, "mixed research" (in the sense of including what we, today, would call qualitative and quantitative data) can be seen in the work of cultural anthropologists and, especially, the fieldwork sociologists (e.g., Gans, 1963; Hollingshead, 1949; Jahoda, Lazarsfeld, & Zeisel, 1931/2003; Lynd & Lynd, 1929/1959). However, the mixed methods label would not be coined until many years later. It is interesting to browse the books written by these earlier social scientists to see how they blended qualitative and quantitative data as they studied their communities. Although mixed methods research is not new, it is a new movement, or discourse, or research paradigm (with a growing number of members) that has arisen in response to the currents of *quantitative research* and *qualitative research*. In the history of ideas, new antitheses and syntheses continually develop in response to current theses. Mixed research is a synthesis that includes ideas from qualitative and quantitative research.

In the social science methodological literature, Campbell and Fiske's (1959) article sometimes is viewed as formalizing the practice of using multiple research methods. In this 1959 article, Campbell and Fiske introduced the idea of triangulation, referring to "multiple operationalism," in which more than one method is used as part of a validation process that ensures that the explained variance is the result of the underlying phenomenon or trait and not of the method (e.g., quantitative or qualitative). It was argued that the convergence of findings stemming from two or more methods "enhances our beliefs that the results are valid and not a methodological artifact" (Bouchard, 1976, p. 268). Interestingly, during the early 1950s, even though he did not use the term *multiple operationalism*, Boring (1953) foreshadowed this concept as follows:

> As long as a new construct has only the single operational definition that is received at birth, it is just a construct. When it gets two alternative operational definitions, it is beginning to be validated. When the defining operations, because of proven correlations, are many, then it becomes reified. (p. 222)

As can be seen, however, the idea of multiple operationalism is more of a measurement and construct validation technique, in its original formulation, than it is a full research methodology. Furthermore, early researchers' idea of multiple operationalism follows more closely what today is called *multimethod research*, in contrast to what currently is called *mixed methods research*. However, Campbell and Fiske (1959) are rightfully credited as being the first to show explicitly how to use multiple research methods for validation purposes.

The ideas of Campbell and Fiske (1959) were extended further by Webb, Campbell, Schwartz, and Sechrest (1966), who defined multiple operationalism as representing the use of multiple measures that "are hypothesized to share in the theoretically relevant components but have different patterns of irrelevant components" (p. 3). According to Webb et al.,

> Once a proposition has been confirmed by two or more independent measurement processes, the uncertainty of its interpretation is greatly reduced. The most persuasive evidence comes through a *triangulation* [italics added] of measurement processes. If a proposition can survive the onslaught of a series of imperfect measures, with all their irrelevant error, confidence should be placed in it. Of course, this confidence is increased by minimizing error in each instrument and by a reasonable belief in the different and divergent effects of the sources of error. (p. 3)

Thus, Webb et al. are credited with being the first to coin the term *triangulation*. This type of triangulation is referred to as between- or across-method triangulation.

It was Denzin (1978) who first outlined how to triangulate methods. Denzin defined triangulation as "the combination of methodologies in the study of the same phenomenon" (p. 291). Denzin outlined the following four types of triangulation: (a) data triangulation (i.e., use of a variety of sources in a study), (b) investigator triangulation (i.e., use of several different researchers), (c) theory triangulation (i.e., use of multiple perspectives and theories to interpret the results of a study), and (d) methodological triangulation (i.e., use of multiple methods to study a research problem). Denzin also distinguished *within-methods* triangulation, which refers to the use of either multiple quantitative or multiple qualitative approaches, from *between-methods* triangulation, which involves the use of both quantitative and qualitative approaches. Denzin surmised that within-methods triangulation had limited value because essentially only one paradigm (e.g., quantitative) is being used such that any inherent weakness stemming from the paradigmatic approach used (e.g., inability to explain why an observed causal relationship exists) will prevail regardless of the specific research design (e.g., experimental) used within a methodological paradigm.[3]

Denzin (1978) recommended the use of between-method triangulation, contending that by utilizing mixed methods, "the bias inherent in any particular data source, investigators, and particularly method will be canceled out when used in conjunction with other data sources, investigators, and methods" (p. 14); and (b) "the result will be a convergence upon the truth about some social phenomenon" (p. 14). According to Denzin, three outcomes arise from triangulation: convergence, inconsistency, and contradiction. Whichever of these outcomes prevail, the researcher can construct superior explanations of the observed social phenomena.

Although acknowledging that triangulation may not be suitable for all research purposes, Jick (1979) noted the following advantages of triangulation: (a) it allows researchers to be more confident of their results; (b) it stimulates the development of creative ways of collecting data; (c) it can lead to thicker, richer data; (d) it can lead to the synthesis or integration of theories; (e) it can uncover contradictions, and (f) by virtue of its comprehensiveness, it may serve as the litmus test for competing theories.

Morse (1991) outlined two types of methodological triangulation: simultaneous or sequential. According to Morse, simultaneous triangulation represents the simultaneous use of qualitative and quantitative methods in which there is limited interaction between the two sources of data during the data collection stage, but the findings complement one another at the data interpretation stage. On the other hand, sequential triangulation is utilized when the results of one approach are necessary for planning the next method.

While Denzin (1978), Jick (1979), and others were promoting triangulation, Sieber (1973) provided a list of reasons to combine quantitative and qualitative research. He outlined how such a combination can be effective at the research design, data collection, and data analysis stages of the research process. For example, at the research design stage, quantitative data can assist the qualitative component by identifying representative sample members, as well as outlying (i.e., deviant) cases. Conversely, at the design stage, qualitative data can assist the quantitative component of a study by helping with conceptual and instrument development. At the data collection stage, quantitative data can play a role in providing baseline information and helping to avoid "elite bias" (talking only to high-status individuals). On the other hand, at the data collection stage, qualitative data can help in facilitating the data collection process. During the data analysis stage, quantitative data can facilitate the assessment of generalizability of the qualitative data and shed new light on qualitative findings.[4] Alternatively, during the data analysis stage, qualitative data can play an important role by interpreting, clarifying, describing, and validating quantitative results, as well as through grounding and modifying.

Rossman and Wilson (1985) identified three reasons for combining quantitative and qualitative research. First, combinations are used to enable confirmation or corroboration of each other through triangulation. Second, combinations are used to enable or to develop analysis in order to provide richer data. Third, combinations are used to initiate new modes of thinking by attending to paradoxes that emerge from the two data sources.

By examining published research, Greene, Caracelli, and Graham (1989) inductively identified the following five broad purposes or rationales of mixed methodological studies: (a) triangulation (i.e., seeking convergence and corroboration of results from different methods studying the same phenomenon), (b) complementarity (i.e., seeking elaboration, enhancement, illustration, clarification of the results from one method with results from the other method), (c) development (i.e., using the results from one method to help inform the other method), (d) initiation (i.e., discovering paradoxes and contradictions that lead to a reframing of the research question), and (e) expansion (i.e., seeking to expand the breadth and range of inquiry by using different methods for different inquiry components).

In 1979, Reichardt and Cook made a plea for program evaluators to use both quantitative and qualitative "methodological paradigms." They pointed out that although specific research methods and techniques are sometimes linked to methodological paradigms, it is nonetheless "our view that the paradigmatic perspective which promotes this incompatibility between the method-types is in error" (p. 11). They also pointed out that

> one will often want to sample attributes from each paradigm *on the same dimension*. For instance, comprehensive evaluations should be process-oriented as well as outcome oriented, exploratory as well as confirmatory. There is no reason for researchers to be constrained to either one of the traditional, though largely arbitrary, paradigms when they can have the best from both. (pp. 18-19)

Cook (1985) coined the term *critical multiplism* (also see Houts, Cook, & Shadish, 1986) to refer to the ideas that research questions can be examined from different perspectives and it is often useful to combine different methods with different biases. Generally speaking, evaluation as a field has moved more quickly into the use of mixed methods research than has psychological and, even, educational research, perhaps because of the very practical nature of evaluation research and the need for multiple sources of evidence when judging social programs.

Sechrest and Sidana (1995) listed four reasons for methodological pluralism: (a) for verification purposes, (b) to provide some basis for estimating possible error in the underlying measures, (c) to facilitate the monitoring of data collected, and (d) to probe a data set to determine its meaning. Also, Dzurec and Abraham (1993, pp. 76-77) identified the following six "pursuits" that link qualitative and quantitative research: (a) the pursuit of mastery over self and the world, (b) the pursuit of understanding through recomposition, (c) the pursuit of complexity reduction to enhance understanding, (d) the pursuit of innovation, (e) the pursuit of meaningfulness, and (f) the pursuit of truthfulness.

Most recently, Collins, Onwuegbuzie, and Sutton (2006) identified four rationales for conducting mixed research: participant enrichment (e.g., mixing quantitative and qualitative research to optimize the sample using techniques that include recruiting participants, engaging in activities such as institutional review board debriefings, ensuring that each participant selected is appropriate for inclusion), instrument fidelity (e.g., assessing the appropriateness and/or utility of existing instruments, creating new instruments, monitoring performance of human instruments), treatment integrity (i.e., assessing fidelity of intervention), and significance enhancement (e.g., facilitating thickness and richness of data, augmenting interpretation and usefulness of findings).

Meanwhile, in recent years, some of the strongest supporters of qualitative research, such as Denzin, Lincoln, and Guba, have, at times, made statements that appear to give credence to mixed methods research. For example, Lincoln and Guba (1985) acknowledged that "indeed, there are many opportunities for the naturalistic investigator to utilize quantitative data—probably more than are appreciated" (pp. 198-199) Also, Guba and Lincoln (1989) stated that "the information may be quantitative or qualitative. Responsive evaluation does not rule out quantitative modes, as is mistakenly believed by many, but deals with whatever information is responsive to the unresolved claim, concern, or issue" (p. 174). Further, Guba and Lincoln (1994) noted that "Both qualitative and quantitative methods may be used appropriately with any research paradigm" (p. 105). Similarly, Guba and Lincoln (2005) reiterated that "within each paradigm, mixed methodologies (strategies) may make perfectly good sense" (p. 200). They also declared, "As we tried to make it clear, the 'argument' arising in the social sciences was *not about method*, although many critics of the new naturalistic, ethnographic, phenomenological, and/or case study approaches assumed it was" (p. 200). Guba and Lincoln (2005) posed and answered the following question:

> Is it possible to blend elements of one paradigm into another, so that one is engaging in research that represents the best of both worldviews? The answer, from our perspective, has to be a cautious *yes*. This is especially so if the models (paradigms) share axiomatic elements that are similar, or that resonate strongly between them. (p. 201)

Schwandt (2000, 2006) has taken a stronger position on the "paradigm wars," calling into question the need for the divisions or differentiation and the defining through opposition of qualitative (and other) research. He has pointed out that "it is highly questionable whether such a distinction [between qualitative inquiry and quantitative inquiry] is any longer meaningful for helping us understand the purpose and means of human inquiry" (2000, p. 210). Schwandt (2000) also declared the following:

> All research is interpretive, and we face a multiplicity of methods that are suitable for different kinds of understandings. So the traditional means of coming to grips with one's identity as a researcher by aligning oneself with a particular set of methods (or being defined in one's department as a student of "qualitative" or "quantitative" methods) is no longer very useful. If we are to go forward, we need to get rid of that distinction. (p. 210)

We agree with Schwandt that the dividing lines are *much* fuzzier than typically suggested in the literature and that antagonism between paradigms is unproductive. The paradigm warriors also too frequently ignore the presence of many intraparadigmatic differences. At the same time, we still believe that it is useful to identify three research paradigms to signify three general clusters of methodological and philosophical positions. However, these positions are not nearly as "logical" and as distinct as is frequently suggested in the literature.

In sum, the 20th century started with some use of what later came to be called mixed research, but social and psychological research quickly became primarily quantitative (e.g., as influenced by logical positivism and a reinvigorated scientism). Partially in reaction, many qualitative currents developed throughout the century, coalescing into a qualitative research paradigm in the 1980s and 1990s (e.g., Guba, 1990). In reaction to the polarization between quantitative and qualitative research, another intellectual movement (focusing on synthesis) occurred and it has come to be called mixed methods research. We currently are in a three methodological or research paradigm world, with quantitative, qualitative, and mixed methods research all thriving and coexisting. In contrast to Thomas Kuhn's (1962) expectation for single paradigms characterizing "normal science," we suggest that a three-paradigm *methodological* world might be healthy because each approach has its strengths and weaknesses and times and places of need. Perhaps normal science is not best for social research; that is, perhaps a continual interaction between Kuhn's normal *and* revolutionary science will best keep us all in check and balanced.

Current Definitions of Mixed Methods Research

In addition to multiple operationalism and triangulation, the third methodological movement (an intellectual and practical *synthesis*) has been given many names. Here are a few: blended research (Thomas, 2003), integrative research (Johnson & Onwuegbuzie, 2004), multimethod research (e.g., Hunter & Brewer, 2003; Morse, 2003), multiple methods (Smith, in press), triangulated studies (cf. Sandelowski, 2003), ethnographic residual analysis (Fry, Chantavanich, & Chantavanich, 1981), and mixed research (Johnson, 2006; Johnson & Christensen, 2004). An advantage of the broader term *mixed research*, as well as *integrative research*, is that it does not suggest a limitation of mixing to methods only.

Mixed methods research has become the most popular term used to describe this movement.[5] It is important to keep in one's mind, however, that the word *methods* should be viewed broadly. Greene (2006) provided an excellent description of the way we viewed the word *methods* in this term (i.e., we see it as meaning "methodology" as conceived and outlined by Greene, 2006). We believe that a broad interpretation and use of the word methods (in mixed methods) allows inclusion of issues and strategies surrounding methods of data collection (e.g., questionnaires, interviews, observations), methods of research (e.g., experiments, ethnography), and related philosophical issues (e.g., ontology, epistemology, axiology). In our view, each of the three major approaches to research include assumptions, principles, and values about these kinds of methodology and practice-related issues as parts of the research paradigm (Johnson & Onwuegbuzie, 2004; Morgan, 2006). Now we will examine how leaders in the field define mixed methods research.

Because, in recent years, the concept of mixed methods research has been defined in a number of ways, we felt that it was important to examine the criteria leaders in the field currently consider important for defining mixed methods research. Our sampling frame (i.e., politically important case sampling; Miles & Huberman, 1994) started with a list of 31 leading mixed methods research methodologists from Tashakkori's "Bridges Web site" (see People Links at http://www.fiu.edu/~bridges/); we later added 5 additional leaders (i.e., contributors to a special journal issue on mixed methods research; see Johnson, 2006). We asked (via e-mail) all of these methodologists if they would share their current definitions of mixed methods research. The 19 definitions provided by the participating methodologists are presented in Table 1. The unit of analysis is definition rather than participant (because 2 definitions were provided by pairs of methodologists).

As can be seen in Table 1, these definitions have varying levels of specificity. A cross-case analysis (Miles & Huberman, 1994) was undertaken to compare and contrast the 19 separate definitions. Specifically, the method of constant comparison was used (Glaser & Strauss, 1967), wherein we compared each subsequent significant statement (i.e., definition or parts of a definition) with previous statements such that similar clusters were labeled with the same code. After all the statements had been coded, the codes were grouped by similarity, and a theme was identified and documented based on each grouping. This analysis revealed five themes. We quantitized (Tashakkori & Teddlie, 1998) some of the themes to provide information about quantity in addition to quality. That is, the themes (i.e., qualitative data) were transformed to numerical form (Onwuegbuzie & Teddlie, 2003) to indicate the number of definitions that contributed to each theme.

According to 15 of the 19 definitions, quantitative research and qualitative research is *what is mixed* (i.e., Theme 1). According to one definition (Hunter's), mixing also includes

Table 1
Definitions of Mixed Methods Research by Leaders in the Field Responding

Pat Bazeley:
I tend to distinguish between mixed methods and multimethod, although if I need a generic term, I used mixed methods. Multimethod research is when different approaches or methods are used in parallel or sequence but are not integrated until inferences are being made. Mixed methods research involves the use of more than one approach to or method of design, data collection or data analysis within a single program of study, with integration of the different approaches or methods occurring during the program of study, and not just at its concluding point. Note that I am not limiting this to a combination of qualitative and quantitative research only, but more broadly, combinations of any different approaches/methods/data/analyses.

Valerie Caracelli:
A mixed method study is one that planfully juxtaposes or combines methods of different types (qualitative and quantitative) to provide a more elaborated understanding of the phenomenon of interest (including its context) and, as well, to gain greater confidence in the conclusions generated by the evaluation study.

Huey Chen:
Mixed methods research is a systematic integration of quantitative and qualitative methods in a single study for purposes of obtaining a fuller picture and deeper understanding of a phenomenon. Mixed methods can be integrated in such a way that qualitative and quantitative methods retain their original structures and procedures (pure form mixed methods). Alternatively, these two methods can be adapted, altered, or synthesized to fit the research and cost situations of the study (modified form mixed methods).

John Creswell:
Mixed methods research is a research design (or methodology) in which the researcher collects, analyzes, and mixes (integrates or connects) both quantitative and qualitative data in a single study or a multiphase program of inquiry.

Steve Currall:
Mixed methods research involves the sequential or simultaneous use of both qualitative and quantitative data collection and/or data analysis techniques.

Marvin Formosa:
Mixed methods research is the utilitization of two or more different methods to meet the aims of a research project as best as one can. The research project may be conducted from either one or two paradigmatic standpoints (mixed methodology study).

Jennifer Greene:
Mixed method inquiry is an approach to investigating the social world that ideally involves more than one methodological tradition and thus more than one way of knowing, along with more than one kind of technique for gathering, analyzing, and representing human phenomena, all for the purpose of better understanding.

Al Hunter:
Mixed methods is a term that is usually used to designate combining qualitative and quantitative research methods in the same research project. I prefer the term *multimethod research* to indicate that different styles of research may be combined in the same research project. These need not be restricted to quantitative and qualitative; but may include, for example, qualitative participant observation with qualitative in-depth interviewing. Alternatively it could include quantitative survey research with quantitative experimental research. And of course it would include quantitative with qualitative styles.

(continued)

Table 1 (continued)

Burke Johnson and Anthony Onwuegbuzie:
Mixed methods research is the class of research where the researcher mixes or combines quantitative and qualitative research techniques, methods, approaches, concepts or language into a single study or set of related studies.

Udo Kelle:
Mixed methods means the combination of different qualitative and quantitative methods of data collection and data analysis in one empirical research project. This combination can serve for two different purposes: it can help to discover and to handle threats for validity arising from the use of qualitative or quantitative research by applying methods from the alternative methodological tradition and can thus ensure good scientific practice by enhancing the validity of methods and research findings. Or it can be used to gain a fuller picture and deeper understanding of the investigated phenomenon by relating complementary findings to each other which result from the use of methods from the different methodological traditions of qualitative and quantitative research.

Donna Mertens:
Mixed methods research, when undertaken from a transformative stance, is the use of qualitative and quantitative methods that allow for the collection of data about historical and contextual factors, with special emphasis on issues of power that can influence the achievement of social justice and avoidance of oppression.

Steven Miller:
Mixed methods is a form of evolving methodological inquiry, primarily directed to the human sciences, which attempts to combine in some logical order the differing techniques and procedures of quantitative, qualitative and historical approaches. At present mixed methods must devote itself to resolving a set of issues, both epistemological and ontological. The first must devote itself to what Miller and Gatta (2006) call the "epistemological link," that is the rules and rationales which "permit" one to proceed mixed methodologically. The second must adhere to some form of "minimal realist" ontology, where either social reality is "One" but can be accessed by different methods separately or working in conjunction, or social reality is multiple in nature and can ONLY be accessed through mixed methods. Present day attempts to couch mixed methods within some broad notion of pragmatism are not satisfactory.

Janice Morse:
A mixed method design is a plan for a scientifically rigorous research process comprised of a qualitative or quantitative *core component* that directs the theoretical drive, with qualitative or quantitative *supplementary component(s)*. These components of the research fit together to enhance description, understanding and can either be conducted simultaneously or sequentially.

Isadore Newman:
Mixed methods research is a set of procedures that should be used when integrating qualitative and quantitative procedures reflects the research question(s) better than each can independently. The combining of quantitative and qualitative methods should better inform the researcher and the effectiveness of mixed methods should be evaluated based upon how the approach enables the investigator to answer the research question(s) embedded in the purpose(s) (why the study is being conducted or is needed; the justification) of the study. (See Newman, Ridenour, Newman & DeMarco, 2003.)

Michael Q. Patton:
I consider mixed methods to be inquiring into a question using different data sources and design elements in such a way as to bring different perspectives to bear in the inquiry and therefore support triangulation of the findings. In this regard, using different methods to examine different questions in the same overall study is not mixed methods.

Table 1 (continued)

Hallie Preskill:
Mixed methods research refers to the use of data collection methods that collect both quantitative and qualitative data. Mixed methods research acknowledges that all methods have inherent biases and weaknesses; that using a mixed method approach increases the likelihood that the sum of the data collected will be richer, more meaningful, and ultimately more useful in answering the research questions.

Margarete Sandelowski:
First, I think of this in terms of either a single primary research study or as a program of research. Then, I see mixed methods as something of a misnomer as mixing implies blending together. Mixed methods research, though, is more the use of different methodological approaches TOGETHER in a single study or single program of research. One cannot blend methods in the sense of assimilating one into the other. I use methods here to refer to larger inquiry approaches (e.g., experiments and grounded theory) which are themselves based in distinctive theoretical perspectives. Yet this sets up a problem too, as grounded theory, for example, can be "positivist" (a la Strauss & Corbin), "constructivist" (a la Charmaz), or "postmodern" (a la Clarke) in sensibility or influence. So, if a researcher is doing grounded theory (positivist style) and an experiment (positivist influence), are any methods actually being mixed? In other words, mixed methods research can be defined at the technique level as the combination of, e.g., purposeful & probability sampling, open-ended and closed-ended data collection techniques, and narrative and mutivariable analyses—i.e., in which anything can be used together (linked or assimilated into each other)—or it can be defined at a larger theoretical/paradigmatic level as using divergent approaches to inquiry together. I would not define mixed methods research as constituting ANY combination of 2 or more things, as any research involves the use of 2 or more of something and the use of experiment and survey is 2 things, but they are informed by one mind (typically positivist/objectivist/realist). We get tangled in words, do we not?

Lyn Shulha:
By collaborative mixed method research, we will mean the purposeful application of a multiple person, multiple perspective approach to questions of research and evaluation. Decisions about how methods are combined and how analyses are conducted are grounded in the needs and emerging complexity of each project rather than in preordinate methodological conventions. . . . Within this context, methods can be "mixed" in a variety of ways. Sometimes, one method serves another in validating and explicating findings that emerge from a dominant approach. On other occasions, different methods are used for different parts of the issues being investigated, and in an independent way. In more complex cases, the methods and perspectives are deliberately mixed from the beginning of the process. The resulting interaction of problem, method, and results produce a more comprehensive, internally consistent, and ultimately, more valid general approach. What sets the most complex forms of collaborative mixed method research apart from other forms of inquiry is that findings depend as much on the researchers' capacities to learn through joint effort and to construct joint meaning as on their expertise in conventional data collection and analysis techniques.

Abbas Tashakkori and Charles Teddlie:
Mixed methods research is a type of research design in which QUAL and QUAN approaches are used in type of questions, research methods, data collection and analysis procedures, or in inferences.

Note: QUAL = qualitative research; QUAN = quantitative research.

within research paradigm mixing (e.g., QUAL + QUAL). One definition includes historical research in addition to quantitative and qualitative research. In other words, there is strong agreement that mixed research involves both quantitative and qualitative research, although one person specifically recommends a broadening of mixed research to include within-research-paradigm mixing.

When or where in the design mixing is carried out (i.e., the *mixing stage*) is another theme (i.e., Theme 2). This theme involves the stage at which mixing is said to take place. For example, three definitions indicate that mixing occurs in the data collection stage. Two definitions indicate that mixing occurs at the data collection and data analysis stages. At least four (and perhaps all of the other definitions indirectly) suggest that mixing can occur at all of the stages of research. According to one definition, mixed methods must include quantitative and qualitative perspectives in the examination of the same research question. Although this was not frequently mentioned, we agree that this is an important point for consideration; Yin (2006) provides explicit argument for this point in his article in a special issue on mixed methods research (for the special issue, see Johnson, 2006).

A related issue is that of the *breadth* of mixed research (i.e., Theme 3). This theme can be regarded as lying on a continuum from those who define mixed methods research as by definition entailing the collection of both qualitative and qualitative data (e.g., Creswell) to those who define mixed methods research as potentially involving mixing at all stages (e.g., Bazeley, Tashakkori and Teddlie), to those who include in their definition the mixing of methodological worldviews and language (i.e., Johnson & Onwuegbuzie, 2004). In fact, the last part of the Johnson and Onwuegbuzie (2004) definition includes a very broad criterion: the mixing of qualitative (kind, type) and quantitative (amount) *language or discourse* (e.g., in one's methodological worldview, in forming interpretations, and in writing and communicating research findings). Viewed in this very broad way, much published research would involve this sort of mixing. Our goal, at the time, in including the criterion of language (while recognizing the importance of pure qualitative research, pure quantitative research, and "pure" mixed methods research) was to provide a very broad middle position for mixed methods research rather than a more narrow middle position. When viewed on the criterion of language or discourse, mixing is a very natural and commonplace process.

The next major theme is *why* mixing is carried out in research (i.e., Theme 4). Many of the definitions included one or more purpose(s) for conducting mixed research. A key purpose mentioned by a number of people was breadth (7) and/or corroboration (5). Comments reflecting breadth or depth included (a) provide better understanding, (b) provide a fuller picture and deeper understanding, and (c) enhance description and understanding. Corroboration was reflected in the definition that focused on providing triangulation of the findings. A number of methodologists included both of these purposes (breadth and corroboration) in their definitions including (a) validate and explicate findings from another approach and produce more comprehensive, internally consistent, and valid findings; (b) provide more elaborated understanding and greater confidence in conclusions; (c) handle threats to validity and gain a fuller and deeper understanding; and (d) provide richer/more meaningful/more useful answers to research questions. However, for a small number of researchers, the theme of why was not limited to providing breadth and/or corroborations. Other purposes included (a) meet the aims of the research project and (b) achieve social justice and avoid oppression.

A final major theme pertains to the *orientation* of the mixed methods research (i.e., Theme 5). Whereas some definitions (e.g., Newman) are consistent with what Tashakkori (2006) labeled a "bottom-up" approach wherein the research question drives the mixed methods research approach, at least one of the definitions (i.e., Mertens) can be classified as representing a "top-down" approach in which the mixed methods approach is not driven by the research question; rather, it is driven by the researcher's quest to conduct research that is emancipatory, antidiscriminatory, participatory, and the like, which focuses squarely on the lives and experiences of marginalized persons or groups such as women; ethnic/racial/cultural minorities; religious minorities; individuals with disabilities/exceptionalities; and members of gay, lesbian, bisexual, and transsexual communities (i.e., transformative-emancipatory research; Mertens, 2003). In fact, rather than representing a dichotomy (Tashakkori, 2006), we believe that every mixed methods research study is situated somewhere along this bottom-up/top-down conceptualization continuum.

Homogeneity and heterogeneity can be seen in the definitions shown in Table 1. On one hand, we hoped to find some consensus about the core of mixed methods research, and we did. On the other hand, heterogeneity also is natural and should be valued positively, because mixed methods research can include a large group of researchers and a large number of research projects. In short, we view agreement *and* difference in the definitions as good for this emerging research paradigm and recommend that readers examine the definitions for both of these characteristics.

Based on our analysis of the definitions in Table 1, we offer the following general definition:

> Mixed methods research is the type of research in which a researcher or team of researchers combines elements of qualitative and quantitative research approaches (e.g., use of qualitative and quantitative viewpoints, data collection, analysis, inference techniques) for the broad purposes of breadth and depth of understanding and corroboration.

This definition refers to mixed methods research as a type of research:

> A mixed methods study would involve mixing within a single study; a mixed method program would involve mixing within a program of research and the mixing might occur across a closely related set of studies.

Defining Different Types of Mixed Methods Research

Looking at the qualitative-quantitative continuum in Figure 1, mixed research can be viewed as incorporating several overlapping groups of mixed methods researchers or types of mixed methods research. The area in the center of the figure, moving outward in both directions (and excluding the area near the poles), is where mixed methods research, broadly speaking, falls, with the center representing the strongest or "pure" form. It makes sense that a researcher might have one primary home (out of the three major homes: qualitative research, mixed research, and quantitative research). Because we argue for a contingency theory of research methodology, however, it also makes sense for the researcher to visit other homes when his or her research can benefit from such a visit (Johnson & Onwuegbuzie, 2004).

The area around the center of the continuum, *equal status*, is the home for the person that self-identifies as a mixed methods researcher. This researcher takes as his or her starting point the logic and philosophy of mixed methods research. These mixed methods researchers are likely to believe that qualitative and quantitative data and approaches will add insights as one considers most, if not all, research questions.

Figure 1
Graphic of the Three Major Research Paradigms, Including Subtypes of Mixed Methods Research

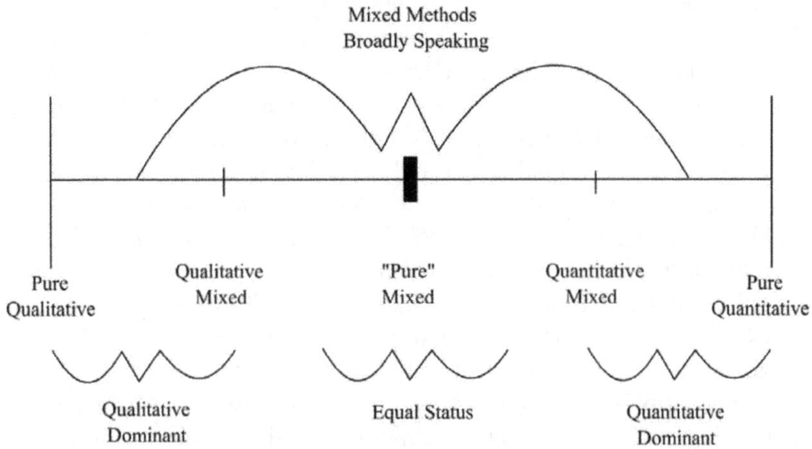

Another type of mixed methods research that results from the continuum shown in Figure 1 is labeled *qualitative dominant* mixed methods research. This type of research is symbolized as QUAL +quan research.[6] This area on the continuum would fit qualitative or mixed methods researchers who believe it is important to include quantitative data and approaches into their otherwise qualitative research projects. Here is a potential definition:

> Qualitative dominant mixed methods research is the type of mixed research in which one relies on a qualitative, constructivist-poststructuralist-critical view of the research process, while concurrently recognizing that the addition of quantitative data and approaches are likely to benefit most research projects.

Another type of mixed methods research that results from the continuum shown in Figure 1 is labeled *quantitative dominant* mixed methods research. This type of research is symbolized as QUAN+qual research. This area on the continuum would fit quantitative or mixed methods researchers who believe it is important to include qualitative data and approaches into their otherwise quantitative research projects. Here is a potential definition:

> Quantitative dominant mixed methods research is the type of mixed research in which one relies on a quantitative, postpositivist view of the research process, while concurrently recognizing that the addition of qualitative data and approaches are likely to benefit most research projects.

Some Current Issues for Mixed Methods Research

After considering the definitions provided in this article, several issues emerged as potentially needing additional consideration in future methodological works. Our purpose here is briefly to introduce a few issues, not to provide extensive discussion or final solutions. First, can we (i.e., researchers and methodologists situated near the middle of the continuum in Figure 1) reach broad agreement about the stages of the research process at which mixing can occur? Is it oftentimes more important to mix at some stages rather than at other stages? What are the gains from mixing at the different stages?

Second, what are effective strategies for integration at different stages of the research process? For example, Bazeley (2006) has carefully examined how to integrate qualitative and quantitative data using data analysis software. Teddlie and Tashakkori (2006) and Tashakkori and Teddlie (2006) discussed the process of making metainferences (that are based on the integration of qualitative and quantitative strands in research studies). Onwuegbuzie and Johnson (2006) also have explored the concept of integration in several ways, including, most directly, what we labeled commensurability legitimation (see below). The key idea that mixed methods research requires some form of integration is clear; still, however, additional research is needed to further explicate this process.

Third, what philosophy of science, or set of philosophical positions, will best partner with mixed methods research? Constructivism and poststructuralism are connected to qualitative research, and postpositivism is connected to quantitative research. Many (or most) mixed methods writers have argued for some version of pragmatism as the most useful philosophy to support mixed methods research. We agree that pragmatism is a well-developed and attractive philosophy for integrating perspectives and approaches. Pragmatism offers an epistemological justification (i.e., via pragmatic epistemic values or standards) and logic (i.e., use the combination of methods and ideas that helps one best frame, address, and provide tentative answers to one's research question[s]) for mixing approaches and methods. A pragmatist would reject a incompatibility thesis and would claim that research paradigms can remain separate, but they also can be mixed into another research paradigm. He or she also likely would be content with making what Dewey called warranted assertions. Another attractive feature of pragmatism for mixed methods research is that pragmatism includes a wide range of theorists that mixed methods researchers can consider. For example, Rescher (2000) and Putnam (2002) offered what Rescher calls *pragmatism of the right* (where "right" is not a political concept but refers to holding a moderately strong form of realism, and a weak form of pluralism). Rorty (see Brandom, 2000) and Maxcy (2003) offered what we call called *pragmatism of the left* (where "left" implies antirealism and strong pluralism; Brandom, 2000; also see Maxcy, 2003). We generally argue for what we call *pragmatism of the middle* as an especially useful philosophy for mixed methods. We have constructed a version of this kind of pragmatism around the ideas of Charles Sanders Peirce, William James, and John Dewey. We (i.e., Johnson & Onwuegbuzie, 2004, especially Table 1) have previously outlined this version of pragmatism. We believe that one or more of the pragmatisms can provide a philosophy that supports paradigm integration and helps mixed research to peacefully coexist with the philosophies of quantitative and qualitative research.

Fourth, does mixed methods need a particular, detailed set of philosophical and methodological positions? For example, does the field need to come up with specific positions that would fit into the classification scheme popularized by Guba and Lincoln (i.e., listing a particular ontological commitment, a particular epistemology, and specific stances toward axiology and appropriate methodology)? In our view, variation in particular philosophical commitments should be welcome in mixed methods research, and we should embrace these differences as an important part of the mixed methods research paradigm—a view shared by Greene (2006). At the same time, it is important that arguments and discussion about "appropriate" philosophical commitments continue so that the field is self-reflexive and continues to grow (philosophically).

Fifth, are equal status designs (equal use of quantitative and qualitative epistemologies) possible? We have asked this because one of the experts suggests that mixed methods research must come from either a quantitative or a qualitative dominant paradigm (Morse). Although we disagree with this position, the position should fit well within mixed methods research "broadly conceived." Our disagreement is based on our observation or interpretation that many philosophers of epistemology and/or science hold nuanced positions that *typically* involve a blending of assumptions, beliefs, and preferred analytical techniques (Johnson, Meeker, Loomis, & Onwuegbuzie, 2004). To address specifically the issue of mixing ideas associated with research paradigms, we have introduced a concept called commensurability validity or legitimation, which is "the extent to which the meta-inferences made [in a mixed methods study] reflect a mixed worldview based on the cognitive process of Gestalt switching and integration" (Onwuegbuzie & Johnson, 2006, p. 57). Commensurability legitimation will not be possible for many researchers, and it is difficult to learn how to switch perspectives and create new perspectives, but we believe that it is possible and desired. The strong (or fully) mixed methods position, we argue, is developed only after explicit and systematic consideration of qualitative and quantitative perspectives. In future work, we hope to draw on ideas from cognitive psychology, counseling psychology (e.g., role-playing), and philosophy and linguistics (intertranslatability of different languages) as we continue to work on the commensurability legitimation issue. Fortunately, commensurability is not always required within an individual because commensurability also can be obtained through the use of research teams that carefully interact and produce joint constructions.

Sixth, the credibility or trustworthiness or validity of mixed research is an important issue. Although this issue tended not to be explicitly mentioned in the definitions, it might be useful to address this in a fuller definition. Several methodologists have started addressing this important issue (cf. Onwuegbuzie & Johnson, 2006; Tashakkori & Teddlie, 2006). In Onwuegbuzie and Johnson (2006), we provided a typology of nine types of validity or legitimation for mixed methods researchers to consider (i.e., inside-outside, sample integration, weakness minimization, sequential, conversion, paradigmatic mixing, commensurability, multiple validities, and political validity). Additional work in this important area is needed. A closely related issue is that of standards for mixed methods research. Patton (2002) has provided an excellent set of standards that should work well in a contingency theory of mixed research (where different standards will be appropriate for different communities and situations). Patton presented five sets of standards, including what he calls traditional scientific research criteria, social construction and constructivist criteria, artistic and evocative criteria, critical change criteria, and evaluation standards and principles (see Exhibit 9.1, pp. 544-545). Additional issues for future consideration might be whether additional sets of standards are needed and how to determine which set or combination of standards would apply to a particular circumstance.

Seventh, should and how might qualitative dominant, equal status, and quantitative dominant mixed methods research be more fully developed and differentiated? Will the qualitative and quantitative dominant mixed research be explicitly incorporated into the qualitative and quantitative research paradigms or will they develop as distinct types? This should be an exciting area for future research as researchers and methodologists coming from different epistemological perspectives construct and systematize these subtypes.

Eighth, what are the details of a full contingency theory for the conduct of human research? That is, exactly (a) when and under what conditions should qualitative research be considered the appropriate approach, (b) when and under what conditions should quantitative research be considered the appropriate approach, and (c) when and under what conditions should mixed research be considered the appropriate approach? A strength of a *contingency theory* of research is that the strengths and weaknesses of qualitative, quantitative, and mixed research are recognized, and all three approaches are considered to be important and needed, albeit in different circumstances. A contingency theory also needs to be carefully developed to help the mixed methods researcher make wise decisions about how to mix methods and approaches in relation to situational contingencies (e.g., given limited resources, what is the best combination to maximize usefulness of information and evidence?). A fully general contingency theory of human research would suggest that researchers need to understand all three research paradigms. The contingency theory also would explain how to make decisions about mixing quantitative and qualitative methods and approaches. This theory, when more fully developed, will help researchers understand how to combine research components in a way that provides a reasonable opportunity to answer the research question(s), and it will require that researchers tailor their designs to unique, and sometimes emergent, research situations.

McLafferty and Onwuegbuzie (2006) have attempted to provide a form of mixed methods contingency theory by proposing a dimensional framework that allows for the coexistence of quantitative and qualitative research approaches and, by extension, provides a philosophical foundation for mixed methods research. Under their framework, the quantitative and qualitative research paradigms are no longer dichotomous—rather, they are *dimensionally different*. According to these authors, research can be methodologically legitimated by recognizing the dimensionality of a study's research question (its what?), purpose (why?), process (how?), and potential (scope of results).

Ninth, a fuller definition of mixed methods research might include reference to the logic of mixed research. We believe that additional work is needed to explicate this logic or set of logics. We have begun addressing this issue in what we have labeled the *fundamental principle of mixed research* (Johnson & Onwuegbuzie, 2004; Johnson & Turner, 2003). When designing a mixed study, according to this "logic," the research should strategically combine qualitative and quantitative methods, approaches, and concepts in a way that produces complementary strengths and nonoverlapping weaknesses. Consideration of the strengths and weaknesses of different approaches is required in relation to situational contingencies. Our intention is for the principle to be viewed very broadly. The principle is *not* limited to triangulation. The "complementary strengths" component of the principle means data should be collected that will provide all of the information that is potentially relevant to the purpose(s) of the study. The complementary strengths component, for example, includes any or all of the major purposes identified by Greene et al. (1989; i.e., triangulation, expansion, complementarity, development, and initiation). The second component of the principle suggests that researchers also attempt to eliminate potential design weaknesses by combining methods that have different weaknesses. The fundamental principle (and its resulting logic of research) should be a point on which researchers from different paradigms can reach agreement because the principle is a general restatement of an idea that is used in qualitative research (e.g., Denzin & Lincoln, 2005; Lincoln & Guba, 1985, used the metaphor of putting together a new, superior, fishnet that is constructed from multiple flawed fishnets), quantitative research (e.g., Campbell & Fiske, 1959; Mark, Henry, & Julnes, 2000), *and* mixed methods research (Brewer & Hunter, 2006; Tashakkori & Teddlie, 1998, 2003). The logic suggests designing studies to diverge, where needed, and converge, where needed, in a way that results in overall or total design viability and usefulness.

Another consideration for mixed methods research logic is provided in our (Onwuegbuzie & Johnson, 2006) concept of multiple validities legitimation. According to "multiple validities legitimation," researchers should attempt the difficult task of designing and conducting studies that are based on consideration of the types of "validity" presented in the qualitative research literature (e.g., Kvale, 1995; Lather, 1986, 1993; Maxwell, 1992; Onwuegbuzie & Leech, in press), the quantitative research literature (e.g., Bracht & Glass 1968; Campbell, 1957; Campbell & Stanley, 1963; Cook & Campbell 1979; Messick, 1989, 1995; Onwuegbuzie, 2003; Smith & Glass, 1987), *and* the mixed methods research literature (Onwuegbuzie & Johnson, 2006; Tashakkori & Teddlie, 2006). Obviously, mixed methods research, when well conducted, is a very intensive and difficult task. Given the alternative, however, it is a challenge we are implored to undertake.

Tenth, will the field be able to develop a typology of mixed methods designs that can be broadly agreed upon? Currently, several typologies are available including, for example, Creswell and Plano Clark (2007), Morgan (1998), and Teddlie and Tashakkori (2006). Do the qualitative dominant, quantitative dominant, and pure mixed methods research need separate sets of designs? We tentatively suggest that the answer is yes.

Eleventh, and last, if one were to view mixed methods research, metaphorically, as the trunk of a tree, then what are its branches? For example, should the major branches be labeled QUAL+quan, QUAN+qual, and QUAN+QUAL? What other branches or specialized types might develop over time (e.g., transformative mixed methods, collaborative mixed methods, reflective mixed methods)? We expect many more specific types of mixed methods research and designs to crystallize in the future as researchers relate mixed methods research concepts and thinking to new and reoccurring research problems and situations.

Conclusion

We believe that Greene (2006) has offered a useful framework for thinking about mixed methods research as a methodological or research paradigm, which she called "Mixed Methods Social Inquiry." She divided mixed methods social inquiry or mixed methods *methodology* (broadly viewed) into four domains: (a) philosophical assumptions and stances (i.e., what are the fundamental philosophical or epistemological assumptions of the methodology?), (b) inquiry logics (i.e., what traditionally is called "methodology" and refers to broad inquiry purposes and questions, logic, quality standards, writing forms that guide the researcher's "gaze"), (c) guidelines for practice (i.e., specific procedures and tools used to conduct research; the "how to" part of research methodology), and (d) sociopolitical commitments (i.e., interests, commitments, and power relations surrounding the location in society in which an inquiry is situated). The five definitional themes identified in the present article (i.e., what is mixed, when/where, breadth, why, and orientation) partially overlap Greene's four domains of methodological development. Specifically, Domain 1 (i.e., philosophical assumptions and stances) overlaps the *breadth* theme; Domain 2 (i.e., inquiry logics) overlaps both by the *when/where* theme and the *why* theme; Domain 3 (i.e., guidelines for practice) overlaps the *what is* mixed theme; and Domain 4 (i.e., sociopolitical commitments) overlaps the *orientation* theme. However, no definition provided by the leaders represented all four of Greene's domains. Yet as noted by Greene, the development of mixed methods research—as is the case for the quantitative and qualitative research paradigms—requires consideration of all four domains. Thus, we believe that a more comprehensive definition might be helpful to the field of mixed methods research.

In an attempt to integrate the ideas discussed in this article including Greene's (2006) domains of methodology, the leaders' general definitions of mixed methods research, and some of the potential gaps in definitions we identified in the previous section, we decided to conclude by offering a tentative and first approximation of a more comprehensive definition or summary of what is called mixed methods. Our new "definition" is as follows: Mixed methods research is an intellectual and practical synthesis based on qualitative and quantitative research; it is the third methodological or research paradigm (along with qualitative and quantitative research). It recognizes the importance of traditional quantitative and qualitative research but also offers a powerful third paradigm choice that often will provide the most informative, complete, balanced, and useful research results. Mixed methods research is the research paradigm that (a) partners with the philosophy of pragmatism in one of its forms (left, right, middle); (b) follows the logic of mixed methods research (including the logic of the fundamental principle and any other useful logics imported from qualitative or quantitative research that are helpful for producing defensible and usable research findings); (c) relies on qualitative and quantitative viewpoints, data collection, analysis, and inference techniques combined according to the logic of mixed methods research to address one's research question(s); and (d) is cognizant, appreciative, and inclusive of local and broader sociopolitical realities, resources, and needs. Furthermore, the mixed methods research paradigm offers an important approach for *generating* important research questions *and* providing warranted answers to those questions. This type of research should be used when the nexus of contingencies in a situation, in relation to one's research question(s), suggests that mixed methods research is likely to provide superior research findings and outcomes.

Notes

1. Thomas Kuhn (1962) coined the term *paradigm*. In a recent article we coined a term we thought might work for delineating the three major research approaches in the social and behavioral sciences: qualitative research, quantitative research, and mixed research (or mixed methods research). We used the term *research paradigm* (Johnson & Onwuegbuzie, 2004) as follows:

> Thomas Kuhn (1962) popularized the idea of a paradigm. Later, when he was asked to explain more precisely what he meant by the term, he pointed out that it was a general concept and that it included a group of researchers having a common education and an agreement on "exemplars" of high quality research or thinking (Kuhn, 1977). In this article, by *research paradigm* we mean a set of beliefs, values, and assumptions that a community of researchers has in common regarding the nature and conduct of

research. The beliefs include, but are not limited to, ontological beliefs, epistemological beliefs, axiological beliefs, aesthetic beliefs, and methodological beliefs. In short, as we use the term, a research paradigm refers to a research culture. We will be arguing that there is now a trilogy of major research paradigms: qualitative research, quantitative research, and mixed methods research. (p. 24)

A synonym for our concept of "research paradigm" would be the term *methodological* paradigm. The point is that a paradigm can develop around what it means to conduct research and how it is undertaken. For Kuhn, the term *paradigm* was clearly not limited to epistemology, which is one of several popular usages today, but not ours. We find it convenient to speak of research or methodological paradigms as a way of separating organizing qualitative, quantitative, and mixed research.

2. Here are the approximate dates of these classical philosophers' lives: Protagoras (c. 490-420 B.C.E), Socrates (470-399 B.C.E), Plato (429-347 B.C.E), Aristotle (384-322 B.C.E), Gorgias (483-375 B.C.E), Cicero (c. 106-43 B.C.E), and Sextus Empiricus (c. late first century C.E. to mid–2nd century).

3. It is questionable whether Denzin currently holds this viewpoint.

4. This is contingent, for example, on an equal probability selection method (EPSEM) being used, a sufficient response rate being obtained, and attrition not being a serious problem.

5. For example, Collins, Onwuegbuzie, and Jiao (in press), who examined 14 major electronic databases (e.g., PsycINFO, CINAHL, ERIC) that represented the fields of psychology, education, sociology, social services, nursing and allied health, and business, identified 496 mixed methods articles (for each database, they examined all the years for which records existed)—representing a conceptual, methodological, theoretical, or applied article in the area of mixed methods—in which the term *mixed methods* or *mixed methodology* was used. A search using other terms did not yield such a large number of articles. For example, the phrase *blended research* yielded only 1 article.

6. The word *Qual* stands for qualitative research, *Quan* stands for quantitative research, and the use of capital letters denotes the dominant approach.

References

Bazeley, P. (2006). The contribution of computer software to integrating qualitative and quantitative data analyses. *Research in the Schools, 13*(1), 64-74.

Boring, E. G. (1953). The role of theory in experimental psychology. *American Journal of Psychology, 66,* 169-184.

Bouchard, T. J., Jr. (1976). Unobtrusive measures: An inventory of uses. *Sociological Methodsand Research, 4,* 267-300.

Bracht, G. H., & Glass, G. V. (1968). The external validity of experiments. *American Educational Research Journal, 5,* 437-474.

Brandom, R. B. (Ed.). (2000). *Rorty and his critics.* Malden, MA: Blackwell.

Brewer, J., & Hunter, A. (2006). *Foundations of multimethod research: Synthesizing styles.* Thousand Oaks, CA: Sage.

Campbell, D. T. (1957). Factors relevant to the validity of experiments in social settings. *Psychological Bulletin, 54,* 297-312.

Campbell, D. T., & Fiske, D. W. (1959). Convergent and discriminant validation by the multitrait-multimethod matrix. *Psychological Bulletin, 56,* 81-105.

Campbell, D. T., & Stanley, J. C. (1963). *Experimental and quasi-experimental designs for research.* Chicago: Rand McNally.

Collins, K. M. T., Onwuegbuzie, A. J., & Jiao, Q. G. (in press). A mixed methods investigation of mixed methods sampling designs in social and health science research. *Journal of Mixed Methods Research.*

Collins, K. M. T., Onwuegbuzie, A. J., & Sutton, I. L. (2006). A model incorporating the rationale and purpose for conducting mixed methods research in special education and beyond. *Learning Disabilities: A Contemporary Journal, 4,* 67-100.

Cook, T. D. (1985). Postpositivist critical multiplism. In L. Shotland & M. M. Mark (Eds.), *Social science and social policy* (pp. 21-62). Beverly Hills, CA: Sage.

Cook, T. D., & Campbell, D. T. (1979). *Quasi-experimentation: Design and analysis issues for field settings.* Chicago: Rand McNally.

Creswell, J. W., & Plano Clark, V. L. (in press). *Designing and conducting mixed methods research.* Thousand Oaks, CA: Sage.

Denzin, N. K. (1978). *The research act: A theoretical introduction to sociological methods.* New York: Praeger.

Denzin, N. K., & Lincoln, Y. S. (2005). Introduction: The discipline and practice of qualitative research. In N. K. Denzin & Y. S. Lincoln (Eds.), *The Sage handbook of qualitative research* (3rd ed., pp. 1-28). Thousand Oaks, CA: Sage.

Dzurec, L. C., & Abraham, J. L. (1993). The nature of inquiry: Linking quantitative and qualitative research. *Advances in Nursing Science, 16,* 73-79.

Fry, G., Chantavanich, S., & Chantavanich, A. (1981). Merging quantitative and qualitative research techniques: Toward a new research paradigm. *Anthropology and Education Quarterly, 12,* 145-158.

Gans, H. J. (1963). *Urban villagers: Group life and class in the life of Italian-Americans.* New York: Free Press.

Glaser, B. G., & Strauss, A. L. (1967). *The discovery of grounded theory: Strategies for qualitative research.* Chicago: Aldine.

Greene, J. C. (2006). Toward a methodology of mixed methods social inquiry. *Research in the Schools, 13*(1), 93-98.

Greene, J. C., Caracelli, V. J., & Graham, W. F. (1989). Toward a conceptual framework for mixed-method evaluation designs. *Educational Evaluation and Policy Analysis, 11,* 255-274.

Guba, E. G. (Ed.). (1990). *The paradigm dialog.* Newbury Park, CA: Sage.

Guba, E. G., & Lincoln, Y. S. (1989). *Fourth generation evaluation.* Newbury Park, CA: Sage.

Guba, E. G., & Lincoln, Y. S. (1994). Competing paradigms in qualitative research. In N. K. Denzin & Y. S. Lincoln (Eds.), *Handbook of qualitative research* (pp. 105-117). Thousand Oaks, CA: Sage.

Guba, E. G., & Lincoln, Y. S. (2005). Paradigmatic controversies, contradictions, and emerging confluences. In N. K. Denzin & Y. S. Lincoln (Eds.), *The Sage handbook of qualitative research* (3rd ed., pp. 191-215). Thousand Oaks, CA: Sage.

Hollingshead, A. B. (1949). *Elmtown's youth.* New York: John Wiley.

Houts, A. C., Cook, T. D., & Shadish, W. R. (1986). The person-situation debate: A critical multiplist perspective. *Journal of Personality, 54*(1), 52-105.

Hunter, A., & Brewer, J. (2003). Multimethod research in sociology. In A. Tashakkori & C. Teddlie (Eds.), *Handbook of mixed methods in social and behavioral research* (pp. 577-594). Thousand Oaks, CA: Sage.

Jahoda, M., Lazarsfeld, P. F., & Zeisel, H. (1931/2003). *Marienthal: The sociography of an unemployed community.* New Brunswick, NJ: Transaction Publishers.

Jick, T. D. (1979). Mixing qualitative and quantitative methods: Triangulation in action. *Administrative Science Quarterly, 24,* 602-611.

Johnson, R. B. (Ed.). (2006). New directions in mixed methods research [Special issue]. *Research in the Schools, 13*(1). Available online at http://www.msera.org/rits_131.htm

Johnson, R. B., & Christensen, L. B. (2004). *Educational research: Quantitative, qualitative, and mixed approaches.* Boston, MA: Allyn & Bacon.

Johnson, R. B., Meeker, K., Loomis, E., & Onwuegbuzie, A. J. (2004, April). *Development of the Philosophical and Methodological Beliefs Inventory.* Paper presented at the annual meeting of the American Educational Research Association, San Diego, CA.

Johnson, R. B., & Onwuegbuzie, A. J. (2004). Mixed methods research: A research paradigm whose time has come. *Educational Researcher, 33*(7), 14-26.

Johnson, R. B., & Turner, L. A. (2003). Data collection strategies in mixed methods research. In A. Tashakkori & C. Teddlie (Eds.), *Handbook of mixed methods in social and behavioral research* (pp. 297-319). Thousand Oaks, CA: Sage.

Kuhn, T. S. (1962). *The structure of scientific revolutions.* Chicago: University of Chicago Press.

Kuhn, T. S. (1977). *The essential tension: Selected studies in scientific tradition and change.* Chicago: University of Chicago Press.

Kvale, S. (1995). The social construction of validity. *Qualitative Inquiry, 1,* 19-40.

Lather, P. (1986). Issues of validity in openly ideological research: Between a rock and a soft place. *Interchange, 17,* 63-84.

Lather, P. (1993). Fertile obsession: Validity after poststructuralism. *Sociological Quarterly, 34,* 673-693.

Lincoln, Y. S., & Guba, E. G. (1985). *Naturalistic inquiry*. Beverly Hills, CA: Sage.

Lynd, R. S., & Lynd, H. M. (1929/1959). *Middletown: A study in modern American culture*. Orlando, FL: Harcourt Brace.

Mark, M. M., Henry, G. T., & Julnes, G. (2000). *Evaluation: An integrated framework for understanding, guiding, and improving policies and programs*. San Francisco: Jossey-Bass.

Maxcy, S. J. (2003). Pragmatic threads in mixed methods research in the social sciences: The search for multiple modes of inquiry and the end of the philosophy of formalism. In A. Tashakkori & C. Teddlie (Eds.), *Handbook of mixed methods in social and behavioral research* (pp. 51-89). Thousand Oaks, CA: Sage.

Maxwell, J. A. (1992). Understanding and validity in qualitative research. *Harvard Educational Review, 62,* 279-299.

McLafferty, C., & Onwuegbuzie, A. J (2006, November). *A dimensional resolution of the qualitative-quantitative dichotomy: Implications for theory, praxis, and national research policy*. Paper presented at the annual meeting of the Mid-South Educational Research Association, Birmingham, AL.

Mertens, D. (2003). Mixed methods and the politics of human research: The transformative-emancipatory perspective. In A. Tashakkori & C. Teddlie (Eds.), *Handbook of mixed methods in social and behavioral research* (pp. 135-164). Thousand Oaks, CA: Sage.

Messick, S. (1989). Validity. In R. L. Linn (Ed.), *Educational measurement* (3rd ed., pp. 13-103). Old Tappan, NJ: Macmillan.

Messick, S. (1995). Validity of psychological assessment: Validation of inferences from persons' responses and performances as scientific inquiry into score meaning. *American Psychologist, 50,* 741-749.

Miles, M. B., & Huberman, A. M. (1994). *Qualitative data analysis: A sourcebook of new methods*. Thousand Oaks, CA: Sage.

Miller, S., & Gatta, J. (2006). The use of mixed methods models and designs in the human sciences: Problems and prospects. *Quality & Quantity, 40*(4), 595-610.

Morgan, D. L. (1998). Practical strategies for combining qualitative and quantitative methods: Applications to health research. *Qualitative Health Research, 8,* 362-376.

Morgan, D. L. (2006). Paradigms lost and pragmatism regained: Methodological implications of combining qualitative and quantitative methods. *Journal of Mixed Methods Research, 1,* 48-76.

Morse, J. (1991). Approaches to qualitative-quantitative methodological triangulation. *Nursing Research, 40,* 120-123.

Morse, J. M. (2003). Principles of mixed methods and multimethod research design. In A. Tashakkori & C. Teddlie (Eds.), *Handbook of mixed methods in social and behavioral research* (pp. 189-208). Thousand Oaks, CA: Sage.

Newman, I., Ridenour, C. S., Newman, C., & DeMarco, G. M. P. (2003). A typology of research purposes and its relationship to mixed methods. In A. Tashakkori & C. Teddlie (Eds.), *Handbook of mixed methods in social and behavioral research* (pp. 189-208). Thousand Oaks, CA: Sage.

Onwuegbuzie, A. J. (2003). Expanding the framework of internal and external validity in quantitative research. *Research in the Schools, 10*(1), 71-90.

Onwuegbuzie, A. J., & Johnson, R. B. (2006). The validity issue in mixed research. *Research in the Schools, 13*(1), 48-63.

Onwuegbuzie, A. J., & Leech, N. L. (in press). Validity and qualitative research: An oxymoron? *Quality & Quantity: International Journal of Methodology*.

Onwuegbuzie, A. J., & Teddlie, C. (2003). A framework for analyzing data in mixed methods research. In A. Tashakkori & C. Teddlie (Eds.), *Handbook of mixed methods in social and behavioral research* (pp. 351-383). Thousand Oaks, CA: Sage.

Patton, M. Q. (2002). *Qualitative research and evaluation methods* (3rd ed.). Thousand Oaks, CA: Sage.

Putnam, H. (2002). *The collapse of the fact/value dichotomy and other essays*. Cambridge, MA: Harvard University Press.

Reichardt, D. S., & Cook, T. D. (1979). Beyond qualitative *versus* quantitative methods. In T. D. Cook & C. S. Reichardt (Eds.), *Qualitative and quantitative methods in evaluation research* (pp. 7-32). Beverly Hills, CA: Sage.

Rescher, N. (2000). *Realistic pragmatism: An introduction to pragmatic philosophy*. Albany: State University of New York Press.

Rossman, G. B., & Wilson, B. L. (1985). Numbers and words: Combining quantitative and qualitative methods in a single large-scale evaluation study. *Evaluation Review, 9,* 627-643.

Sandelowski, M. (2003). Tables or tableaux? The challenges of writing and reading mixed methods studies. In A. Tashakkori & C. Teddlie (Eds.), *Handbook of mixed methods in social and behavioral research* (pp. 321-350). Thousand Oaks, CA: Sage.

Schwandt, T. (2006). Opposition redirected. *International Journal of Qualitative Studies in Education, 19,* 803-810.

Schwandt, T. A. (2000). Three epistemological stances for qualitative inquiry. In N. K. Denzin & Y. S. Lincoln (Eds.), *Handbook of qualitative research* (2nd ed., pp. 189-213). Thousand Oaks, CA: Sage.

Sechrest, L., & Sidana, S. (1995). Quantitative and qualitative methods: Is there an alternative? *Evaluation and Program Planning, 18,* 77-87.

Sieber, S. D. (1973). The integration of fieldwork and survey methods. *American Journal of Sociology, 73,* 1335-1359.

Smith, M. L. (in press). Multiple methodology in education. In J. Green, G. Camilli, & P. Elmore (Eds.), *Complementary methods for research in education*. Washington, DC: American Educational Research Association.

Smith, M. L., & Glass, G. V. (1987). *Research and evaluation in education and the social sciences*. Englewood Cliffs, NJ: Prentice Hall.

Tashakkori, A. (2006, July). *Growing pains? Agreements, disagreements, and new directions in conceptualizing mixed methods*. Keynote address presented at the 2nd annual Mixed Methods Conference, Humerton School of Health Studies, Cambridge, UK.

Tashakkori, A., & Teddlie, C. (1998). *Mixed methodology: Combining qualitative and quantitative approaches* (Applied Social Research Methods Series, Vol. 46). Thousand Oaks, CA: Sage.

Tashakkori, A., & Teddlie, C. (Eds.). (2003). *Handbook of mixed methods in social and behavioral research*. Thousand Oaks, CA: Sage.

Tashakkori, A., & Teddlie, C. (2006, April). *Validity issues in mixed methods research: Calling for an integrative framework*. Paper presented at the annual meeting of the American Educational Research Association, San Francisco.

Teddlie, C., & Tashakkori, A. (2006). A general typology of research designs featuring mixed methods. *Research in the Schools, 13*(1), 12-28.

Thomas, R. M. (2003). *Blending qualitative and quantitative research methods in theses and dissertations*. Thousand Oaks, CA: Corwin.

Webb, E. J., Campbell, D. T., Schwartz, R. D., & Sechrest, L. (1966). *Unobtrusive measures*. Chicago: Rand McNally.

Yin, R. K. (2006). Mixed methods research: Are methods genuinely integrated or merely parallel? *Research in the Schools, 13*(1), 41-47.